10650590

DATE DUE

THE
ENGLISH
NOVEL

Background Readings

edited by

LYNN C. BARTLETT
WILLIAM R. SHERWOOD

Vassar College

J. B. LIPPINCOTT COMPANY
Philadelphia • New York

Copyright © 1967 by J. B. Lippincott Company
Library of Congress Catalog Card Number: 67–15508
Printed in the United States of America

THE LIPPINCOTT COLLEGE ENGLISH SERIES
Under the editorship of Albert J. Guerard
Stanford University

823.03
B284e

ॐ PREFACE

THE ENGLISH NOVEL: BACKGROUND READINGS, a collection of materials taken from letters, notebooks, reviews, works of literature, and other sources, is intended as supplementary reading in the study of the history of the eighteenth and nineteenth century English novel. We have confined ourselves to selections which are significantly related, in one way or another, to ten novels generally included in standard college courses in this subject: Fielding's *Tom Jones*, Richardson's *Clarissa Harlowe*, Sterne's *Tristram Shandy*, Jane Austen's *Emma*, Scott's *The Heart of Midlothian*, Emily Brontë's *Wuthering Heights*, Thackeray's *Vanity Fair*, Dickens' *Bleak House*, George Eliot's *Middlemarch*, and Hardy's *Jude the Obscure*—a list, we think, which notably represents the range, the variety, and the stages of development of classic English prose fiction.

This anthology, the only one of its kind, has various important uses. Most obviously, it makes accessible to a large number of students materials that either are unavailable at all in most college libraries or, even in the best of libraries, exist in but one or two

55809

copies. In effect, THE ENGLISH NOVEL: BACKGROUND READINGS is a portable library reserve-shelf designed for a specific course and bringing before a student audience many items ordinarily known only to specialists. Because it is a supplementary text, we have not thought it necessary to include the kinds of introductions found in most classroom editions of the novels themselves, and we have assumed that standard biographical information and the facts of publication of these novels are readily and widely available and can be supplied by the instructor to the extent that he wishes. We have likewise refrained from making specific suggestions as to how to use these readings in the classroom. Our purpose is not to pre-empt, even indirectly, the position of the instructor, but simply to supply him with more to teach with and the student with more to learn from.

With this aim in mind, we have deliberately restricted our selections to material from the eighteenth and nineteenth centuries, for we have observed that collections of twentieth-century criticisms, useful as they may be in some respects, do tempt students to substitute the opinions of "authorities" for their own thinking. In addition, we wanted to devote as much space as possible to illustrating the tastes, conventions, and assumptions of the times within which these novels were written. As teachers of this course, we have found that students have particular difficulty understanding and even believing in the existence of opinions about literature that are substantially different from their own. But when confronted with reactions contemporary with the original publication, reactions opposed—sometimes violently—to one another, and opposed, in many cases, to the student's own, the student will, we believe, gain perspective on the particular novel itself, on the period in which it appeared, and, finally, on the expectations which he, as a member of a modern American audience, has brought to it. We also hope that comparing a novelist's statement of his intentions (in cases where such statements are available) with the first critical responses to his work will dramatize for the student that interaction between private artistic purpose and public expectation which is one of the principal concerns of any course in the history of prose fiction. This is not to say, however, that the critical comments collected in this anthology are useful only as historical documents; many of them still have considerable validity in their own right. Moreover, because this course, as we conceive it, is a unified treatment of the development of the novel as a *genre,* we have not limited our selections to the criticisms, favorable or unfavorable, which greeted these novels upon their first appearance but have also included comments by later writers reflecting their awareness of the emergence and growth of a new artistic form and literary tradition. Thus we have Coleridge on Fielding and Sterne, Hazlitt on Richardson, Thackeray on Fielding, George Henry Lewes on Jane Austen, Swinburne on Emily Brontë.

Since the novel is, after all, a work of art, our collection, in addition to illustrating changes in literary theory and public preference, contains a variety of materials chosen to help the student to appreciate the workings of the creative imagination, including the ways in which the novelist makes use of history and literature as well as daily experience and the ways in which he comes to terms with the practical demands of editing and publishing. Some of the items that will serve this purpose are comments by the novelists themselves on the intentions and reception of their work—such as Richardson's on *Clarissa* and Hardy's on *Jude the Obscure.* Others are excerpts from notes and plans—such as Dickens' for *Bleak House* and George Eliot's for *Middlemarch.* Still others are historical and literary "sources"—such as portions of the record of William Maclauchlane's trial, for *The Heart of Midlothian;* "The Bridegroom of Barna," for *Wuthering Heights;* and Gleig's *Story of the Battle of Waterloo,* for *Vanity Fair.*

It is only honest to admit that in some cases one simply cannot find as much of certain kinds of material as could usefully be included in a collection such as this one. In other cases, where material is abundant, much that might have been included has had to be omitted because of limitations of space. The verbosity of some writers has been a problem, for if one cuts out too much of a review, for instance, one is in danger of losing not only a desirable "period" flavor but also valuable subtleties. While some of our selections are necessarily short—extracts from letters, for instance—we have tried to avoid scrappiness. In the space at our command, we have attempted to achieve as much variety as possible; on the other hand, we have had to keep in mind the demands of context. Our goals have been range and relevance. If we have reached them, THE ENGLISH NOVEL: BACKGROUND READINGS will provide opportunity for teachers of the history of English fiction to exercise their ingenuity and their imagination in any number of ways.

We should like to express our gratitude to Vassar College for the extensive use we were permitted to make of Vassar's facilities in doing the research for this book. We owe a particular debt to the members of the staff of the Vassar College Library for all the services which they rendered so cheerfully and competently. Our demands upon them were great, but we were never made to feel so, and the hard work which they did made our own work much easier than it might have been. To the various publishers who gave us permission to use copyrighted materials we also offer general thanks; individual acknowledgments appear at appropriate places in the body of the book.

L.C.B.
W.R.S.

❦ CONTENTS

❦ Henry Fielding
Tom Jones • 1749

Samuel Richardson
Clarissa Harlowe · 1748

Laurence Sterne
Tristram Shandy · 1767

Jane Austen
Emma · 1815

Sir Walter Scott
The Heart of Midlothian · 1818

Emily Bronte
Wuthering Heights · 1847

William Makepeace Thackeray
Vanity Fair · 1848

Charles Dickens
Bleak House · 1853

George Eliot
Middlemarch · 1871–72

Thomas Hardy
Jude the Obscure · 1895

Henry Fielding
Tom Jones
1749

1 Thomas Cawthorn

"To Henry Fielding Esq. on Reading His Inimitable History of *Tom Jones*," *Gentleman's Magazine*, August, 1749[1]

—neque
Si charae fileant, quod bene feceris,
Mercedem tuleris.

Hor. Lib. IV. Ode VIII

Long, thro' the mimic scenes of motly life,
Neglected *Nature* lost th' unequal strife;
Studious to show, in mad, fantastic shape,
Each grinning gesture of his kindred ape,
Man lost the name: while each, in artful dress,
Appear'd still something more or something less:

1. Vol. XIX, p. 371.

Virtue and vice, unmix'd, in fancy stood,
And all were vilely bad, or greatly good;
Eternal distance ever made to keep,
Exciting horrour, or promoting sleep:
    Sick of her fools, great *Nature* broke the jest,
And *Truth* held out each character to test,
When *Genius* spoke: Let *Fielding* take the pen!
Life dropt her mask, and all mankind were men.

2 *Samuel Taylor Coleridge*

FROM "Table Talk,"[1] July 5, 1834

What a master of composition Fielding was! Upon my word, I think the Oedipus Tyrannus, the Alchemist, and Tom Jones, the three most perfect plots ever planned. And how charming, how wholesome, Fielding always is! To take him up after Richardson, is like emerging from a sick room heated by stoves, into an open lawn, on a breezy day in May.

3 *Samuel Richardson*

FROM A Letter to Aaron Hill, July 12, 1749[2]

While the Taste of the Age can be gratified by a Tom Jones (Dear Sir, have you read Tom Jones?) I am not to expect that the World will bestow two Readings, or one indeed attentive one, on such a grave Story as Clarissa, which is designed to make those think of Death, who endeavour all they can to banish it from their

1. Reprinted, by permission of the editor, from Thomas Middleton Raysor, ed., *Coleridge's Miscellaneous Criticism,* London: Constable, 1936, p. 437.
2. Reprinted, by permission of the publisher from Alan Dougald McKillop, *Samuel Richardson, Printer and Novelist,* Chapel Hill: The University of North Carolina Press, 1936, p. 172.

Thoughts. I have found neither Leisure nor Inclination yet to read that Piece, and the less Inclination, as several good Judges of my Acquaintance condemn it and the general Taste together. I could wish to know the Sentiments of your Ladies upon it. If favourable they would induce me to open the Six Volumes; the rather, as they will be so soon read.

FROM A Letter to Astrea and Minerva Hill, August 4, 1749[1]

I must confess, that I have been prejudiced by the Opinion of Several judicious Friends against the truly coarse-titled Tom Jones: and so have been discouraged from reading it.—I was told, that it was a rambling Collection of Waking Dreams, in which Probability was not observed: And that it had a very bad Tendency. And I had Reason to think that the Author intended for his Second View (His *first*, to fill his Pocket, by accommodating it to the reigning Taste) in writing it, to whiten a vicious Character, and to make Morality bend to his Practices. What Reason had he to make his Tom illegitimate, in an Age when Keeping is become a Fashion? Why did he make him a common—What shall I call it? And a Kept Fellow, the Lowest of all Fellows, yet in Love With a Young Creature who was trapsing after him, a Fugitive from her Father's House?—Why did he draw his Heroine so fond, so foolish, and so insipid?—Indeed he has one Excuse—he knows not how to draw a delicate Woman—he has not been accustomed to such Company—And is too prescribing, too impetuous, too immoral, I will venture to say, to take any other Byass than that a perverse and cooked Nature has given him; or Evil Habits, at least, have confirm'd in him. Do Men expect Grapes of Thorns, and Figs of Thistles? But, perhaps, I think the worse of the Piece because I know the Writer, and dislike his Principles both Public and Private, tho' I wish well to the *Man*, and Love Four worthy Sisters of his with whom I am well acquainted. And indeed should admire him, did he make the Use of his Talents which I wish him to make; For the Vein of Humour, and Ridicule, which he is

1. Ibid, pp. 172–173.

Master of, might, if properly turned, do great Service to ye Cause of
Virtue.

4 Lady Bradsheigh

FROM Letters to Samuel Richardson[1]

(December 16, 1749)

The character of Sophia is so very trifling and insipid, that I
never heard a dispute about it.

The girls are certainly fond of Tom Jones, as I told you before,
and they do not scruple declaring it in the company of your incog-
nita; for, alas! I am no awful body to them; they just say the same
before me as if I were but twenty; tho' I give you my word, I never
let a faulty word or action pass me without a visible disapprobation;
and many a round battle have I had with them concerning Tom
Jones, as soft and as gentle as you seem to think my blame; and you
repeat my pretty words with a sort of contempt. Now, if you would
only lay a little stronger emphasis upon those words, you would
not find them so gentle; at least, I did not mean them to be so;
for I designed the condemnation strongly from my heart.

* * *

(undated)

As to Tom Jones, I am fatigued with the name, having lately
fallen into the company of several young ladies, who had each a
Tom Jones in some part of the world, for so they call their favourites; and ladies, you know, are for ever talking of their

1. Reprinted from Anna L. Barbauld, ed., *The Correspondence of Samuel Richardson,* London: R. Phillips, 1804, vol. IV, pp. 280–281, 295–296.

favourites. Last post I received a letter from a lady, who laments the loss of her Tom Jones; and from another, who was happy in the company of her Tom Jones. In like manner, the gentlemen have their Sophias. A few days ago, in a circle of gentlemen and ladies, who had their Tom Jones's and their Sophias, a friend of mine told me he must shew me his Sophia, the sweetest creature in the world, and immediately produced a Dutch mastiff puppy.

5 *Lady Mary Wortley Montague*

FROM A Letter to the Countess of Bute, July or August 23, 1755[1]

H. Fielding has given a true picture of himself and his first wife, in the characters of Mr. and Mrs. Booth,[2] some compliments to his own figure excepted; and, I am persuaded, several of the incidents he mentions are real matters of fact. I wonder he does not perceive Tom Jones and Mr. Booth are sorry scoundrels. All these sort of books have the same fault, which I cannot easily pardon, being very mischievous. They place a merit in extravagant passions, and encourage young people to hope for impossible events, to draw them out of the misery they chose to plunge themselves into, expecting legacies from unknown relations, and generous benefactors to distressed virtue, as much out of nature as fairy treasures. Fielding has really a fund of true humour, and was to be pitied at his first entrance into the world, having no choice, as he said himself, but to be a hackney writer, or a hackney coachman. His genius deserved a better fate; but I cannot help blaming that continued indiscretion, to give it the softest name, that has run through his life, and I am afraid still remains.

1. Reprinted from Lord Wharncliff and W. Moy Thomas, eds., *The Letters and Works of Lady Mary Wortley Montague,* London: George Bell and Sons, 1887, vol. II, p. 289.
2. Characters from Fielding's *Amelia*.

6 Samuel Johnson & James Boswell

FROM *Boswell's Life of Johnson*[1]

(Spring, 1768)

'Sir, (continued he,) there is all the difference in the world between characters of nature and characters of manners; and *there* is the difference between the characters of Fielding and those of Richardson. Characters of manners are very entertaining; but they are to be understood, by a more superficial observer, than characters of nature, where a man must dive into the recesses of the human heart.'

It always appeared to me that he estimated the compositions of Richardson too highly, and that he had an unreasonable prejudice against Fielding. In comparing those two writers, he used this expression; 'that there was as great a difference between them as between a man who knew how a watch was made, and a man who could tell the hour by looking on the dial-plate.' This was a short and figurative state of his distinction between drawing characters of nature and characters only of manners. But I cannot help being of opinion, that the neat watches of Fielding are as well constructed as the large clocks of Richardson, and that his dial-plates are brighter. Fielding's characters, though they do not expand themselves so widely in dissertation, are as just pictures of human nature, and I will venture to say, have more striking features, and nicer touches of the pencil; and though Johnson used to quote with approbation a saying of Richardson's, 'that the virtues of Fielding's heroes were the vices of a truly good man,' I will venture to add, that the moral tendency of Fielding's writings, though it does not encourage a strained and rarely possible virtue, is ever favourable to honour and honesty, and cherishes the benevolent and generous affections. He who is as good as Fielding would make him, is an amiable member of society, and may be led on by more regulated instructors, to a higher state of ethical perfection.

* * *

1. Reprinted from G. B. Hill, ed., as revised by L. F. Powell, *Boswell's Life of Johnson*, London: Clarendon Press, 1934, vol. II, pp. 48–49, 173–175.

(April 6, 1772)

Fielding being mentioned, Johnson exclaimed, 'he was a blockhead;' and upon my expressing my astonishment at so strange an assertion, he said, 'What I mean by his being a blockhead is that he was a barren rascal.' BOSWELL. 'Will you not allow, Sir, that he draws very natural pictures of human life?' JOHNSON. 'Why, Sir, it is of very low life. Richardson used to say, that had he not known who Fielding was, he should have believed he was an ostler. Sir, there is more knowledge of the heart in one letter of Richardson's, than in all "Tom Jones." I, indeed, never read "Joseph Andrews"'. ERSKINE, 'Surely, Sir, Richardson is very tedious.' JOHNSON. 'Why, Sir, if you were to read Richardson for the story, your impatience would be so much fretted that you would hang yourself. But you must read him for the sentiment, and consider the story as only giving occasion to the sentiment.'—I have already given my opinion of Fielding; but I cannot refrain from repeating here my wonder at Johnson's excessive and unaccountable depreciation of one of the best writers that England has produced. "Tom Jones" has stood the test of publick opinion with such success, as to have established its great merit, both for the story, the sentiments, and the manners, and also the varieties of diction, so as to leave no doubt of its having an animated truth of execution throughout.

 7

FROM "A Literary Article from Paris," *Gentleman's Magazine,* March, 1750[1]

A LITERARY ARTICLE FROM PARIS.

Histoire de Tom Jones, *ou* L' Enfant *trouvé;* the History of *T. Jones,* or the *Foundling,* translated into *French* by M. *de la Place,* and adorned with cuts designed by M. *Gravelot.*

If we believe the epistle dedicatory addressed to a commissioner

1. Vol. XX, pp. 117–118.

of the *British* treasury *(George Lyttelton,* Esq;) "The strictest regard to religion and virtue has been observed throughout the whole course of this history, and the reader will find nothing in it contrary to the severest rules of decency, or offensive to the most tender imagination*." We must here suppose that, by *virtue,* M. *Fielding* would not have us understand a rigorous observation of all the precepts in the christian system of morality, but only the practice of the principal offices of justice and humanity; otherwise the loose manners of his heroe might give occasion to upbraid the author with neglecting to fulfil exactly the first of his promises. And that we may have room to discharge him from the breach of the last, it is necessary to imagine yourself transported to the country where the scene is laid. In *France* the ladies would be shock'd at the repeated breaches of faith in *Tom Jones* to his mistress, and fathers and mothers would exclaim against that resolute boldness with which *Miss Western* abandons her father's house to preserve herself inviolate to her lover. In *England* they are not so rigorous; every father and mother indeed, in *London* as well as *Paris,* would be glad to have their children perfectly obedient to their will; but the love of liberty in the *English,* renders them generally more disposed to forgive the disobedience of a daughter, when her obedience might make her miserable. Inconstancy in a lover, will no more be pardon'd by an *English* than a *French* woman, but the first will sooner pass by a slight neglect; in general, the *English* ladies are more jealous of a man's sentiments, the *French* of his actions. M. *de la Place,* the translator of this piece, would have done well perhaps to have inserted these remarks, which we have ventur'd to make, in his *preliminary discourse,* in order to prevent those objections which some cavillers might make against M. *Fielding.*

A synopsis of so long a series of events as the history of *Tom Jones,* would take up too much room in this collection; we shall therefore only endeavour to shew the merit of this ingenious work of imagination. The public has not for a long time been entertain'd

---

* "The *English* editor says,—*From the name of my patron,* I hope my reader will be convinced, at his very entrance on this work, that he will find in the whole course of it nothing prejudicial to the cause of religion and virtue; nothing inconsistent with the strictest rules of decency, nor which can offend even the chastest eye in the perusal, On the contrary, I declare, that to recommend goodness and innocence hath been my sincere endeavour in this history."

with a piece where the principal persons are more engaging or more interesting, the episodes better connected with the principal action, the characters more equally sustained, the incidents more artfully prepared, or more naturally arising one out of another. Miss *Western* is a truly admirable character; *Tom Jones*, as much a libertine as he is, engages all sensible hearts by his candor, generosity, humanity, his gratitude to his benefactors, his tender compassion, and readiness to assist the distressed. The name of *Allworthy*, which in *English* signifies *supereminently good*, could never be more justly bestow'd than on the respectable uncle of *Jones*. The character of *Blifil*, in opposition to that of the *Foundling*, presents us with an admirable contrast, and is dress'd up with singular art. The author has employ'd no less skill about his other characters, in assigning to every one his station and business, so that, among so great a number, they all, except one, appear necessary to the action. *Sancho Pancho* was the original by which M. *Fielding* drew his *Partridge*, who indeed is not so entertaining as the 'Squire of *Don Quixote*, but however cannot fail of pleasing an *English* taste.

Whether the author's imitating the manner of *Cervantes, Scarron*, and *le Sage*, in the titles of his chapters, is approved by his countrymen, we cannot say; but if we may give our opinion, how proper soever it seems in works of fancy designed for delight and amusement, it is altogether as improper in a piece whose principal design is interesting and instructive.

8 Orbilius [*pseudonym*]

FROM *An Examen of the History of Tom Jones, a Foundling*, 1750[1]

INTRODUCTION

The Task of examining Mr. *F*.'s late celebrated Performance, called *The History of a Foundling*, chiefly with a View to Morals,

1. London: printed for W. Owen near Temple-Bar, 1750, pp. 1–5, 7–9, 23–25, 27–28, 36, 43–44, 46, 51, 53–54, 61–64, 73–76, 88–94, 111–112, 118–119.

at your Request, I willingly undertake. But as, in attending my Author in every Stage, and through every Inn he drives to (where I shall at least be sure of good Chear), I foresee that I shall be obliged to run to some Length, I will not take up your Time by a longer Introduction. . . .

The present Work, it seems, is the *Labour of some Years*. Can that be? *Some Years* about such a Performance as *Tom Jones!*—We all took Mr. *F.* to be endowed with quicker Parts than this *Labour of his Brain* warrants our ascribing to him; since, instead of a *Minerva*, he has only been delivered of her *Owl*. If a Man presents his Readers with his *Dreams*, need he take up *Years* in telling them? *John Bunyan* perform'd, as it seems, a Work infinitely superior and more useful, with much greater Ease. And *John Bunyan's* Performance was a Work of Genius: But *John Bunyan was* a Genius, though a grave one. Mr. *F.* on the contrary, is so volatile, that I dare say he never pursued any one thing for a Year together; much less such a *skipping* Work as this before us; which, though it comprehends an unmeasurable Length of Time, need not have cost much in writing, if we may guess by the Correctness of the Style. *John Dryden*, otherwise an incomparable Writer, boasted of his having produced a bad Play in a Fortnight: Mr. *F.* more inconsistently, of having spent *some Years* (which others may enterpret *many*) in corrupting Youth, *i. e.* in writing *Tom Jones*. Yet *the Reader*, Mr. *F* tells us, will find *nothing in the whole Course* of his Performance, *prejudicial to the Cause of* RELIGION *and* VIRTUE: *Nothing inconsistent with the* STRICTEST RULES *of* DECENCY; that is, according to Mr. *F.*'s Notions of Decency, we may presume; *nor which can offend even the* CHASTEST *Eye in the Perusal.*—TO RECOMMEND GOODNESS AND INNOCENCE, HATH BEEN the Author's SINCERE ENDEAVOUR IN THIS HISTORY. How unhappy, if he should fail in an Endeavour *so sincere!* . . .

Tom Jones, then, the spurious or misbegotten Issue of Miss *Bridget Allworthy*, and dropt by that Lady in her Brother Mr. *Allworthy's* Bed, is by this Gentleman, in order, I suppose, to illustrate his Prudence, as well as Morality, educated in so *genteel*, or rather loose a Manner, between the contrary Disciplines of the rigid Churchman Mr. *Thwackum*, and the Moral Philosopher Mr. *Square*, as gives an unhappy Prognostic of his future Follies and Vices;

since a Man, who in his Youth has not had the Advantage of some settled Principles of Religion, rarely settles himself afterwards in right Principles or Practices (who better than our Author should have known that?) This being the Case, it is no Wonder that *Tom* scarce finds himself released from the too slack Government under which he had been educated, but he plunges into every Debauchery. Add to this, That *Allworthy,* though a Man of Virtue himself, had not the Prudence to instill into his vicious Foster-Son a Remembrance of his disadvantageous Birth, which might have restrained him from many Enormities; nor even to give him any Employment, which might teach him, that he was not born merely to gratify his natural Propensity, which led him headlong into an early Commerce with Women. . . .

Sophia herself is with great Pomp introduced to the Veneration of the Reader for her Modesty, and other good Qualities; but as it is certain, that Mr. *F.* is utterly unable (as we see in all his Pieces, but most flagrantly in this) to draw a Woman of true Virtue and Modesty; so in nothing is she so illustrious as in her Partiality to the well-known Debaucheries of *Jones,* and in her Elopement from her Father's House, on Pretence of avoiding a disgustful Match with *Blifil,* the legitimate Son of *Allworthy's* Sister, which nevertheless she had no just Ground to fear, as we shall hereafter shew. . . .

And now arrives the Time, when our Author, being at a Loss to contrive Ways and Means to raise the Character of his Hero, since he could not in Merit, and would not at *Tyburn,* reconciles him to *Allworthy* by the Means before mentioned; *Allworthy* reconciles him to *Sophia;* and the Fiddles strike up (not without the Melody of Marrow-bones and Cleavers, we presume) to the Joy of every Fortune-hunter and rathe-ripe Virgin in the Kingdom.

[There follows a meticulous chapter-by-chapter analysis of *Tom Jones,* sections of which are given below.]

BOOK ONE

CHAPTER I. Mr. *F.*'s *Ordinary,* unless we should unhappily choose *another,* or a *better,* if such there *can* be ; and if we must be forced to *d—n our French and Italian Hashes and Ragoûts;* which our Author inconsistently dignifies by saying, that they are *no other than* HUMAN NATURE. But what then is Nature? It is indeed the *Nature* of a HOG to wallow in the Mire, and to lick up all the Filth he can any-where meet with : And perhaps this is also the *Nature* of *some Authors.* But, for the Honour of the Creator, as well as of the Creature, let us not suppose this to be HUMAN NATURE in the Abstract. Mr. *F.* indeed acknowledges, that *true Nature is as difficult to be met with in Authors, as the Bayonne-Ham, or Bologna Sausage* [by which Similes he seems to be a Person of most exquisite Relish] *is to be found in the Shops;* and of this we shall see that he has given almost as many Instances as Chapters.

CHAPTER III. Mrs. *Deborah Wilkins* is introduced, doing the first Offices to our filthy Author's stinking Hero: *Faugh! how it stinks!* saith *she* here, as I doubt the Reader will say hereafter. *It doth not smell like a Christian,* adds *Deborah.* But if this fetid Foundling *maketh* no worse a Figure in the rest of the Book, than he *now* doth, bad, however, as that is, he may, for aught I know, prove a very innocent Person. If he *doth* not now *smell like a Christian,* how will he smell hereafter?

CHAPTER VII. ... But here follows what I have much greater Objections to, as it overthrows a moral Doctrine of the highest Importance, relating to Friendship: The Author tells us, That "Men of *true Wisdom* and *Goodness* are contented to take Persons and Things as they are, without complaining of their Imperfections, or attempting to *amend* them." Heavens! Is it not then the Part of Humanity, as well as of Friendship, to take notice of the Imperfections of those with whom we converse, in order to their Amendment? The contrary Practice ought to be branded with the Name of vile Dissimulation, Flattery, or Cowardice.

... I think it is now clear, that, far from admitting our Author's Rule, which would only encourage a supine Continuance in Vice, and weaken all Attempts of Reformation, we ought to conclude, that we are NOT *to take Persons and Things as they are;* but strive, with the quickest Eye, and the warmest Zeal, to observe and amend the *Imperfections* of both. "Forgiveness of Faults," adds Mr. *F.* "we must bestow without DESIRE of Amendment." If so, we should very plainly demonstrate, that we had no Concern at all

about them: Which, instead of true Friendship, is the utmost
Cruelty to those we pretend to love.

BOOK TWO

CHAPTER III. There are Plenty of *Squares* in this Land of
Liberty, who by their perpetually applying the Cant Terms, *un-
alterable Rule of Right,* and *eternal Fitness of Things,* have almost
disputed both Right and Fitness out of the world. The Sceptical
Manner, in which these Gentlemen argue, is exposed in their own
Language: But I am persuaded we must agree with *Thwackum,* not
only in holding the Necessity of chastising young *Tom,* but also in
maintaining (as we are well warranted by Revelation, and by a strict
Scrutiny into the Propensities of our own Hearts), *that the human
Mind, since the Fall, is nothing but a Sink of Iniquity, till purified
and redeemed by Grace;* as also, that there is no *true Honour* without *Religion;* or rather, that these are convertible Terms. Those
groundless Notions of the natural Generosity of the human Mind,
and the Love of Virtue for its own Sake, are owing to too careless
an Inspection into human Nature. And therefore I am surprised,
that a Person who pretends to have studied it, and to have given us
a Picture of Nature, as it were, *in puris Naturalibus,* has not
enough weighed the above Points, which are the Foundation of all
Morality.

BOOK FOUR

CHAPTER V. The Relation of *Tom Jones's* obstinate Lye, and
his Heroism in suffering for *Black George,* is so extremely prevalent
with *Sophia,* that, for no other Reason whatever, she makes him a
present of her Heart. A worthy Example to young Ladies in the like
Situation! We are here a second time informed (as we had been
in the last Chapter of the preceding Book) that Tom *was become
a great Favourite of the 'Squire.* And the Behaviour of *Sophia*
(far from any Discouragement to the Hero, which one would have
expected from this delicate Interview) shews him to be as great a
Favourite of the Daughter, as Libertines generally are with *sprightly*
Ladies, of which Class *Sophia* was. But that her *Sprightliness* should
increase whenever she was in Company with Tom, was a Demonstra-
tion, not of her *Modesty,* for which she is celebrated by our Author ;

nor of her Love, which, if not of the lowest Sort, would surely at first have been reserved, ceremonious, and fearful; but of her Giddiness and Precipitancy, . . .

BOOK FIVE

CHAPTER I. . . . whose [Fielding's] last Question is "Hath any one living attempted to explain what the modern Judges of our Theatres mean by the Word *low?*" Mr. *F* can best explain it, and seems to be conscious how fitly it has been applied to his Works. But his Question may be further answer'd by informing him, that *low* Characters are those in which Nature is degraded beneath the Standard at which it of right ought to be placed, by making them too much, or too little, what they should be; some Examples of which we have given, and are afraid, in the Course of this our laborious Criticism, of being able to give many more. . . .

The Critics have in this Chapter incurred our Author's heavy Displeasure: And natural it is, that they should: For does not the Culprit hate the Sight of a Judge? The Questions put by him I, as *Clerk* to the Court of Criticism, have answered: And tho' the Author should *unfortunately not be able to see* the Validity of the Reasons given, this ought not to avail in Arrest of Judgment, since, if the Court is satisfied, the Prisoner may be as blind as Mr *F*.'s Blind Man *in likening* Bombast *and* Fustian *to the Sound of a Trumpet;* and yet Sentence be given agreeable to Justice.

CHAPTER IV. The *little Incident* of the Muff, on which Mrs *Honour,* or the Author, so profusely wantons, is at the same time a *great* one against *Sophia*'s Delicacy, who could value it the more for Mr. *Jones*'s egregious fooling with it; and conveys to young Gentlemen and Ladies admirable Instructions in the Art of Toying. But whether these Instructions contain *nothing inconsistent with the strictest Rules of Decency,* according to the Author's early Declaration, must be left to the *chaste Eye* of the Reader, and need not be further dwelt upon here.

BOOK SIX

CHAPTER I. That there are *such things as Virtue and Goodness really existing in human Nature,* I agree with the Author; supposing he understands uncorrupted Nature; since we are told by an Apostle, that *the* Gentiles, *which have not the Law, do by* NATURE *the things contained in the Law* (Rom. ii. 14.). But if he only means by *Nature*, what he has described in several Parts of this Performance, most of his intelligent Readers, I believe, will be tempted to doubt, whether his *Nature* will not be found to be the same with what himself calls in the same Paragraph A BAD MIND, from which both Virtue and Goodness must of course be excluded.

CHAPTER IV. This calm Villain *Blifil* may have all the ill Qualities ascribed to him: But how is it, that one more Vice was not added to the rest, I mean that, which Mr. *F.* had called *Hungering after Women*, Chap. I. of this Book? to which he had such Excitements in the Beauty of *Sophia*. The Author paints him as without Desires of this Sort; which how he will make agreeable to Nature, I know not. He seems indeed to have this cold Temper allotted to him, to detract from the Value of the Virtue of Chastity, by representing it only as constitutional; which is the Character of an Eunuch; and the contrary Vice to be so largely distributed to *Jones*, to advance in like manner the Credit of Incontinence, which few, besides our Author, will think at too low an Ebb in this Age and Nation.

CHAPTER V. "I Know none with such Perfections," says Miss *Western* to her Aunt, meaning Mr. *Jones*. "So brave, and yet so gentle; so *witty*, yet so *inoffensive;* so *humane*, so *civil*, so genteel, so handsome." Of his *Wit* we have heard little as yet; of his *Inoffensiveness* less. Let *Blifil* answer for his *Civility*, whom Mr. *Jones* d—ns for a Rascal, Book V. Chap. IX. and his Schoolmaster *Thwackum* for his *Humanity*, whom he insults, and leaves for dead, Chap. XI. of the same Book, to screen himself, and his Partner, in their infamous Commerce. Yet in the Author's Judgment, as well as in *Sophia*'s, who cannot be thought *Recta in Curia*, "balancing his Faults with his Perfections, the latter seemed rather to preponderate," Book IV. Chap. XI. In the same Chapter the Author says, *he was no hardened Sinner:* Which will be seen as the Story proceeds, by observing whether he meets with any Temptation which he overcomes.

CHAPTER VI. What an idle loitering Fellow is this *Jones!* No less than two Hours at the Canal! Ought not Mr. *Allworthy* in common Prudence, as he was cast upon him in the Sport of Fortune, and entertained by him on a Principle of Humanity, to have endeavoured to make him an useful Member of the Community, rather than by an unrestrained Liberty to have laid him open to the Assaults of every Vice, which usually attacks those who are not employed in some serious Occupation, with Success?

BOOK NINE.

CHAPTER I. Ominous surely was Mr. *F.*'s Prophecy concerning *foolish Novels, and monstrous Romances,* which are to be *produced —— to the great Loss of Time, and Depravation of Morals in the Reader.* And never was human Oracle better fulfilled, than in the present Work, especially when we consider, that tho' Mr. *F.* requires in his Historian, that his *Conversation* must be *universal,* yet he himself is far better skilled in the Manners of the *inferior Part of Mankind,* than he is in those of the *superior:* As will be abundantly manifest, not only in the Sequel of this Book, but almost in every Page of the Work.

CHAPTER II. Mr. *F.* in summing up the Qualifications which make a Man look like an Angel, has unhappily forgot that only Ingredient which constitutes the Essence of an Angel, as far as the Nature of those glorious Beings can be made known to us: This is, VIRTUE. As to *Person, Features, Youth, Health, Strength, Freshness, Spirit,* and *Good-nature* in the popular Sense, some of these are ridiculous, when applied to Angels; and they were all possessed perhaps in as eminent a Degree by Captain *Macheath,* as by our Hero. Yet Captain *Macheath*'s Author was not so conceited as to imagine his infamous Hero resembled one of that beatified Order, who *Are happier than Mankind, because they're better* — But, with the strictest Poetical Justice, dooms him to Death for his Villainies, tho' the Royal Mercy interposes to save the Criminal, and prevent the Damnation of Mr. *Gay*'s Comic Opera. And whoever compares that Opera (bad as it is) with Mr. *F.*'s Production, will find the former infinitely surpass the latter in Morality, as well as in *all* that *Wit and Humour,* with which our Author supposes he hath cloathed his dirty Characters, purely with a Design to conceal their Turpitude from the Eye of the less discerning Reader.

CHAPTER V. Three times are we told of Mr. *Jones*'s Good-nature: 1st, *His Face shewed most apparent Marks of Good-nature.*

2dly, In the same Paragraph, *Good-nature was strongly painted in his Look*. 3dly, In the next, He was *good-humoured*. In the former Paragraph, His Face was *the Picture of Health:* In the latter, he had a very fine *Complexion*. Why this Redundancy of Ornament, but to shew the Power of his Charms over the infamous Mrs. *Waters?* But in what Degree does all this advance any of his mental Accomplishments? Good-nature may be owing to his *Flow of animal Spirits:* And is more conspicuous in the Rake, and jolly Debauchee, who, as the Phrase is, are nobody's Enemies but their own, than in the Man of strict Sobriety and Virtue; tho', in the genuine Fruits of Good-nature, the latter always excels the former. *Here,* says Mr. *F.* after drawing *Jones's* and Mrs. *Waters's* detestable Impurity, *the Graces think proper to end their Description*. And well it was for them, that so they did; otherwise they were no longer *Graces,* but those obscene Birds the *Harpyes;* and, notwithstanding Mr. *F.* thinks such Transmutations improbable, as not well relishing a plain Allegory, would have squirted their Ordure in the Faces of every modest Reader. But let Mr. *F.* be warned by this to take heed of dancing on the Edge of a Precipice; in other Words, that his Readers, by his loose Descriptions, be not tempted to peep behind the Curtain.

BOOK ELEVEN

CHAPTER I. If modern Critics are to be represented as *common Slanderers of the Reputation of Books,* let it be observed, on the other side, that there are certain Books which have no Reputation to lose, against which therefore no Slander can militate. Such Books, I mean, as paint modern Vices as if they were Peccadilloes; and by that means endeavour to overthrow the Boundaries of Virtue and Vice. Whether the present Work will come under this Predicament, is apparent to the Reader, from what has been already said. . . . I agree, that "to depreciate a Book maliciously, or even wantonly, is —an ill-natured Office; and a morose, snarling Critic may—be suspected to be a bad Man." But, with regard to my elaborate Endeavours to expose the Author's Morality, Wit, and Religious Principles, I am not conscious of any-thing but of having strictly followed the Advice of the critical, but not ill-natured Mr. *Addison,* who, in *Spect.* Vol. VI. No. 445. says, "For my own part, I have endeavoured to make nothing ridiculous, that is not in some measure criminal. I have set up the immoral Man as the Object of Derision: In short, if I have not formed a new Weapon against Vice and Irreligion, I have at least shewn how that Weapon may be put to a right Use, which has *so often fought the Battles of Impiety and Profaneness.*"

CHAPTERS IV. V. VI. VII. I Shall, as before, with regard to the *Man of the Hill,* throw Mrs. *Fitzpatrick*'s History into one View. Weak she was by her own Acknowledgement: but she had little Reason to be angry with her Husband for preferring his own Seat to *dirty Lodgings at* Bath: Less, to *despise* him for living in an hospitable manner with the neighbouring Gentlemen. If he was *surly,* she ought to have ascribed this to her own discontented Temper; and not to have arraigned him for *maintaining a constant Lye* in his Actions abroad, when compared to his Behaviour at home. On the contrary, that Temper, in which a Man spends most of his Hours, ought to denominate his Character, not *vice versa;* especially since so good a Reason might be given for the Change. But Mrs. *Fitzpatrick,* had she known her Cousin's Story, might easily have retorted upon her, instead of her Question, "Why, why, would you marry an *Irishman?*" in the last of these Chapters, the following just Reproof, "Why, why, would you marry a Whoremaster, and a Vagabond?"

BOOK THIRTEEN

CHAPTER VIII. Fifty Pounds given to *Jones* for his Gallantry is a most excellent Instance of *Christian Charity! Jones*'s indeed to *Anderson* is praiseworthy. But this impudent Quality-Whore's is beneath Censure. Can anything be more odious, than for a Woman of Figure to divest herself of her Dignity for a vile Satisfaction, and heap on her Partner in Guilt so ample a Reward of his Baseness? Where is Female Decency, that seeks to be courted, even when its own Inclination forwards the Courtship? Can any *English* Lady of Quality be so gross a Sensualist?—Perhaps she may: But is this corrupted Scene to be called Nature? And shall an Author glory in describing the Jakes of an human Mind, and say that he drew his Character from the *original Book of Nature,* as he expresses himself Book VII. Chap. XII.? Ought he not rather to conclude with *Thwackum,* Book III. Chap. III. *that the human Mind; since the Fall, is nothing but a Sink of Iniquity?* Now then is the Time that the worthy Mr. *Jones* is *Right Honourably* taken into Keeping: In which he will make as illustrious a Figure as any-where else in this Work.

CHAPTER X. That so great a Voluptuary as Mr. *Jones* should be alternately committing Acts of Debauchery, and tasting, by conferring, the Pleasures of Beneficence (which he does in this Chapter by leaving his Beneficiary, to attend the Call of the infamous Lady *Bellaston*), is an Inconsistency in Character never before heard of. To *earn the Wages of Iniquity,* in order with those Wages to merit Heaven by Acts of disinterested Beneficence, may qualify him indeed for a Place in the *Roman* Calendar of Saints, but in no other Chair of Beatification, I doubt. And Mr. *F.* must certainly have searched the Breviary to find so mixt a Character, where Instances of Oddity are easily to be met with, which, in any less grave Book, might perhaps pass for Instances of Humour also.

CHAPTER XI. The apropos Distinction of the *Heart* being absent from the rest of the Body in that prompt Apology of *Jones* for his unfaithful Behaviour at *Upton* ("My *Heart* was never unfaithful to you: *That* had no Share in the Folly I was guilty of") is an Apology which might be made with equal Justice by the most abandoned Libertine that ever haunted the Purlieus of *Drury-Lane* or *Covent-Garden.* They must all therefore be excused alike: And a Lady of Honour, who has once assured herself of her Lover's *Heart,* never need be concerned for what becomes of the rest of his Body. This is Doctrine fit to be preached to the *Grand Turk*'s favourite Sultana: But dismal will be the Condition of this Island, and its dazling Beauties, who might rival any of the Gems of the Orient, when it comes to be endured here. But why say I, *endured?* Is it not more than this already? Is it not liked, applauded, devoured? *O Tempora! O Mores!* If this is admired, then may also *Sophia's* yielding and foolishly fond Behaviour in this Scene (not resenting *Jones*'s Infidelity, but only her being made a Talk in Inns) be applauded too.

BOOK FOURTEEN

CHAPTER I. After a long Repetition of the Doctrine already laid down in several of these initial Chapters, concerning the Learning necessary in writing a History *of the comic Class,* our Author advances a Proposition or two, which I shall beg leave to controvert. "There is not," says he, "a greater Error, than that which universally prevails among the VULGAR, who, borrowing their Opinion from some *ignorant Satirists,* have affixed the Character of Lewdness to these Times." As I am one of the *Vulgar,* whom the Author here condemns, I shall endeavour to support the Opinion of my Brethren, not by a long Train of Reasoning (which it is not in the Power of the *Vulgar* to comprehend), but from this single Consideration; That, were not the prevailing Character of this Age *Lewdness,* Mr. *F.* would never have found Readers enough in high Life to take off his numerous Editions of the present Work; in which if Lewdness doth not prevail, neither doth it in this Age and Nation. And upon this I rest the Issue of the Cause. . . . Therefore we must, I am afraid, agree with the aforesaid *Vulgar,* that Lewdness is indisputably *the Character of these Times.* And therefore our Author's Conclusion must also be false; and, inverted, ought to run thus: That "the true Characteristic of the present *Beau Monde* is *Vice* as well as *Folly;* and the Epithet which it deserves is not only that of *Frivolous,* but that of equally *vain* and *vicious.*"

CHAPTER IV. "I have been guilty with Women," says *Jones;* "but am not conscious, that I have ever *injured* any." What Sophistry is this! Is it not the greatest Injury Men can do to their Fellow-creatures, either to incite or consent to Acts of Wickedness? Is not the Soul (If there is a Futurity!) equally endangered by both? And can the Soul be at all endangered, where there is no sort of Injury committed? Let Mr. *F.* solve these Theses, *in Foro Conscientiæ,* and then I will acknowlege, that Mr. *Jones* may be *guilty with* a Woman, without doing an *Injury to* her.

BOOK EIGHTEEN

CHAPTER I. Good Mr. *F.* since you are at last come to be *plain and serious,* and to lay *aside* your *Jokes and Raillery,* let me ask you one *plain and serious* Question: Which is, Pray, what *obliged you to cram into this Book* so great a *Variety of Matter?* Were you not at Liberty to omit any of your Episodes, that of the *Man of the Hill,* that of Mrs. *Fitzpatrick's* History, or that of

Partridge at *Hamlet,* which ever you thought least entertaining, that so you might have found room to move, and that nevertheless your Readers might not have been disappointed in paying for an even Six? If thus you play, you are always sure of the Game, and your Competitors can only throw Deux-Ace. I therefore admire your *Policy* in choosing a perfect Number, as an Omen of your Success: Which your Bookseller can tell hath been well answered. You teach us also to admire you for your *Brevity,* when you say, that the Reader will *think the Number of Pages contained in* this Book *scarce sufficient to tell the Story.* But you forget, that you ought before this time so to have conducted your Story, as not to have been in Danger of *cramming.* If you take your Readers indeed for so many Chickens, you are extremely right in *cramming* them, before you eat your Dinner on them. If you have been treated with *Scurrility,* I condole with you on the Occasion: But hath not your Pen well revenged you? If you wrote once against the Court, and your Brother-Writers have hit you in the Teeth with your temporizing, do you not enjoy the Sweets of such a Conversion, and laugh, in a whole Skin, at those who only bark at you, because you outran them?

CONCLUSION

And now, Sir, upon the Whole, I must acknowledge, that, were it not for the bad Morals, which, especially in the earlier Parts of this Work, are insinuated, I should hardly have troubled you or myself with so long a Course of Criticism: An Office, from which, as it is principally conversant in finding Faults, I am extremely averse. Had not these Faults been so glaring, the Author's *counterfeit* Wit might have pass'd for *true,* and dazled the Eyes of our Beaux and Belles with its tinsel Lustre, for any thing I should have done to prevent it. But so much Notice has been taken of this Performance, as an **inimitable* one, that, when I was opposing the Author's Scheme of Morality, I could not avoid lifting up the censorial Rod against

* See certain Verses to *Henry Fielding,* Esq; *on reading his* INIMITABLE *History of* Tom Jones, published in the *Gentleman*'s Magazine for *August,* 1749, which have been wisely disowned by a Gentleman of the same Name with their Author by a public Advertisement.

the other also. Yet have I no personal Pique against this Gentleman; but admire some irregular Touches of Wit and Morality, which, like the few fertile Spots to be seen among the most barren Parts of the *Alps,* may be found in travelling thro' his Volumes. But these are so over-balanced by their Contraries, and by what we have Reason to fear (from comparing our Author's former Works with his latter) of his future Degeneracy from the *Milk of human Kindness* to the Pap of infantile Insipidity, that we cannot help exclaiming with *Horace,*

> Aetas parentum, pejor avis, tulit
> Nos nequiores, mox daturos
> Progeniem vitiofiorem.

Carm. III. vi. 46, 47, 48.

I am, SIR,

Your most humble Servant,

ORBILIUS

9 *William Hazlitt*

FROM "Letters of Horace Walpole"[1]

To come, however, to the better side of our subject.—Walpole is, as we have said, an inimitable gossip,—a most vivacious garrulous historian of fair-haired women, and curious blue china. His garrulity, moreover, hath a genius of its own—and a transparent tea-cup lets in the light of inspiration upon it, and makes it shine with colours nigh divine. An inlaid commode is, with him, the mind's easy chair. We shall select a few passages from the letters before us, which, for pleasantry, ease and alertness, are by far the gayest *morceau* of

---

1. Reprinted, by permission of the publisher, from P. P. Howe, ed., from *The Complete Works of William Hazlitt,* London: J. M. Dent & Sons, 1930–34, vol. XVI, pp. 146–147.

description we have read of late. We may begin with a curious anecdote of Fielding, which is almost as interesting as any thing in the book. Thus it is—

"Take sentiments out of their pantoufles, and reduce them to the infirmities of mortality, what a falling off there is! I could not help laughing in myself t'other day, as I went through Holborn in a very hot day, at the dignity of human nature. All those foul old-clothes women panting without handkerchiefs, and mopping themselves all the way down within their loose jumps. Rigby gave me as strong a picture of nature. He and Peter Bathurst, t'other night, carried a servant of the latter's, who had attempted to shoot him, before Fielding; who, to all his other vocations, has, by the grace of Mr. Lyttleton, added that of Middlesex Justice. He sent them word that he was at supper; that they must come next morning. They did not understand that freedom, and ran up, where they found him banqueting with a blind man, a w———, and three Irishmen, on some cold mutton and a bone of ham, both in one dish, and the dirtiest cloth. He never stirred, nor asked them to sit. Rigby, who had seen him so often come to beg a guinea of Sir. C. Williams, and Bathurst, at whose father's he had lived for victuals, understood that dignity as little, and pulled themselves chairs,—on which he civilized."

It is very certain that the writings of men are coloured by their indolence, their amusements, and their occupations; and this little peep into Fielding's private hours, lets us at once into his course of studies, and is an admirable illustration of his Tom Jones, Jonathan Wild, and other novels. We are taken into the artist's workshop, and shown the models from which he works; or rather, we break in upon him at a time when he is copying from the *life*. It is a very idle piece of morality, to lament over Fielding for this low indulgence of his appetite for character. If he had been found quietly at his tea, he would never have left behind him the name he has done. There is nothing of a tea inspiration in any of his novels. They are assuredly the finest things of the kind in the language; and we are Englishmen enough to consider them the best in any language. They are indubitably the most English of all the works of Englishmen.

FROM "Lectures on the English Comic Writers"[1]

It has been usual to class our own great novelists as imitators of one or other of these two writers. Fielding, no doubt, is more like Don Quixote than Gil Blas; Smollett is more like Gil Blas than Don Quixote; but there is not much resemblance in either case. Sterne's Tristram Shandy is a more direct instance of imitation. Richardson can scarcely be called an imitator of anyone; or if he is, it is of the sentimental refinement of Marivaux, or of the verbose gallantry of the writers of the seventeenth century.

There is very little to warrant the common idea that Fielding was an imitator of Cervantes, except his own declaration of such an intention in the title-page of Joseph Andrews, the romantic turn of the character of Parson Adams (the only romantic character in his works), and the proverbial humour of Partridge, which is kept up only for a few pages. Fielding's novels are, in general, thoroughly his own; and they are thoroughly English. What they are most remarkable for, is neither sentiment, nor imagination, nor wit, nor even humour, though there is an immense deal of this last quality; but profound knowledge of human nature, at least of English nature; and masterly pictures of the characters of men as he saw them existing. This quality distinguishes all his works, and is shown almost equally in all of them. As a painter of real life, he was equal to Hogarth; as a mere observer of human nature, he was little inferior to Shakspeare, though without any of the genius and poetical qualities of his mind. His humour is less rich and laughable than Smollett's; his wit as often misses as hits; he has none of the fine pathos of Richardson or Sterne; but he has brought together a greater variety of characters in common life, marked with more distinct peculiarities, and without an atom of caricature, than any other novel writer whatever. The extreme subtlety of observation on the springs of human conduct in ordinary characters, is only equalled by the ingenuity of contrivance in bringing those springs into play, in such a manner as to lay open their smallest irregularity. The detection is always complete, and made with the certainty and skill of a philosophical experiment, and the obviousness and familiarity of a

1. Vol. VI, pp. 112–114.

casual observation. The truth of the imitation is indeed so great, that it has been argued that Fielding must have had his materials ready-made to his hands, and was merely a transcriber of local manners and individual habits. For this conjecture, however, there seems to be no foundation. His representations, it is true, are local and individual; but they are not the less profound and conclusive. The feeling of the general principles of human nature operating in particular circumstances, is always intense, and uppermost in his mind; and he makes use of incident and situation only to bring out character.

It is scarcely necessary to give any illustrations. Tom Jones is full of them. There is the account, for example, of the gratitude of the elder Blifil to his brother, for assisting him to obtain the fortune of Miss Bridget Alworthy by marriage; and of the gratitude of the poor in his neighbourhood to Alworthy himself, who had done so much good in the country that he had made every one in it his enemy. There is the account of the Latin dialogues between Partridge and his maid, of the assault made on him during one of these by Mrs. Partridge, and the severe bruises he patiently received on that occasion, after which the parish of Little Baddington rung with the story, that the school-master had killed his wife. There is the exquisite keeping in the character of Blifil, and the want of it in that of Jones. There is the gradation in the lovers of Molly Sea-grim; the philosopher Square succeeding to Tom Jones, who again finds that he himself had succeeded to the accomplished Will Barnes, who had the first possession of her person, and had still possession of her heart, Jones being only the instrument of her vanity, as Square was of her interest. Then there is the discreet honesty of Black George, the learning of Thwackum and Square, and the profundity of Squire Western, who considered it as a physical impossibility that his daughter should fall in love with Tom Jones. We have also that gentleman's disputes with his sister, and the inimitable appeal of that lady to her niece.—'I was never so hand-some as you, Sophy: yet I had something of you formerly. I was called the cruel Parthenissa. Kingdoms and states, as Tully Cicero says, undergo alteration, and so must the human form!' The adven-ture of the same lady with the highwayman, who robbed her of her jewels, while he complimented her beauty, ought not to be passed over, nor that of Sophia and her muff, nor the reserved coquetry of her cousin Fitzpatrick, nor the description of Lady Bellaston, nor the modest overtures of the pretty widow Hunt, nor the indiscreet babblings of Mrs. Honour. The moral of this book has been objected to, without much reason; but a more serious objection has been made to the want of refinement and elegance in two principal characters. We never feel this objection, indeed, while we are reading the book: but at other times, we have something like a lurking suspicion that Jones was but an awkward fellow, and Sophia a pretty simpleton. I do not know how to account for this effect, unless it is that Fielding's constantly assuring us of the beauty of his hero, and the good sense of his heroine, at last produces a distrust of both. The story of Tom Jones is allowed to be unrivalled: and it is this circumstance, together with the vast variety of characters, that has given the history of a Foundling so decided a preference over Fielding's other novels.

FROM "Why Heroes of Romance Are Insipid"[1]

Many people find fault with Fielding's Tom Jones as gross and immoral. For my part, I have doubts of his being so very handsome from the author's always talking about his beauty, and I suspect he was a clown, from being constantly assured he was so very genteel. Otherwise, I think Jones acquits himself very well both in his actions and speeches, as a lover and as a *trencher-man* whenever he is called upon. Some persons, from their antipathy to that headlong impulse, of which Jones was the slave, and to that morality of good-nature which in him is made a foil to principle, have gone so far as to prefer Blifil as the *prettier fellow* of the two. I certainly cannot subscribe to this opinion, which perhaps was never meant to have followers, and has nothing but its singularity to recommend it. . . . If Fielding could have made virtue as admirable as he could make vice detestable, he would have been a greater master even than he was. I do not understand what those critics mean who say he got all his characters out of alehouses. It is true he did some of them.

1. Vol. XVII, p. 250.

10 Samuel Taylor Coleridge

FROM "Notes on Tom Jones"[1]

Manners change from generation to generation, and with manners morals appear to change,—actually change with some, but appear to change with all but the abandoned. A young man of the present day who should act as Tom Jones is supposed to act at Upton, with Lady Bellaston, &c. would not be a Tom Jones; and a Tom Jones of the present day, without perhaps being in the ground a better man, would have perished rather than submit to be kept by a harridan of fortune. Therefore this novel is, and, indeed, pretends to be, no exemplar of conduct. But, notwithstanding all this, I do loathe the cant which can recommend Pamela and Clarissa Harlowe as strictly moral, though they poison the imagination of the young with continued doses of *tinct. lyttae,* while Tom Jones is prohibited as loose. I do not speak of young women;—but a young man whose heart or feelings can be injured, or even his passions excited, by aught in this novel, is already thoroughly corrupt. There is a cheerful, sun-shiny, breezy spirit that prevails every where, strongly contrasted with the close, hot, day-dreamy continuity of Richardson. Every indiscretion, every immoral act, of Tom Jones, (and it must be remembered that he is in every one taken by surprise—his inward principles remaining firm—) is so instantly punished by embarrassment and unanticipated evil consequences of his folly, that the reader's mind is not left for a moment to dwell or run riot on the criminal indulgence itself. In short, let the requisite allowance be made for the increased refinement of our manners,—and then I dare believe that no young man who consulted his heart and conscience only, without adverting to what the world would say —could rise from the perusal of Fielding's Tom Jones, Joseph Andrews, or Amelia, without feeling himself a better man;—at least without an intense conviction that he could not be guilty of a base act.

1. Reprinted, by permission of the editor, from Thomas Middleton Raysor, ed., *Coleridge's Miscellaneous Criticism,* London: Constable, 1936, pp. 302–304.

If I want a servant or mechanic, I wish to know what he does: —but of a friend, I must know what he is. And in no writer is this momentous distinction so finely brought forward as by Fielding. We do not care what Blifil does;—the deed, as separate from the agent, may be good or ill;—but Blifil is a villain;—and we feel him to be so from the very moment he, the boy Blifil, restores Sophia's poor captive bird to its native and rightful liberty.

Book xiv. ch. 8.

Notwithstanding the sentiment of the Roman satirist, which denies the divinity of fortune; and the opinion of Seneca to the same purpose; Cicero, who was, I believe, a wiser man than either of them, expressly holds the contrary; and certain it is there are some incidents in life so very strange and unaccountable, that it seems to require more than human skill and foresight in producing them.

Surely Juvenal, Seneca, and Cicero, all meant the same thing, namely, that there was no chance, but instead of it providence, either human or divine.

Book xv. ch. 9.

The rupture with Lady Bellaston.

Even in the most questionable part of Tom Jones, I cannot but think, after frequent reflection, that an additional paragraph, more fully and forcibly unfolding Tom Jones's sense of self-degradation on the discovery of the true character of the relation in which he had stood to Lady Bellaston, and his awakened feeling of the dignity of manly chastity, would have removed in great measure any just objections,—at all events relatively to Fielding himself, and with regard to the state of manners in his time.

Book xvi. ch. 5.

That refined degree of Platonic affection which is absolutely detached from the flesh, and is indeed entirely and purely spiritual, is a gift confined to the female part of the creation; many of whom I have heard declare (and doubtless with great truth) that they would, with the utmost readiness, resign a lover to a rival, when such resignation was proved to be necessary for the temporal interest of such lover.

I firmly believe that there are men capable of such a sacrifice, and this, without pretending to, or even admiring or seeing any virtue in, this absolute detachment from the flesh.

11 Sir Walter Scott

FROM "Henry Fielding,"[1] 1821[2]

The general merits of this popular and delightful work have been so often dwelt upon, and its imperfections so frequently censured, that we can do little more than hastily run over ground which has been repeatedly occupied. The felicitous contrivance, and happy extrication of the story, where every incident tells upon and advances the catastrophe, while, at the time time, it illustrates the characters of those interested in its approach, cannot too often be mentioned with the highest approbation. The attention of the reader is never diverted or puzzled by unnecessary digressions, or recalled to the main story by abrupt and startling recurrences; he glides down the narrative like a boat on the surface of some broad navigable stream, which only winds enough to gratify the voyager with the varied beauty of its banks. One exception to this praise, otherwise so well merited, occurs in the story of the "Old Man of the Hill;" an episode, which, in compliance with a custom introduced by Cervantes, and followed by Le Sage, Fielding has thrust into the midst of his narrative, as he had formerly introduced the history of Leonora, equally unnecessarily and inartificially, into that of "Joseph Andrews." It has also been wondered, why Fielding should have chosen to leave the stain of illegitimacy on the birth of his hero; and it has been surmised, that he did so in allusion to his own first wife, who was also a natural child. A better reason may be discovered in the story itself; for had Miss Bridget been privately married to the father of Tom Jones, there could have been no adequate motive assigned for keeping his birth secret from a man so reasonable and compassionate as Allworthy.

1. Reprinted from *Lives of Eminent Novelists and Dramatists,* London: Frederick Warne & Co., pp. 430–433.
2. This essay was written originally as a preface to the first volume of Ballantyne's *Novelist's Library* series and appeared in 1821.

But even the high praise due to the construction and arrangement of the story, is inferior to that claimed by the truth, force, and spirit of the characters, from Tom Jones himself, down to Black George the game-keeper, and his family. Amongst these, Squire Western stands alone; imitated from no prototype, and in himself an inimitable picture of ignorance, prejudice, irascibility, and rusticity, united with natural shrewdness, constitutional good-humour, and an instinctive affection for his daughter,—all which qualities, good and bad, are grounded upon that basis of thorough selfishness, natural to one bred up, from infancy, where no one dared to contradict his arguments, or to control his conduct. In one incident alone, Fielding has departed from this admirable sketch. As an English squire, Western ought not to have taken a beating so unresistingly from the friend of Lord Fellamar. We half suspect that the passage is an interpolation. It is inconsistent with the Squire's readiness to engage in rustic affrays. We grant a pistol or sword might have appalled him; but Squire Western should have yielded to no one in the use of the English horsewhip; and as, with all his brutalities, we have a sneaking interest in the honest jolly country gentleman, we would willingly hope there is some mistake in this matter.

The character of Jones, otherwise a model of generosity, openness, and manly spirit, mingled with thoughtless dissipation, is, in like manner, unnecessarily degraded by the nature of his intercourse with Lady Bellaston; and this is one of the circumstances which incline us to believe, that Fielding's ideas of what was gentleman-like and honourable had sustained some depreciation, in consequence of the unhappy circumstances of his life, and of the society to which they condemned him.

A more sweeping and general objection was made against the "History of a Foundling" by the admirers of Richardson, and has been often repeated since. It is alleged, that the ultimate moral of "Tom Jones," which conducts to happiness, and holds up to our sympathy and esteem, a youth who gives way to licentious habits, is detrimental to society, and tends to encourage the youthful reader in the practice of those follies, to which his natural passions, and the usual course of the world, but too much direct him. French delicacy, which, on so many occasions, has strained at a gnat, and swallowed a camel, saw this fatal tendency in the work, and by an *arrêt* prohibited the circulation of a bungled abridgment by De Laplace, entitled a translation. To this charge Fielding himself might probably have replied, that the vices into which Jones suffers himself to fall, are made the direct cause of placing him in the distressful situation, which he occupies during the greater part of the narrative; while his generosity, his charity, and his amiable qualities, become the means of saving him from the consequences of his folly. But we suspect with Dr. Johnson, that there is something of cant both in the objection, and in the answer to it. "Men," says that moralist, "will not become highwaymen, because Macheath is acquitted on the stage;" and we add, they will not become swindlers and thieves, because they sympathize with the fortunes of the witty picaroon Gil Blas, or licentious debauchées, because they read "Tom Jones." The professed moral of a piece is usually what the reader is least interested in; it is like the mendicant, who cripples after some splendid and gay procession, and in vain solicits the attention of those who have been gazing upon it. Excluding from consideration those infamous works, which address themselves directly to awakening the grosser passions of our nature, we are inclined to think, the worst evil to be apprehended from the perusal of novels is, that the habit is apt to generate an indisposition to real history, and useful literature; and that the best which can be hoped is, that they may sometimes instruct the youthful mind by real pictures of life, and sometimes awaken their better feelings and sympathies by strains of generous sentiment, and tales of fictitious woe. Beyond this point they are a mere elegance, a luxury contrived for the amusement of polished life, and the gratification of that half love of literature, which pervades all ranks in an advanced stage of society, and are read much more for amusement, than with the least hope of deriving instruction from them. The vices and follies of Tom Jones, are those which the world soon teaches to all who enter on the career of life, and to which society is unhappily but too indulgent; nor do we believe, that, in any one instance, the perusal of Fielding's Novel has added one libertine to the large list, who would not have been such, had it never crossed the press. And it is with concern we add our sincere belief, that the fine picture of frankness and generosity, exhibited in that fictitious character, has had as few imitators as the career of his follies. Let it not be supposed that we are indifferent to morality, because we treat with scorn that affectation, which, while, in common life, it connives at the open practice of libertinism, pretends to detest the memory of an author, who painted life as it was, with all its shades, and more than all the lights which it occasionally exhibits, to relieve them. For particular passages of the work, the author can only be defended under the custom of his age, which permitted, in certain cases, much stronger language than ours. He has himself said, that there is nothing which can offend the chastest eye in the perusal; and he spoke probably according to the ideas of his time. But in modern estimation, there are several passages at which delicacy may justly take offence; and we can only say, that they may be termed rather jocularly coarse than seductive; and that they are atoned for by the admirable mixture of wit and argument, by which, in others, the cause of true religion and virtue is supported and advanced.

Fielding considered his works as an experiment in British literature; and, therefore, he chose to prefix a preliminary Chapter to each Book, explanatory of his own views, and of the rules attached to this mode of composition. Those critical introductions, which rather interrupt the course of the story, and the flow of the interest at the first perusal, are found, on a second or third, the most entertaining chapters of the whole work.

12 William Makepeace Thackeray

FROM The English Humorists of the Eighteenth Century, 1853[1]

"Hogarth, Smollett, and Fielding"

I cannot offer or hope to make a hero of Harry Fielding. Why hide his faults? Why conceal his weaknesses in a cloud of peri-

1. Reprinted from *The Works of William Thackeray*, The Biographical Edition, New York and London: Harper, 1898–99, vol. VII, pp. 578–582.

phrasis? Why not show him, like him as he is, not robed in a marble toga, and draped and polished in a heroic attitude, but with inked ruffles, and claret stains on his tarnished laced coat, and on his manly face the marks of good fellowship, of illness, of kindness, of care, and wine? Stained as you see him, and worn by care and dissipation, that man retains some of the most precious and splendid human qualities and endowments. He has an admirable natural love of truth, the keenest instinctive antipathy to hypocrisy, the happiest satirical gift of laughing it to scorn. His wit is wonderfully wise and detective; it flashes upon a rogue and lightens up a rascal like a policeman's lantern. He is one of the manliest and kindliest of human beings: in the midst of all his imperfections, he respects female innocence and infantine tenderness, as you would suppose such a great-hearted, courageous soul would respect and care for them. He could not be so brave, generous, truth-telling as he is, were he not infinitely merciful, pitiful, and tender. He will give any man his purse—he can't help kindness and profusion. He may have low tastes, but not a mean mind; he admires with all his heart good and virtuous men, stoops to no flattery, bears no rancour, disdains all disloyal arts, does his public duty uprightly, is fondly loved by his family, and dies at his work. . . .

Fielding, no doubt, began to write this novel [*Joseph Andrews*] in ridicule of "Pamela," for which work one can understand the hearty contempt and antipathy which such an athletic and boisterous genius as Fielding's must have entertained. He couldn't do otherwise than laugh at the puny, cockney bookseller, pouring out endless volumes of sentimental twaddle, and hold him up to scorn as a mollcoddle and a milksop. *His* genius had been nursed on sackposset, and not on dishes of tea. *His* muse had sung the loudest in tavern choruses, had seen the daylight streaming in over thousands of emptied bowls, and reeled home to chambers on the shoulders of the watchman. Richardson's goddess was attended by old maids and dowagers, and fed on muffins and bohea. "Milksop!" roars Harry Fielding, clattering at the timid shop-shutters. "Wretch! Monster! Mohock!" shrieks the sentimental author of "Pamela;" and all the ladies of his court cackle out an affrighted chorus. Fielding proposes to write a book in ridicule of the author, whom he disliked and utterly scorned and laughed at; but he is himself of so generous, jovial, and kindly a turn that he begins to like the characters which he invents, can't help making them manly and pleasant as well as ridiculous, and before he has done with them all loves them heartily every one.

Richardson's sickening antipathy for Harry Fielding is quite as natural as the other's laughter and contempt at the sentimentalist. I have not learned that these likings and dislikings have ceased in the present day: and every author must lay his account not only to misrepresentation, but to honest enmity among critics, and to being hated and abused for good as well as for bad reasons. Richardson disliked Fielding's works quite honestly: Walpole quite honestly spoke of them as vulgar and stupid. Their squeamish stomachs sickened at the rough fare and the rough guests assembled at Fielding's jolly revel. Indeed the cloth might have been cleaner: and the dinner and the company were scarce such as suited a dandy. The kind and wise old Johnson would not sit down with him. But a greater scholar than Johnson could afford to admire that astonishing genius of Harry Fielding: and we all know the lofty panegyric which Gibbon wrote of him, and which remains a towering monument to the great novelist's memory. "Our immortal Fielding," Gibbon writes, "was of the younger branch of the Earls of Denbigh, who drew their origin from the Counts of Hapsburgh. The successors of Charles V. may disdain their brethren of England: but the romance of 'Tom Jones,' that exquisite picture of human manners, will outlive the palace of the Escurial and the Imperial Eagle of Austria."

There can be no gainsaying the sentence of this great judge. To have your name mentioned by Gibbon, is like having it written on the dome of St. Peter's. Pilgrims from all the world admire and behold it.

As a picture of manners, the novel of "Tom Jones" is indeed exquisite: as a work of construction quite a wonder: the by-play of wisdom; the power of observation; the multiplied felicitous turns and thoughts; the varied character of the great Comic Epic: keep the reader in a perpetual admiration and curiosity. But against Mr. Thomas Jones himself we have a right to put in a protest, and quarrel with the esteem the author evidently has for that character. Charles Lamb says finely of Jones, that a single hearty laugh from him "clears the air"—but then it is in a certain state of the atmosphere. It might clear the air when such personages as Blifil or Lady Bellaston poison it. But I fear very much that (except until the very last scene of the story), when Mr. Jones enters Sophia's drawing-room, the pure air there is rather tainted with the young gentleman's tobacco-pipe and punch. I can't say that I think Mr. Jones a virtuous character; I can't say but that I think Fielding's evident liking and admiration for Mr. Jones, shows that the great humourist's moral sense was blunted by his life, and that here in Art and Ethics, there is a great error. If it is right to have a hero whom we may admire, let us at least take care that he is admirable: if, as is the plan of some authors (a plan decidedly against their interests, be it said), it is propounded that there exists in life no such being, and therefore that in novels, the picture of life, there should appear no such character; then Mr. Thomas Jones becomes an admissible person, and we examine his defects and good qualities, as we do those of Parson Thwackum, or Miss Seagrim. But a hero with a flawed reputation; a hero spunging for a guinea; a hero who cannot pay his landlady, and is obliged to let his honour out to hire, is absurd, and his claim to heroic rank untenable. I protest against Mr. Thomas Jones holding such rank at all. I protest even against his being considered a more than ordinary young fellow, ruddy-cheeked, broad-shouldered, and fond of wine and pleasure. He would not rob a church, but that is all; and a pretty long argument may be debated, as to which of these old types—the spendthrift, the hypocrite, Jones and Blifil, Charles and Joseph Surface,—is the worst member of society and the most deserving of censure. The prodigal Captain Booth is a better man than his predecessor Mr. Jones, in so far as he thinks much more humbly of himself than Jones did: goes down on his knees, and owns his weaknesses, and cries out "Not for my sake, but for the sake of my pure and sweet and beautiful wife Amelia, I pray you, O critical reader, to forgive me."

Samuel Richardson
Clarissa Harlowe
1748

1 *Lady Mary Wortley Montague*

FROM Letters to her daughter, the Countess of Bute,[1]

(September 22, 1755)

This letter is as long and as dull as any of Richardson's. I am ashamed of it, notwithstanding my maternal privilege of being tiresome. . . .

This Richardson is a strange fellow. I heartily despise him, and eagerly read him, nay, sob over his works in a most scandalous manner.

* * *

1. Reprinted from Lord Wharncliff and W. Moy Thomas, eds., *The Letters and Works of Lady Mary Wortley Montague*, London: George Bell and Sons, 1887, vol. II, pp. 232–233, 293–294, 300.

(March 1, 1752)

. . . I was such an old fool as to weep over Clarissa Harlowe, like any milkmaid of sixteen over the ballad of the Lady's Fall. To say truth, the first volume softened me by a near resemblance of my maiden days; but on the whole 'tis most miserable stuff. Miss How, who is called a young lady of sense and honour, is not only extreme silly, but a more vicious character than Sally Martin, whose crimes are owing at first to seduction, and afterwards to necessity; while this virtuous damsel, without any reason, insults her mother at home and ridicules her abroad; abuses the man she marries; and is impertinent and impudent with great applause. Even that model of affection, Clarissa, is so faulty in her behaviour as to deserve little compassion. Any girl that runs away with a young fellow, without intending to marry him, should be carried to Bridewell or to Bedlam the next day. Yet the circumstances are so laid, as to inspire tenderness, notwithstanding the low style and absurd incidents; and I look upon this and Pamela to be two books that will do more general mischief than the works of Lord Rochester.

* * *

(October 20, 1755)

Her[1] whole behaviour, which he designs to be exemplary, is equally blamable and ridiculous. She follows the maxim of Clarissa, of declaring all she thinks to all the people she sees, without reflecting that in this mortal state of imperfection, fig-leaves are as necessary for our minds as our bodies, and 'tis as indecent to show all we think, as all we have. He has no idea of the manners of high life: his old Lord M. talks in the style of a country justice, and his virtuous young ladies romp like the wenches round a maypole. Such liberties as pass between Mr. Lovelace and his cousins, are not to be excused by the relation. I should have been much astonished if Lord Denbigh[2] should have offered to kiss me; and I dare swear Lord Trentham[3] never attempted such an impertinence to you.

1. Harriet's, in *Sir Charles Grandison.*
2. Lady Mary's cousin.—Thomas' note.
3. Son of Lady Mary's sister, Lady Gower, and, therefore, a cousin of Lady Bute.—Thomas' note.

2 *Samuel Richardson*

Correspondence with Lady Bradsheigh [Belfour[1]]

FROM A letter from Lady Bradsheigh
October 10, 1748[2]

I am pressed, Sir, by a multitude of your admirers, to plead in behalf of your amiable Clarissa: having too much reason, from hints given in your four volumes, from a certain advertisement, and from your forbearing to write, after promising all endeavours should be used towards satisfying the discontented; from all these, I say, I have but too much reason to apprehend a fatal catastrophe. I have heard that some of your advisers, who delight in horror, (detestable wretches!) insisted upon rapes, ruin, and destruction; others, who feel for the virtuous in distress, (blessings for ever attend them!) pleaded for the contrary. Could you be deaf to these, and comply with those? Is it possible, that he who has the art to please in softness, in the most natural, easy, humorous, and sensible manner, can resolve to give joy only to the ill-natured reader, and heave the compassionate breast with tears for irremediable woes? Tears I would choose to shed for virtue in distress; but still would suffer to flow, in greater abundance, for unexpected turns of happiness, in which, Sir, you excel any other author I ever read! where nature ought to be touched, you make the very soul feel. . . . Therefore, Sir, after you have brought the divine Clarissa to the very brink of destruction, let me intreat (may I say, insist upon) a turn, that will make your almost despairing readers half mad with joy. I know you cannot help doing it, to give yourself satisfac-

1. "The correspondence with Lady Bradsheigh began in the following manner: a lady, calling herself Belfour, wrote to the author of Clarissa, after reading the four first volumes, acquainting him that a report prevailed, that The History of Clarissa was to end in a most tragical manner, and, expressing her abhorrence of such a catastrophe, begged to be satisfied of the truth by a few lines inserted in the Whitehall Evening Post. Mr. Richardson complied with her request; in consequence of which many letters passed between them, the lady's under her assumed name."—Barbauld's note.

2. Reprinted from Anna L. Barbauld, ed., *The Correspondence of Samuel Richardson*, London: R. Phillips, 1804, vol. IV, pp. 177–181.

tion; for I pretend to know your heart so well, that you must think it a crime, never to be forgiven, to leave vice triumphant, and virtue depressed. . . .

I have all this time pleaded only in behalf of Clarissa; but you must know, (though I shall blush again,) that if I was to die for it, I cannot help being fond of Lovelace. A sad dog! why would you make him so wicked, and yet so agreeable? He says, sometime or other he designs being a good man, from which words I have great hopes; and, in excuse for my liking him, I must say, I have made him so, up to my own heart's wish; a faultless husband have I made him, even without danger of a relapse. A foolish rake may die one; but a sensible rake must reform, at least in the hands of a sensible author it ought to be so, and will, I hope.

If you disappoint me, attend to my curse:—May the hatred of all the young, beautiful, and virtuous, for ever be your portion! and may your eyes never behold any thing but age and deformity! may you meet with applause only from envious old maids, surly bachelors, and tyrannical parents! may you be doomed to the company of such! and, after death, may their ugly souls haunt you!

Now make Lovelace and Clarissa unhappy if you dare.

* * *

FROM Samuel Richardson to Lady Bradsheigh
October 26, 1748[1]

. . . You cannot imagine, how sensibly I am grieved for the Pain the unexpected Turn of my Story has given you! God forbid that anything unhappy, or disastrous, should ever fall to the Lot of a Lady so generously sensible of the Woes of others, as she must be, who can thus be affected by a moral Tale, tho' the Characters (however presumed to be in Nature) existed not in Life.

Indeed you are not *particular* in your Wishes for a happy Ending, as it is called. I had proposed to draw my Girl amiable in order to make her a true Object of Pity, and Example to her Sex. But I find by several other Applications to me, on your side of the Ques-

1. John Carroll, ed., *Selected Letters of Samuel Richardson,* by permission of the Clarendon Press, Oxford, 1964, pp. 90–97.

tion, that I have drawn her too amiable. Nor can I go thro' some of the Scenes myself without being sensibly touched (Did I not say, that I was another Pygmalion?) But yet I had to shew, for Example-sake a young Lady struggling nobly with the greatest Difficulties, and triumphing from the best Motives, in the Course of Distresses the tenth Part of which would have sunk even manly Hearts; Yet tenderly educated, born to Affluence, naturally meek, altho' where an Exertion of Spirit was necessary manifesting herself to be a true Heroine. . . .

And what Madam, is the temporary Happiness we are so fond of? What the long Life we are so apt to covet?—Hear what my Girl says on that Subject, writing to her dear Friend Miss Howe, to comfort her on her apparent Decline.

Do not, my Dear, be concerned, that I call this my last Stage. What is even the long Life which in high Health we wish for? What but as we go along, a Life of Apprehension, sometimes for our Friends, oftener for our selves? And at last, when arrived at the old Age we covet, one heavy Loss or Deprivation having succeeded another, we see ourselves stript, as I may say, of every one we loved; and find ourselves exposed as uncompanionable poor Creatures, to the Slights, the Contempts, of Jesting Youth, who want to push us of[f] the Stage, in hopes to possess what we have. And superadded to all, our own Infirmities every Day increasing; of themselves enough to make the Life we wished for, the greatest Disease of all.

Such are the Lessons I endeavour to inculcate by an Example in natural Life. And the more irksome these Lessons are to the Young, the Gay, and the Healthy, the more necessary are they to be inculcated.

> A Verse may find him who a Sermon flies
> And turn Delight into a Sacrifice[1]

Of this Nature is my Design. Religion never was at so low an Ebb as at present: And if my Work must be supposed of the Novel kind, I was willing to try if a Religious Novel would do good. . . .

1. From George Herbert's "The Church Porch."

And as to reforming and marrying Lovelace, and the Example to be given by it, what but This that follows, would it have been, instead of the amiable one your Good nature and Humanity point out?—Here 'says another Lovelace, may I pass the Flower and Prime of my Youth, in forming and pursuing the most insidious Enterprizes—I may delude and ruin my Miss Betterton, I may form Plots against and destroy my French Countess. As many of the Daughters and Sisters of worthy Families, as I can seduce, may I seduce, Scores perhaps in different Climates—And on their Weakness build my profligate Notions of the whole Sex—I may at last meet with and attempt a Clarissa, a Lady of peerless Virtue. I may try her, vex her, plague and torment her worthy Heart. I may set up all my Batteries against her Virtue. And if I find her Proof against all my Machinations, and myself tired with rambling, I may then reward that Virtue. I may graciously extend my Hand. She may give me hers, and rejoice and thank Heaven for my Condescension in her Favour. The Almighty I may suppose, at the same Time to be as ready with his Mercy, forgoing his Justice on my past Crimes, as if my Nuptials with this meritorious Fair One were to attone for the numerous Distresses and Ruins I have occasioned in other Families: And all the Good-natured the Worthy, the Humane part of the World forgiving me too, because I am a handsome and an humorous Fellow, will clap their Hands with joy and cry out—

'Happy, happy, happy pair!
None but the Rake deserves the Fair!'[1]

You are pleased to tell me, that I have drawn a Character above Nature.—'You mean, say you to do Honour to the Sex by exalting her above it; which in my Opinion will debase instead of doing it Honour.' . . .

There cannot be a more pernicious Notion, than that which is so commonly received, That a reformed Rake makes the best Husband. This Notion it was my Intent to combat and expose, as I mentioned so early as in the Preface to my first Volume. And how could I have answered this End, had I pursued the Plan your benevolent Heart

1. See John Dryden's—"Alexander's Feast," first chorus for Richardson's allusion.

wishes I had pursued? Indeed, indeed, Madam, Reformation is not, can not, be †an easy,†[1] a sudden thing, in a Man long immersed in Vice—The Temptations to it, as from Sex to Sex, so natural; constitution, as in such a Character as Lovelace, so promotive, a Love of Intrigue so predominant—So great a self admirer—so supposedly admired by others—And was it not Nature that I proposed to follow? . . .

But why, as I asked in my former, is Death painted in such shocking Lights, when it is the common Lot? If it is become so terrible to human Nature, it is Time to familiarize it to us—Hence another of my great Ends, as I have hinted—'Don't we lead back,' says my divine Girl on a certain Occasion, which had shocked those about her, 'a starting Steed to the Object he is apt to start at, in order to familiarize him to it, and cure his starting?'

Who but the Persons concerned, should choose for themselves, what would make them happy?—If Clarissa think not an early Death an Evil, but on the contrary, after an exemplary Preparation, looks upon it as her consummating Perfection, who shall grudge it her?—Who shall punish her with Life? *There is no Inquisition in the Grave,* as she quotes, *whether we have lived ten or an hundred Years; and the Day of Death is better than the Day of our Birth.* . . .

But after all it is the Execution must either condemn or acquit me. I am however, discouraged and mortified at what you tell me that you cannot think of accepting of the Volumes when completed if the catastrophe be not as you wish.

I am pained for your apprehended Pain, were you to read to the End, and the more as I own that I have lost my Aim, and judge wrongly from my own Heart and Eyes, if there are not Scenes to come that will affect so tender a Heart as yours. But I think that you cannot bear to read the Fifth Volume only?—That will give you to judge a little of the Management. That will cure you for your Love for the Man—Perhaps however you would not wish to be cured.—But it will still further exalt my Girl in your Eyes.— Burn the Book when you come to the Scenes you cannot go thro.

1. Daggers (†) are placed on each side of words inserted by Richardson in revising letters.—Carroll's note.

All the first part is lively and Humour is aimed at in the savage Man's Letters.

* * *

FROM Samuel Richardson to Lady Bradsheigh
December 15, 1748[1]

Indeed, Madam, I could not think of leaving my Heroine short of Heaven: Nor that I should do well if I punished not so premeditated a Violation; and thereby made Pity on her Account, and Terror on his, join to complete my great End, for the sake of *Example* and *Warning*.

I am not solicitous to establish a private Reputation for Tenderness of Heart, tho' a tender a feeling Heart is what I venerate wherever I find it. If I have drawn hard-hearted Scenes, I have likewise drawn tender ones; and if the *Author* rather than the *Characters* in his Story must be considered, I only hope to be weighed in an equal Balance. . . .

I hope I have every where avoided, All Rant, Horror, indecent Images, inflaming Descriptions, even when Rake writes to Rake, Terror and Fear and Pity are Essentials in a Tragic Performance. . . .

A good Comedy is a fine Performance. But how few are there that can be called good? Even those that are tolerable are so mixed with indecent Levities and with Double Entendres, if not worse (at which Footmen have a Right to insult by their Roars their Ladies in the Boxes) that a modest young Creature hardly knows how to bear the offence to her Ears in the Representation, joined with the Insults given by the Eyes of the young Fellows she is surrounded by!—These Indecencies would be unnaturally shocking in Tragedy, as every one feels in the Tragi Comedy more especially. But †true† Tragedy we must not bear. . . .

You say 'that you are not affected in the same sensible manner by Distresses in unnatural Heroics, as you are when they appear purely in Nature; where the Distresses come nearer one's Self.'

1. Reprinted, by permission of the Clarendon Press, from Carroll, ed., *Selected Letters of Samuel Richardson,* pp. 104–106, 108, 112–113, 116.

This is exceedingly well said. This was one of the principal Reasons of writing the History of Clarissa. . . .

A Writer who follows Nature and pretends to keep the Christian System in his Eye, cannot make a Heaven in this World for his Favourites; or represent this Life otherwise than as a State of Probation. Clarissa I once more averr could not be rewarded in this World. To have given her her Reward here, as in a happy Marriage, would have been as if a Poet had placed his Catastrophe in the Third Act of his Play, when the Audience were *obliged* to expect two more. What greater moral Proof can be given of a World after this, for the rewarding of suffering Virtue, and for the punishing of oppressive Vice, than the Inequalities in the Distribution of Rewards and Punishments here below? . . .

You say, 'You suppose, that I designed that my fair Readers shou'd find out what was worthy and agreeable in Lovelace.' I did, Madam, and I told you in my first Letter that he had some good Qualities given him in Compliment to the Eye and Ear of Clarissa. But little did I think at the time that those Qualities (politically rather than from Principle exerted as some of them evidently were, particularly in his Behaviour to his Rosebud) would have given Women of Virtue and Honour such a liking to him, as I have found to be the Case with many. I thought I had made him too wicked, too Intriguing, too revengeful, (and that in his very first Letters) for him to obtain the Favour and good Wishes of any worthy Heart of *either* Sex. I try'd his Character, as it was first drawn, and his last Exit, on a young Lady of Seventeen. She shewed me by her Tears at the latter that he was not very odious to her for his Vagaries and Inventions. I was surprized; and for fear such a Wretch should induce Pity, I threw into his Character some deeper Shades. And as he now stands, I verily think that had I made him a worse Man, he must have been a Devil.—*For Devils believe and tremble.* . . .

Sometimes you make me apprehend, that you will not read the Story thro: (Remember, Madam, if you do not you are not fairly intituled to condemn the Catastrophe). At other times you give me Hope that you will—'Off, off, thou foolish Softness,' pathetically say you! 'And to make me more perfectly a *Christian* let me *catch* at *Fortitude*—No it will not do—It flies me—Another Tear I protest!'—Charming Sensibility! But by the Words *catch at Fortitude* you seem to suppose it on the Wing. Ah Madam, you have soon done with your Essay to obtain it:—But resolve only to make it a Guest for an Hour in a Day! And it may †quickly† become an Inmate. Tears you must consider as Reliefs from Grief, not as Grief itself. My Story is designed to strengthen the tender Mind, and to enable the worthy Heart to bear up against the Calamities of Life. May no real Evils ever happen to ruffle, to shock, a Mind so beautifully tender! . . .

Read my Story through and you will see †that† in the Example Clarissa sets, Meekness of Heart is intirely consistent with that Dignity of Mind, which on all proper Occasions she exerts with so much distinguishing Excellence, as carries her above the irascible Passions. . . .

* * *

A Postscript
FROM Lady Bradsheigh to Samuel Richardson
undated[1]

P. S. Just as I was sending this to the post, your fifth volume came to my hand; and I am really quite ashamed of receiving such a favour, as I think myself undeserving of it. I long to read it—and yet I dare not. But I have a kind friend who will first look it over; though, God knows, he has a heart tender as my own, but is willing to save me pain, though at the expence of suffering it himself. If I find the dreaded horrid act is not perpetrated, I will promise to read it. There is nothing else I fear; and I will hope still, from your good nature, that you may be moved, and alter your fatal and un-pleasing design. . . .

. . . O, Sir! I have been prevailed upon to read a part of your story, that I thought would have torn my heart in a thousand pieces. You have drawn a villain above nature; and you make that villain

1. Barbauld, *The Correspondence of Samuel Richardson*, vol. IV, pp. 196–197, 199–201.

a sensible man, with many good qualities, and you have declared him not an unbeliever. Indeed, Sir, I am more out of conceit with your scheme than ever; it must do harm, indeed it must. What will any villain care what becomes of a Clarissa, when he has gained his horrid ends, which you have taught him how to gain? Dear Sir, if it be possible—yet, recall the dreadful sentence; bring it as near as you please, but prevent it. Do, dear Sir, it is too shocking and barbarous a story for publication. I wish I could not think of it. Blot out but one night, and the villainous laudanum, and all may be well again.

I opened my letter to add this, and my hand trembles, for I can scarce hold my pen. I am as mad as the poor injured Clarissa; and am afraid I cannot help hating you, if you alter not your scheme.

* * *

FROM Lady Bradsheigh to Samuel Richardson
January 11, 1749[1]

I have, Sir, with much pain, much greater than you imagine, gone thro' your inimitable piece. . . .

It was purely out of gratitude, and to oblige you, I read the three last volumes. I expected to suffer, but not to that degree I have suffered. Had you known me, Sir, your good-nature could not have pressed me to a mortification so great as that I have experienced. But you do not know what a fool I am. What is such a warm constitution good for but to torment me?

Had you seen me, I surely should have moved your pity. When alone, in agonies would I lay down the book, take it up again, walk about the room, let fall a flood of tears, wipe my eyes, read again, perhaps not three lines, throw away the book, crying out, excuse me, good Mr. Richardson, I cannot go on; it is your fault—you have done more than I can bear; threw myself upon my couch to compose, recollecting my promise (which a thousand times I wished had not been made); again I read, again I acted the same part: some-

---

1. Barbauld, *The Correspondence of Samuel Richardson,* vol. IV, pp. 239–243, 246.

times agreeably interrupted by my dear man, who was at that time labouring through the sixth volume with a heart capable of impressions equal to my own, tho' the effects shewn in a more justifiable manner, which I believe may be compared to what Mr. Belford felt when he found the beauteous sufferer in her prison room: "Something rose in my throat, I know not what, which made me guggle as it were for speech."

Seeing me so moved, he begged, for God's sake, I would read no more; kindly threatened to take the book from me, but upon my pleading my promise, suffered me to go on. That promise is now fulfilled, and I am thankful the heavy task is over, tho' the effects are not. Had it been conducted as I wished, instead of being impatient to get through the sad story, how should I have dwelt with pleasure upon every line, and felt loth to come to the conclusion.

My spirits are strangely seized, my sleep is disturbed; waking in the night, I burst into a passion of crying; so I did at breakfast this morning, and just now again. God be merciful to me—what can it mean? Perhaps, Sir, you may attribute it to violent passions, but indeed, if I know myself, I have none such. It is all weakness, downright foolish weakness. I do assure you, I do not aggravate the uneasiness I labour under, no, nor tell the worst. . . .

Much pleasure have I lost, much pain have I endured. Indeed, Sir, I am afraid I cannot forgive you, not heartily, at least, this great while. You do not think perhaps how I have used you. I have called you all sorts of names, both good and bad, sometimes loving, sometimes hating, tho' at all times admiring. . . .

But it is all over. And now I shall fall upon you, for drawing such an irreclaimable monster, and giving such a lover to Clarissa, that her matchless excellence could not have the power to reform. (There I think the glory you designed our sex sinks a little.) Dear soul! she once had set her heart upon it, and who would not have gratified that good heart? Why, you would not. The director of all her fortunes, denied her the enjoyment of all earthly comforts. Barbarous— what shall I call you?—I believe I had best stop here; for why should I say the thing that is not?

* * *

FROM Samuel Richardson to Lady Bradsheigh
undated, but apparently in reply to a letter
of hers dated February 9, 1750[1]

But you would have me set about reforming my own sex. Dear
lady! you make me smile! Why, I attempted to draw a good
woman; and the poor phantom has set half her own sex against her.
The men more generally admire her, indeed, because bad men, as I
have quoted above from Lovelace, admire good women. But with
some of the sex she is a prude; with others a coquet; with more a
saucy creature, whose life, manners, and maxims, are affronts to
them. Mr Fielding's Sophia is a much more eligible character.
What think you, Madam, was my return to two different ladies,
who, unknown to, and but little acquainted with each other, sent
me, the one, a letter, accusing Clarissa for a coquet; the other, taking her to task as a prude? Why, to send to each the other's letter
for a full answer of her's. And so I lost, at setting out, two correspondents, and, what was worse, my two letters; for I never
could get them back, and had taken no copies of them; and there
were some curious strokes in both: but the ladies have ever since
been well acquainted.

* * *

A Postscript
FROM Lady Bradsheigh to Samuel Richardson
March 29, 1751[2]

P.S. The true state of a pity-moving case, recommended to the
author of Clarissa:
The die was cast for chaining a fair young lady to a man she
hated. Clarissa-like, she declared her unconquerable aversion, to
father, mother, and every intimate friend; frankly told her lover, she
would rather die than marry him. This gentleman, blinded by passion, (in every other respect, esteemed a very sensible man) flat-

1. Barbauld, vol. VI, pp. 81–83.
2. Vol. VI, pp. 98–99.

tered himself with imagining he could gain her affections, by making an indulgent, tender husband; and insisted on having the match concluded. Accordingly, this ill-suited couple were yoked together. Her Harlowe-hearted parents, deaf to entreaty, unmoved by the young lady's prayers and tears, forced her to give her hand where she could not bestow a repugnant heart.

This reluctant obedience (fatal marriage!) is attended with miserable consequences—nothing less, on her part, than frantic extravagance and attempted elopement. The unhappy husband's woful distress and deep melancholy is aggravated by a suspicion that his wife intended to poison him. Upon the discovery of this terrible affair, she was closely confined, till a resolution was taken, (not less barbarous than the cruelty that caused her distraction), which was, to banish this object of compassion to some remote part of the world. Accordingly, the poor creature was hurried away—is actually sent to a little town in France—compelled to live there, for, in case she quits that place, she is not to receive one penny, to support her.

3 Samuel Richardson

FROM Letters to Aaron Hill[1]

(October 29, 1746)

This Conduct, [Lovelace's duel with her brother—Ed.] reported to her, and to prevent worse Consequences, induces her to renew a Correspondence by Letters, begun with every one's Knowlege: Her Mother conniving at it, in order to prevent Mischief. Altho' the Antipathy between ye young Gentlemen is founded on their College Disagreements, yet Ambition and Avarice, as is largely mentioned, and the Envy and Apprehension, that the Favour she stood in with

1. Reprinted, by the permission of the Clarendon Press, from Carroll, ed., *Selected Letters of Samuel Richardson*, pp. 72–87.

her Uncles and Father, would make them follow her Grandfather's Example, who left her an Estate, and thinking Lovelace would, by his Birth and Alliances, eclipse him, are the principal Motives of keeping up, and augmenting his Hatred; as Lovelace's Slighting of Arabella for Clarissa, are hers; and this joins in one Interest the two Lovers.

As to Clarissa's being in downright Love, I must acknowlege, that I rather [would]¹ †chose to† have it imputed to her, (his too well-known Character consider'd) by her penetrating Friend, (and then a Reader will be ready enough to believe it, the *more* ready, for her not owning it, or being blind to it herself) than to think *her self* that she is. This gives occasion for much natural Reluctance to believe her self to be in Love, on her Part, and much Raillery (the Talent of Miss Howe) on her [Friend's] †Part†; And as I think the Passion, unless ye Object be undoubtedly worthy, and generous, *ought* to be subdued, and it is a Part of my Instruction from her Example, that Prudence *may* prevail over it, and *should;* and as it is one of my Two principal Views, to admonish Parents agt. forcing their Children's Inclinations, in an Article so essential to their Happiness, as Marriage; I was very desirous, that it should appear to a Reader, that had so excellent a Creature been left to her self, well as she might have liked him had he been a moral Man, she would have overcome her Liking to him; and despised him: And then I was willing to explode, [in her principal Motive,] that pernicious Notion, that a Reformed Rake (one of her now chief, and generous Motives) makes the best Husband.— And this Foundation laid, I conceived it more natural, and of consequence, more *exemplary,* that so noble a Creature, when she had been outrag'd by such a Man (by this Time her Preference of him being more *Self-apparent and avowed)* [that she] should be able to refuse him, against the Advice of her best Friend, and rather refuge her self in ye Arms of Death, than in his.

I had further intended to make her so faultless, that a Reader should find no way to account for the Calamities she met with, and to justify Moral Equity but by looking up to a future Reward; another of my principal Doctrines; and one of my principal Views

---

1. Shaped brackets [ ] enclose words deleted by Richardson.

to inculcate in this Piece. I had not indeed, sat down to scribble on this Subject, but with this View. Going off with a man is, moreover, the Thing I wanted most to make inexcusable; and I thought I ought not to make a Clarissa, give a Sanction to such an highly un-dutiful and disreputable Procedure, from any common Motives.

Lovelace's Character I *intend* to be unamiable, as I hinted: I once read to a young Lady Part of his Character, and then his End; and upon her pitying him, and wishing he had been rather made a Penitent, than to be killed, I made him still more and more odious, by his heighten'd Arrogance and Triumph, as well as by vile Actions, leaving only some Qualities in him, laudable enough to justify her first Liking.

* * *

(January 26, 1747)

I must still say, that I would not have Clarissa in Love, at set-ting out: And that I intended the [Flame] †Passion† should be inspired and grow, unknown to herself, and be more obvious, for a good while, to every-body than to herself; and when it became glowing, that it should be owing more to unreasonable Opposition, than to the Merits of the Man: And yet that her chief Objections to him should be rather from *Hearsay* bad Fame than *personal De-tection*.—I wou'd not give him such a Behaviour to her, as should be shocking: And in his first Letter to his Friend, he acknowleges honourable Love; and has no Intention of other, till he find her in his Power.—Hence my Caution, for a young Woman not to put herself in the Power of her Lover.—In general, I believe, no Woman, who loves, sees the Man's Faults in the Light every-body else sees them in. [They] All †Women† flatter themselves, that even the Man whom they know to have been base to *others,* will not, cannot, be so to *them;* and this from Vanity, as well as good Opinion of the Man they prefer. I must repeat, that I am afraid, that Love-lace's open-hearted Wickedness to his *Friend (not to Clarissa)* is not sufficiently considered, and perhaps will not generally be so.

But I am very greatly mortified, that what I have so much

laboured, as to make it manifest, that Clarissa, tho' provoked as she was by a disgraceful Confinement; by her Brother's and Sister's [Insults] *permitted* Insults; tho' threaten'd to be *forced* into the Arms of a Man she abhorred; tho' thus provoked, I say, to *promise* to go off; yet repenting, and resolving *not* to go off, only to meet him, in order to let him know as much; and to re-assure him personally (for fear of Mischief), that, altho' she wou'd stay, she would die rather than be compelled to be the Man's Wife she hated; That this should be called, by such a clear Discerner; *a rash Elopement with a Man;* and that your Reasoning in this material Place, is built upon the Supposition of her voluntarily *running away from her Father's House, with a worse Man †than Solmes†* of her own choosing! I am very unfortunate, good Sir, let me say, [to be so ill-understood:] To have *given Reason,* [*I should say,*] to be so little understood: And how can I but doubt my own Conduct in this Story, when, if I did not, I must question your Attention to it, in the most material Point of all, respecting my Heroine's Character, and, as I may say, one of the principal Morals that I proposed to be drawn from my Story?

I call this a *laboured* Point with me, because I have consulted two very delicate Minds of the Sex, upon my Conduct of it. They have both confessed, that they think Clarissa had sufficient Provocations to throw herself into Lovelace's Protection (She not knowing him †to be† so bad as he was—And at the time, as I have said, he *meant* her no Evil) That it became her Character, nevertheless, to change her Purpose, and stand ye Event of her Friends next Meeting (determined, as you hint she might be, to say *No* to the last); yet apprized, that they had chosen a [Parson] Clergyman *for their purpose,* instead of one of *Character,* who had refused to be there—Great Cause of Apprehension this!—That her Motives for meeting him (in order to pacify & assure him, that her resolved-upon Stay should not be with ye Purpose he most dreaded) were justifiable and Characteristic—And the two Ladies owned, that, *having met him,* they should not, in her Case, have been able, however reluctant, to avoid being carried off, (tricked off) by so determined, so prepared a Contriver! . . .

* * *

(May 10, 1748)

The Sale is pretty quick for an *imperfect* Work. †Yet† I know not whether it has not suffered [much] by the Catastrophe's being too much known and talked of. I intend another Sort of Happiness (founded on the Xn system) for my Heroine, than that which was to depend upon the Will and Pleasure, and uncertain Reformation and good Behaviour of a vile Libertine, †to† whom I could not think of giving a [person] †Lady† of †such† Excellence. The Sex give too much countenance to Men of this Cast †for any one† to make [them] such a Compliment to their Errors. And to rescue her from a Rake, and give a Triumph to her not only over him but over all her Oppressors, and the World besides, in a triumphant Death (as Death must, †at last,† have been her Lot, had she been ever so prosperous) I thought as noble a View, as it was new. But I find, Sir, by many Letters sent me, and by many Opinions given me, that †some of† the greater Vulgar, as well as all the less, had rather it had had what they call, an Happy Ending. This will be of Prejudice to [me in] the Sale [and has been]: But, as I had an Ambition to attempt what I have the Vanity to think was never yet attempted; and as I think, if Health be spared me, that I shall be able to give an uncommon Turn and Appearance, to common Calamities which, at one time or other, in every Person's Life, may be of some Use, I am not at all concerned about [the Sale; I mean as to] the Profits of [it] the sale; tho' neither in Circumstance nor Philosophy absolutely above attending to that Part.

FROM A Letter to Astrea and Minerva Hill, December 14, 1748[1]

What Pride you give me in your Approbation of my Clarissa! —And how charmingly just is your Correction of Miss Howe! Would you not wonder, were you to hear, that such there are as prefer that lively Girl to her? And still more, were you to be assured, that there are Numbers of your Sex, who pity the Lovelace

1. Reprinted, by permission of the Clarendon Press, from Carroll, ed., *Selected Letters of Samuel Richardson,* pp. 102–103.

you are affrighted at, and call Clarissa perverse, over-delicate, and Hard-hearted; and content, that she ought to have married him?

If two or three Wicked Men are joined to make one Lovelace, and if he be by that means drawn more excessively wicked than any one single Man has been known to be (and yet in a more diffuse Walk there have been, and perhaps there are, worse Men than even Lovelace) do we not see in these Ladies, that there cannot be a Rake so Vile, if he have Form or Figure, an Air of Generosity, and Fire and Flight, and what is called Wit, and Intrepidity but whom, in his worst Actions, be the object of his Attempts ever so worthy, they can forgive?

But is there nothing, Dear Ladies, in my divine Girl, to be corrected, should the Piece come to a Second Impression?—No essential Point of Delicacy in which she is wanting! Scan her Conduct, and judge her by your own Hearts; and when she is corrected by them, she will then more boldly than now she can, claim Attention as an Example to her whole Sex. . . .

FROM A Letter to Edward Moore [1748][1]

But further as to his sufferings,—See the Voiture tho' moving slowly, by its motion getting his wounds bleeding afresh; and again, with difficulty stopt. See him giving Directions afterward for his last devoir to his Friend Belford. See him, contrary to all expectation, as de la Tour says, living over the night, but suffering much, as well from his Impatience and *Disappointment* as from his *Wounds*.—for, adds the honest valet, 'He seemed very unwilling to Die.'—What a farther contrast this to the last Behaviour of the divine Clarissa!—See him in his following Delirium Spectres before his eyes! His lips moving, tho' speechless—*wanting* therefore to speak—'See him in convulsions, and fainting away at nine in the morning.' A Quarter of an hour in them; yet recovering to more Terror. The *Ultimate Composure* mentioned by de la Tour, rather mentioned to comfort his surviving Friends than appearing to have reason to suppose it to be so, from his subsequent description of his

1. Reprinted, by permission of the Clarendon Press, from Carroll, ed., *Selected Letters of Samuel Richardson*, p. 122.

last Agonies. *Blessed,* his word—interrupted by another strong Convulsion—*Blessed* again repeated, when he recovered from it rather to shew the Reader that he felt, than that he was so *Ultimately Composed.* 'Then *seeming* ejaculation,—then speaking inwardly but so as not to be understood—' how affecting such a circumstance in such a Man! And at last with his wonted haughtiness of spirit— *LET THIS EXPIATE* all his apparent Invocation and address to the *SUPREME.* Have I not then given rather a dreadful than a hopeful Exit, with respect to Futurity, to the unhappy Lovelace!— I protest I have been unable to reperuse the acct: of his Death *with this great Circumstance* in my Head, and to think of the triumphant one of my divine Clarissa, without pity—and I did hope that the contrast if attentively considered would be very striking.

FROM A Letter to Frances Grainger, January 22, 1750[1]

I cannot but be pleased at your Hint that if the Modern Ladies were to allow to the Character of Clarissa its due Merit, they would 'own themselves very weak'—to use your own Words—'and her very Wise.' 'And what Lady,' say you, 'would chuse to do that?'— This is the very Reason by which I have taken the Liberty to account, elsewhere, for the good Reception the Character of the weak, the insipid, the Runaway, the Inn-frequenting Sophia has met with. In that, as in the Character of her illegitimate Tom, there is nothing that very Common Persons may not attain to; Nothing that will reproach the Conduct or Actions of very ordinary Capacities, and very free Livers: while Clarissa's Character, as it might appear unattainable by them, might be supposed Prudish, too delicate, and a silent Reproach to themselves. Had I been at Leisure to examine *The History of Tom Jones,* But I might have been at Leisure indeed to set about such a Task! And yet I am sure I should have been able to do the Author Impartial Justice. But I should have known whom by the Examination to have called Sophias and whom Clarissas. . . .

1. Reprinted, by permission of the Clarendon Press, from Carroll, ed., *Selected Letters of Samuel Richardson,* pp. 143–145.

Be pleased, Madam, always to remember this Great Rule, in-culcated thro'out the History of Clarissa, That in all reciprocal Duties the Non-Performance of the Duty on one Part is not an excuse for the Failure of the other. Why, think you, are future Rewards promised and future Punishments threatened? But the one to induce us to Persevere in our Duties here, the other to Punish our Deviation from them. She was not bid to *obey* even unjust *Powers not only for Wrath but for Conscience Sake*. No one that disapproves of the Conduct of Clarissa and of her Principles but must find fault with the Doctrines laid down in the Bible, or know not what they are. For is not hers the Conduct laid down for Pursuit in the Sacred Books? *The Bear and Forbear,* the uncontentious *Giving up the Cloak* also, rather than to dispute or litigate for the *Coat*—The *turning* the unsmitten *Cheek*—The *Forgiveness of those that hate us and despitefully use us*—The *Praying for our Enemies* —The Christian Meekness—The Affiance in God's Mercy, Power, and Goodness, as what shall infallibly reward us hereafter for our Patience and Suffering here. Read, but read everywhere in her character, all this and more. Why should I point out particular Places?

And as to the other Part of the Christian Doctrine of Terror-menaced Punishment, see it set forth in the Punishment of Love-lace and of the whole Harlowe Family, even in this World. And shall not a Clarissa, shall not a Christian Heroine trust to Heaven for her own Reward? shall she elbow, scuffle, contend, and be vin-dictive, rather than intitle herself to the Blessings held in Store for the Patient, the resigned, the persevering mind? Parents and Sov-ereigns must in general be left for God to Punish, and seldom do faulty ones escape their Share of Punishment in this Life, and that even Springing from the Seeds sown by themselves. But where would Depravity end if this were to be ye Argument to a Parent? I, Madam, will be the Judge of the Measures of my own Obedience to you; I am Twenty-one—I am free of all Obligation to you. I owe you nothing for all your care of me in my helpless Infancy—For your Expence in my Education, whatever be ye Use I have made of it, for the Fortune you have accumulated for me, for my genteel Maintenance when I could neither contribute to it nor deserve it. And my Children, if I ever have any, I acquit of their Duty and

Observance to me. They will do the same by theirs, no doubt. We will be a Family of Revellers as well as Levellers. Our Examples, I hope, will spread—and then will the World be worth living in; for Children at least. And what is left for you, Parents, to do, but when we have no further Occasion for you, to make your Wills, divide what you have among us, and like the Hottentot Parents retire to the Dens of the Wild Beasts, or live upon such a Pittance as we shall allow you, or allow you to reserve to yourselves, or to be so good natur'd and dutiful, since you owe as much Duty to us as we owe to you, as to lie down and die quietly. Sufficiently returned will be the Obligation for bringing us into ye world, if we take care of you on your Leaving it.

FROM A Letter to Sarah Chapone, March 25, 1751[1]

. . . Pray tell my Miss Sally that Miss Howe as well as Pamela was intirely the Creature of my Fancy. It was my View to draw a lively Woman of Virtue and in the Main of excellent Qualities with a Soul so capable of glowing Friendship as to deserve Clarissa's warmest Love, and this in order to combat the Notion of Rakes and Foplings that Womens Minds are incapable of fervent and steady Friendships, and I threw in a few Shades, a few Failings consequent to so lively a Character and for Clarissa to correct: Such as Flippancy to her Mother and Insolence to the good Man she nevertheless intended to have in order to insinuate the *Faults* and the *Cure* to young Minds.—But tho I have had Ideas of this or that Person before me in *parts* no one Person Man or Woman sat before me for the *Whole* of any of my Pictures so that I was out of Fear of being supposed to have it in my Thought either to flatter or affront any Person breathing. And to say Truth I had my Vanity in hopeing to be able to draw Characters not unnatural and yet to have it to say and to think that no single Person could claim the Good or be disgusted with the Bad.—What a deal of Wickedness may it be infer'd was in my Mind to draw from *thence* such a Man as Lovelace:—Indeed I put the Iniquity of two or three bad Characters togeather in my Mind in order to draw his; and several times as I

---

1. Reprinted, by permission of the Clarendon Press, from Carroll, ed., *Selected Letters of Samuel Richardson*, pp. 180–181.

proceeded I had Thoughts of burning the Ms. for fear of doing Mischief by his Character. Yet takeing in Scoffers and Infidels and Gamesters, and Sporters with other Mens properties as well as with their own I am convinced there are worse Men than even him. But if I have set the Balance even by drawing from the same Source my better Characters it is all I am sollicitous about as to the World for I know that I have many Faults. And this I must say that I have the Felicity to imagine that I have made the Conversations and Correspondence of the Rakes (and more particularly in the Reformation of the one and in the Remorses and the Death of the other) as instructive as any Parts of the Whole Work.—See my Dear Miss Sally how your Questions have run me into Boasting!— But I shall have a still greater Boast my Dear if I can by any meanes flatter my self with deserving yours and your Sisters Love. . . .

4 Henry Fielding

A Letter to Samuel Richardson, October 15, 1748[1]

I have read over your 5th Vol. In all the Accounts which Loveless Gives of the Transactions at Hampstead, you preserve the same vein of Humour which hath run through the preceding Volumes. The new Characters you Introduce are natural and entertaining, and there is much of the true Comic Force in the Widow Bevis. I have seen her often, and I Promise you, you have drawn her with great exactness. The Character of Loveless is heightened with great Judgment. His former Admirers must lose all Regard for him on his Perseverance, and as this Regard Ceases, Compassion for Clarissa rises in the same Proportion. Hence we are admirably prepared for what is to follow.—Shall I tell you? Can I tell you what I think of the latter part of your Volume? Let the Overflowings of a Heart which you have filled brimfull speak for me.

1. Reprinted, by permission of the publisher from E. L. McAdam Jr., "A New Letter from Fielding," *Yale Review,* copyright Yale University Press, vol. XXXVIII (Winter, 1949), pp. 304–306.

"When Clarissa returns to her Lodgings at St. Clairs the Alarm begins, and here my Heart begins its Narrative. I am Shocked; my Terrors ar[e ra]ised, and I have the utmost Apprehensions for the poor betrayed Creature.—But when I see her enter with the Letter in her Hand, and after some natural Effects of Despair, clasping her Arms about the Knees of the Villain, call him her Dear Lovelace, desirous and yet unable to implore his Protection or rather his mercy; I then melt into Compassion, and find what is called an Effeminate Relief for my Terror, to continue to the End of the Scene. When I read the next Letter I am Thunderstruck; nor can many Lines explain what I feel from Two.

"What I shall [sic] say of holding up the Licence? I will say a finer Picture was never imagined. He must be a Glorious Painter who can do it Justice on Canvas, and a most wretched one indeed who could not do much on such a Subject. The Circumstance of the Fragments is Great and Terrible; but her [Clarissa's] Letter to Lovelace is beyond any thing I have ever read. God forbid that the Man who reads this with dry Eyes should be alone with my Daughter when she hath no Assistance within Call. Here my Terror ends and my Grief begins which the Cause of all my Tumultuous Passions soon changes into Raptures of Admiration and Astonishment by a Behaviour the most Elevated I can possibly conceive, and what is at the same time most Gentle and most natural. This Scene I have heard hath been often objected to. It is well for the Critick that My Heart is now writing and not my Head. During the Continuance of this Vol. my Compassion is often moved; but I think my Admiration more. If I had rec'd no Hint or Information of what is to succeed I should perceive you paving the way to load our admiration of your Heroine to the Highest Pitch, as you have before with wonderfull Art prepared us for both Terror and Compassion on her Account. This last seems to come from the Head. Here then I will end: for I assure you nothing but my Heart can force me to say Half of what I think of *the* Book. And yet what hinders me? I cannot be suspected of Flattery. I know the Value of that too much to throw it away, where I have no Obligation, and where I expect no Reward. And sure the World will not suppose me inclined to flatter one whom they will suppose me to hate if the[y] will be pleased to recollect that we are Rivals for that coy Mrs. Fame. Believe me however if your Clarissa had not engaged my

Affections more than this Mrs. all your Art and all your Nature had not been able to extract a single Tear: for as to this Mrs. I have ravished her long ago, and live in a settled cohabitation with her in defiance of that Public Voice which is supposed to be her Guardian, and to have alone the Power of giving her away. To explain this Riddle. It is not that I am less but more addicted to Vanity than others; so much that I can wrap my self up as warmly in my own vanity, as the Ancient could involve himself in his Virtue. If I have any Merit I certainly know it and if the World will not allow it me, I will allow it my self. I would not have you think (I might say know) me *to be* so dishonest as to assert that I despise Fame; but this I solemnly aver that I love her as coldly, as most of us do Heaven, so that I will sacrifice nothing to the Pursuit of her. much less would I bind my self, as all her Passionate Admirers do, to harbour in my Bosom that monster Envy which of all Beings either real or imaginary I most heartily and sincerely abhor. You will begin to think I believe, that I want not much external Commendation. I will conclude then with assuring you. That I heartily wish you Success. That I sincerely think you in the highest manner deserve it. And that if you have it not, it it [*sic*] would be in me unpardonable Presumption to hope for Success, and at the same time almost contemptible Humility [not?] to desire it.

"I am Dear Sͬ yrs. most Affectionately Hen. Ffielding

"I beg you to send me immediately the two remaining Vols:"

5 [*Albrecht von Haller*][1]

FROM "Remarks on the History of CLARISSA," *Gentleman's Magazine*, August, 1749[2]

The method which the author has pursued, in the history of *Clarissa*, is the same as in the life of *Pamela;* both are related in

1. This attribution was made by Laurence M. Price in "On the Reception of Richardson in Germany," *Journal of English and Germanic Philology*, vol. XXV (1926), p. 19.
2. Vol. XIX, pp. 345–349.

familiar letters, by the parties themselves, at the very time in which the events happened; and this method has given the author great advantages, which he could not have drawn from any other species of narration. The minute particulars of events, the sentiments and conversation of the parties, are, upon this plan, exhibited with all the warmth and spirit that the passion, supposed to be predominant at the very time, could produce, and with all the distinguishing characteristicks, which memory can supply, in a history of recent transactions. Romances in general, and *Marivaux's* among others, are wholly improbable; because they suppose the history to be written after the series of events is closed by the catastrophe; a circumstance, which implies a strength of memory, beyond all example and probability, in the persons concerned, enabling them, at the distance of several years, to relate all the particulars of a transient conversation: Or rather it implies a yet more improbable confidence and familiarity between all these persons and the author. There is, however, one difficulty attending the epistolary method, for it is necessary that all the characters should have an uncommon taste for this kind of correspondence, and that they should suffer no event, nor even a remarkable conversation to pass without immediately committing it to writing; but, for the preservation of these letters, once written, the author has provided with great judgment, so as to render this circumstance highly probable.

We shall now proceed to the history itself, to which we shall add some cursory remarks. . . .

The style of *Clarissa* is peculiar to itself; that of *Lovelace* is full of new words, arbitrarily formed in his own manner, which are strongly expressive of his ideas. The style of every letter is excellently adapted to the character of the writer; but there is such a gentility, so easy and natural an elegance preserved in the whole, as would alone render this work valuable. As the greater part of the most interesting scenes are exhibited in dialogue, proper attention must be given to the change of the speakers, the author being, in every sense, above the common way of distinguishing them by putting their names before their respective parts of the conversation.

The pathetic has never been exhibited with equal power, and it is manifest, in a thousand instances, that the most obdurate and insensible tempers have been softened into compassion, and melted into tears, by the death, the sufferings, and the sorrows of *Clarissa*. We have not read any performance, in any language, that so much as approaches to a competition; for here nature is represented with all its circumstances, and nature only can persuade and move. In *Clarissa* we see a virtuous character, in the same station of life with ourselves suffer with an immovable and unshaken constancy. The misfortunes of an *Ariane* move me not at all, those of a Princess of *Cleves* but faintly. The heroes there are beings too different from myself, and the misfortunes which happen to them, bear no proportion to any that may happen to me. I cannot but know it to be a fable, and the necessary effect of this knowledge is insensibility.

The chief ornament of *Clarissa* is the description; there are some in *Pamela* which are excellent, but those of her younger sister are more frequent, more elevated, and more animated. The death of *Belton* is represented with such circumstances of horror, as cannot but intimidate the most daring profligate. The sufferings of *Clarissa* during her injurious imprisonment, the preparations which she makes for her death, her death itself, her noble defence against the second attempt of *Lovelace,* her sorrows, and even her deliriums, her funeral; all this, is drawn with an animated expression, that strikes, persuades, subdues—Such is the unanimous opinion of all readers, however diversified by taste, disposition, and capacity.

But *Clarissa* is rendered almost inestimable, by those exalted sentiments of piety, virtue, generosity, prudence, and humility, which adorn the person of the heroine, and are inculcated by her discourse and conduct. It is impossible to read the three last volumes without being conscious to a secret elation of mind; a species of delight, equally pure and noble, arising from the contemplation of human nature in the highest perfection to which it can attain by the purest virtue, and the most distinguish'd grace.

But has this *Clarissa*, which we thus extol, no faults? This reflexion frequently arises to the reader, whom a journalist too apparently endeavours to prepossess. There is a degree of malignity in the human breast, and we should be inconsolable when our praise is extorted by admiration but for the pleasure of mingling some criticisms with our eulogium; this raises us nearer to a level with those whom we cannot but commend. But to be serious and impartial, *Clarissa* has faults, at least, with respect to *our manners* and *customs;* for, I will not venture to assert, that they can justly be styled faults by an *English* reader.

I do not mean the faults of which *Clarissa* is guilty, and which bring on her ruin: It is, however, certain, that a lady of her prudence, and purity of mind, should have broke off all correspondence with *Lovelace,* the moment it was forbidden by her mother; for the necessity of continuing it, to prevent ill consequences, is apparently no more than a pretence; and a good intention does not justify an evil action.

She is also guilty of another very considerable fault, in consenting to two assignations with a lover, whom she knew to be a rake, and had been forbidden the house by her parents, whom she loved and honoured.

She seems also to take the part of *Lovelace,* against her relations, with too much zeal. She ought rather to have heard their accusations, and to have suffer'd herself to be disabused.

She treats Mr. *Solmes* with too much disrespect; she might laudably have refus'd him, in such terms as might leave him no hope, but she ought not to have insulted him.

On the other hand, she shews too scrupulous a delicacy after she has suffered herself to be carry'd off by *Lovelace:* It then became expedient for her to marry *Lovelace,* who, more than once, offer'd her his hand, in the involuntary transports of his passion.———A lady, who has once put herself into the power of her lover, is no longer to affect distance, or expect the punctilio's of courtship should be observed. . . .

It is also certain, that the author has abused the privilege, which he derives from the unbounded liberty of his country: He has dispersed, in some parts of his book, the particulars of freedoms taken by *Lovelace,* which exceed the bounds of decency. The infamous house into which the heroine is introduced, and in which she is so grossly abused, makes me fear that *Clarissa,* at least in *France,* will share the same fate with the *Theodore* of *Corneille.* All the libertines of *Paris,* all the ladies of gallantry, who feared nothing in the crime itself, were disgusted with the coarseness of the expression, and the piece, though it was the work of *Pierre Corneille,* was not suffer'd to be play'd out. . . .

There is yet another scene which *Belford* has painted in the most offensive colours; a view of the life of common women. It is, indeed, excellently drawn; but can it be exhibited at all without disgusting a delicate reader? . . .

Let us here quit the subject. There never was a book without fault; at least, in which a fault could not be found, if it was diligently sought. Happy are the authors who, with the editor of *Clarissa*, can captivate nations, and to whom the suffrage of some, who are critics by profession, is not deny'd!

6 *The Reverend Philip Skelton*

FROM "Hints of Prefaces for *Clarissa*," c. 1750[1]

They who read Romances and Novels, being accustomed to a Variety of Intrigues and Adventures, thro' which they are hurried to the Catastrophe; when they take up Clarissa, not considering that it is another kind of Work, or rather a new Species of Novel, are apt to think it tedious, towards the Beginning especially, because they have not the same Palate for natural Incidents, as for imaginary Adventures; for the Workings of private and domestic Passions, as for those of Kings, Heroes, Heroines; for a Story English as to its Scenes, Names, Manners, as for one that is foreign: But a Reader of true Taste and Judgment will like it infinitely better, because it comes home to the Heart, and to common Life, in every Line; because it abounds with a surprising Variety of Strokes and Paintings, that seem to be taken from real Life, and of Maxims and Reflections too just, and too useful, to be passed over unnoticed or unremembred [sic] by a Reader of Experience. These, together with the masterly Management of the Characters, serve better to entertain, while they instruct, a judicious Reader, than a Croud of

1. Reprinted from Publication Number 103 (1964) of the Augustan Reprint Society, William Andrews Clark Memorial Library, University of California at Los Angeles, pp. 7–8. The draft of Richardson's preface included Richardson's transcription of Skelton's evaluation of *Clarissa*. Neither the Preface nor the Postscript, for which this draft likewise furnished considerable material, incorporated Skelton's comments.

mere imaginary Amours, Duels, and such-like Events, which abound with Leaves and Flowers, but no Fruits; and therefore cannot be relished but by a vitiated Taste, by the Taste of a Chameleon, not of a Man. Two or three Hours furnish Matter for an excellent Play: Why may not Two or Three Months supply Materials for as many Volumes? Is the History of Thucydides less entertaining or instructive, because its Subject is confined to narrow Bounds, than that of Raleigh, which hath the World for its Subject? Is Clarissa a mere Novel? Whoever considers it as such, does not understand it. It is a System of religious and moral Precepts and Examples, planned on an entertaining Story, which stands or goes forward, as the excellent Design of the Author requires; but never stands without pouring in Incidents, Descriptions, Maxims, that keep Attention alive, that engage and mend the Heart, that play with the Imagination, while they inform the Understanding.

7 Samuel Richardson

FROM Preface to *Clarissa*[1]

The following History is given in a series of letters, written principally in a double yet separate correspondence;

Between two young ladies of virtue and honour, bearing an inviolable friendship for each other, and writing not merely for amusement, but upon most *interesting* subjects; in which every private family, more or less, may find itself concerned: and,

Between two gentlemen of free lives; one of them glorying in his talents for stratagem and invention, and communicating to the other, in confidence, all the secret purposes of an intriguing head and resolute heart.

But here it will be proper to observe, for the sake of such as may apprehend hurt to the morals of youth, from the more freely-written letters, that the gentlemen, though professed libertines as to the

1. Reprinted from *The Novels of Samuel Richardson Esq.*, London: Hurst, Robinson, and Company, 1824, vol. I, pp. 509–510.

female sex, and making it one of their wicked maxims, to keep no faith with any of the individuals of it, who are thrown into their power, are not, however, either infidels or scoffers; nor yet such as think themselves freed from the observance of those other moral duties which bind man to man.

On the contrary, it will be found, in the progress of the work, that they very often make such reflections upon each other, and each upon himself and his own actions, as reasonable beings *must* make, who disbelieve not a future state of rewards and punishments, and who one day propose to reform—one of them actually reforming, and by that means giving an opportunity to censure the freedoms which fall from the gayer pen and lighter heart of the other.

And yet that other, although, in unbosoming himself to a select friend, he discover wickedness enough to entitle him to general detestation, preserves a decency, as well in his images as in his language, which is not always to be found in the works of some of the most celebrated modern writers, whose subjects and characters have less warranted the liberties they have taken.

In the letters of the two young ladies, it is presumed, will be found not only the highest exercise of a reasonable and *practicable* friendship, between minds endowed with the noblest principles of virtue and religion, but occasionally interspersed, such delicacy of sentiments, particularly with regard to the other sex; such instances of impartiality, each freely, as a fundamental principle of their friendship, blaming, praising, and setting right the other, as are strongly to be recommended to the observation of the *younger* part (more specially) of female readers. . . .

All the letters are written while the hearts of the writers must be supposed to be wholly engaged in their subjects (the events at the time generally dubious): so that they abound not only with critical situations, but with what may be called *instantaneous* descriptions and reflections (proper to be brought home to the breast of the youthful reader;) as also with affecting conversations; many of them written in the dialogue or dramatic way.

"*Much more* lively and affecting," says one of the principal characters, "must be the style of those who write in the height of a *present* distress; the mind tortured by the pangs of uncertainty (the events then hidden in the womb of fate;) *than* the dry, narrative,

unanimated style of a person relating difficulties and danger sur-
mounted, can be; the relater perfectly at ease; and if himself
unmoved by his own story, not likely greatly to affect the reader."

8 Samuel Richardson

FROM Postscript to *Clarissa*[1]

The foregoing work having been published at three different periods
of time, the author, in the course of its publication, was favoured
with many anonymous letters, in which the writers differently expressed their wishes with regard to the apprehended catastrophe.

Most of those directed to him by the gentler sex, turned in favour
of what they called a *fortunate ending*. Some of the fair writers,
enamoured, as they declared, with the character of the heroine, were
warmly solicitious to have her made happy; and others, likewise of
their mind, *insisted that poetical justice* required that it should be so.
And when, says one ingenious lady, whose undoubted motive was
good-nature and humanity, it must be concluded, that it is in an
author's power to make his piece end as he pleases, why should he
not give pleasure rather than pain to the reader, whom he has
interested in favour of his principal characters?

Others, and some gentlemen, declared against tragedies in general,
and in favour of comedies, almost in the words of Lovelace, who was
supported in his taste by all the women at Mrs. Sinclair's and by
Sinclair herself. "I have too much *feeling*, said he. There is enough
in the world to make our hearts sad, without carrying grief into our
diversions, and making the distresses of others our own."

And how was this happy ending to be brought about? Why, by
this very easy and trite expedient; to wit, by reforming Lovelace,
and marrying him to Clarissa—not, however, abating her one of
her trials, nor any of her sufferings, [for the sake of the sport her
distresses would give to the *tender-hearted* reader, as she went

1. Reprinted from *The Novels of Samuel Richardson Esq.*, London: Hurst,
Robinson, and Company, 1824, vol. II, pp. 778–779, 782–786.

along,] the last outrage excepted; that, indeed, partly in compliment to Lovelace himself, and partly for delicacy-sake, they were willing to spare her.

But whatever were the fate of his work, the author was resolved to take a different method. He always thought that *sudden conversions,* such, especially, as were left to the candour of the reader to *suppose* and *make out,* had neither *art,* nor *nature,* not even *probability,* in them; and that they were, moreover, of very *bad* example. To have a Lovelace, for a series of years, glory in his wickedness, and think that he had nothing to do, but as an act of grace and favour to hold out his hand to receive that of the best of women, whenever he pleased, and to have it thought that marriage would be a sufficient amends for all his enormities to others as well as to her—he could not bear that. Nor is reformation, as he has shewn in another piece, to be secured by a fine face; by a passion that has sense for its object; nor by the goodness of a wife's heart, nor even example, if the heart of the husband be not graciously touched by the Divine finger.

It will be seen, by this time, that the author had a great end in view. He has lived to see scepticism and infidelity openly avowed, and even endeavoured to be propagated from the *press;* the great doctrines of the Gospel brought into question; those of self-denial and mortification blotted out of the catalogue of Christian virtues; and a taste even to wantonness for outdoor pleasure and luxury, to the general exclusion of domestic as well as public virtue, industriously promoted among all ranks and degrees of people.

In this general depravity, when even the pulpit has lost great part of its weight, and the clergy are considered as a body of *interested* men, the author thought he should be able to answer it to his own heart, be the success what it would, if he threw in his mite towards introducing a reformation so much wanted; and he imagined, that if in an age given up to diversion and entertainment, he could *steal in,* as may be said, and investigate the great doctrines of Christianity under the fashionable guise of an amusement; he should be most likely to serve his purpose, remembering that of the Poet:—

> A verse may find him who a sermon flies,
> And turn delight into a sacrifice.

He was resolved, therefore, to attempt something that never yet
had been done. He considered that the tragic poets have as seldom
made their heroes true objects of pity, as the comic their's laudable
ones of imitation; and still more rarely have made them in their
deaths look forward to a *future hope*. And thus, when they die, they
seem totally to perish. Death, in such instances, must appear terrible.
It must be considered as the greatest evil. But why is death set in
shocking lights, when it is the universal lot?

He has, indeed, thought fit to paint the death of the wicked, as
terrible as he could paint it. But he has endeavoured to draw that
of the good in such an amiable manner, that the very Balaams of
the world should not forbear to wish that their latter end might be
like that of the heroine.

And after all, what is the *poetical justice* so much contended for
by some, as the generality of writers have managed it, but another
sort of dispensation than that with which God, by revelation, teaches
us. He has thought fit to exercise mankind; whom placing here only
in a state of probation, he hath so intermingled good and evil, as to
necessitate us to look forward for a more equal dispensation of both?

The Author of the History (or rather Dramatic Narrative) of
Clarissa, is therefore well justified by the *Christian system,* in
deferring to extricate suffering virtue to the time in which it will
meet with the *completion* of its reward. . . .

Several persons have censured the heroine as too cold in her love,
too haughty, and even sometimes provoking. But we may presume
to say, that this objection has arisen from want of attention to the
story, to the character of Clarissa, and to her particular situation.

It was not intended that she should be *in love,* but *in liking* only,
if that expression may be admitted. It is meant to be everywhere
inculcated in the story for *example sake,* that she never would have
married Mr. Lovelace, because of his immoralities, had she been left
to herself; and that her ruin was principally owing to the persecutions of her friends.

What is too generally called *love,* ought (perhaps *as* generally)
to be called by another name. *Cupidity,* or a *Paphian stimulus,* as
some women, even of condition, have acted, are not words too harsh
to be substituted on the occasion, however grating they may be to

delicate ears. But take the word *love* in the gentlest and most honour-able sense, it would have been thought by some highly improbable, that Clarissa should have been able to shew such a command of her passions, as makes so distinguishing a part of her character, had she been as violently in love, as certain warm and fierce spirits would have had her to be. . . .

It has been thought, by some worthy and ingenious persons, that if Lovelace had been drawn an *infidel* or *scoffer*, his character, ac-cording to the taste of the present worse than sceptical age, would have been more natural. It is, however, too well known, that there are very many persons of his cast, whose actions discredit their belief. And are not the very devils, in Scripture, said to *believe* and *tremble?* . . .

Some have wished that the story had been told in the usual narra-tive way of telling stories, designed to amuse and divert, and not in letters written by the respective persons whose history is given in them. The author thinks he ought not to prescribe to the taste of others, but imagined himself at liberty to follow his own. He perhaps mistrusted his talents for the narrative kind of writing. He had the good fortune to succeed in the epistolary way once before. A story in which so many persons were concerned either principally or collaterally, and of characters and dispositions so various, carried on with tolerable connection and perspicuity, in a series of letters from different persons, without the aid of digressions and episodes foreign to the principal end and design, he thought had *novelty* to be pleaded for it; and that, in the present age, he supposed would not be a slight recommendation. . . . It is very well accounted for in it, how the two principal female characters came to take so great a delight in writing. Their subjects are not merely subjects of amuse-ment; but greatly interesting to both; yet many ladies there are who now laudably correspond, when at distance from each other, on occasions that far less affect their mutual welfare and friendships, than those treated of by these ladies. The two principal gentlemen had motives of gaiety and vain-glory for their inducements. It will generally be found, that persons who have talents for familiar writ-ing, as these correspondents are presumed to have, will not forbear amusing themselves with their pens on less arduous occasions than what offer to these. These FOUR, (whose stories have a connection with each other,) out of the great number of characters which are introduced in this History, are only eminent in the epistolary way; the rest appear but as occasional writers, and as drawn in rather by necessity than choice, from the different relations in which they stand with the four principal persons.

The length of the piece has been objected to by some, who perhaps looked upon it as a mere *novel* or *romance;* and yet of *these* there are not wanting works of equal length.

They were of opinion, that the story moved too slowly, particularly in the first and second volumes, which are chiefly taken up with the altercations between Clarissa and the several persons of her family.

But is it not true, that those altercations are the foundation of the whole, and therefore a necessary part of the work? The letters and conversations, where the story makes the slowest progress, are presumed to be *characteristic.* They give occasion, likewise, to suggest many interesting *personalities,* in which a good deal of the instruction essential to a work of this nature is conveyed. And it will, moreover, be remembered, that the author, at his first setting out, apprized the reader, that the story (interesting as it is generally allowed to be) was to be principally looked upon as the vehicle to the instruction.

To all which we may add, that there was frequently a necessity to be very circumstantial and minute, in order to preserve and maintain that air of probability, which is necessary to be maintained in a story designed to represent real life; and which is rendered extremely busy and active by the plots and contrivances formed and carried on by one of the principal characters.

Some there are, and ladies too! who have supposed that the excellencies of the heroine are carried to an improbable, and even to an impracticable, height in this history. But the education of Clarissa, from *early childhood,* ought to be considered as one of her very great advantages; as, indeed, the foundation of *all* her excellencies; and, it is hoped, for the sake of the doctrine designed to be inculcated by it, that it will. . . .

It must be confessed, that we are not to look for *Clarissas* among the *constant frequenters* of Ranelagh and Vauxhall, nor among those who may be called *Daughters of the card-table*. If we do, the character of our heroine may then, indeed, be justly thought not only improbable, but unattainable. But we have neither room in this place, nor inclination, to pursue a subject so invidious. We quit it, therefore, after we have *repeated* that we *know* there are *some*, and we *hope* there are *many*, in the British dominions, (or they are hardly anywhere in the European world,) who, as far as *occasion* has called upon them to exert the like *humble* and *modest*, yet *steady* and *useful*, virtues, have reached the perfections of a Clarissa.

9 Samuel Richardson

FROM Preface to *Sir Charles Grandison*, 1753[1]

The Editor of the following Letters takes leave to observe, that he has now, in this publication, completed the plan, that was the object of his wishes, rather than of his hopes, to accomplish.

The first collection which he published, entitled 'Pamela,' exhibited the beauty and superiority of virtue in an innocent and unpolished mind, with the reward which often, even in this life, a protecting Providence bestows on goodness. A young woman of low degree, relating to her honest parents the severe trials she met with, from a master who ought to have been the protector, not the assailer, of her honour, shews the character of a libertine in its truly contemptible light. This libertine, however, from the foundation of good principles laid in his early years by an excellent mother; by his passion for a virtuous young woman; and by her amiable example, and unwearied patience, when she became his wife; is, after a length of time, perfectly reclaimed.

The second collection, published under the title of 'Clarissa,' displayed a more melancholy scene. A young lady of higher fortune, and born to happier hopes, is seen involved in such variety of deep

1. Reprinted from *The Novels of Samuel Richardson Esq.*, London: Hurst, Robinson, and Company, 1824, vol. II, p. iii.

distresses, as lead her to an untimely death; affording a warning to parents against forcing the inclinations of their children in the most important article of their lives; and to children, against hoping too far from the fairest assurances of a man void of principle. The heroine, however, as a truly *christian heroine*, proves superior to her trials; and her heart, always excellent, refined and exalted by every one of them, rejoices in the approach of a happy eternity. Her cruel destroyer appears wretched and disappointed, even in the boasted success of his vile machinations: But still (buoyed up with self-conceit and vain presumption) he goes on, after every short fit of imperfect, yet terrifying conviction, hardening himself more and more; till, unreclaimed by the most affecting warnings, and repeated admonitions, he perishes miserably in the bloom of life, and sinks into the grave oppressed with guilt, remorse, and horror. His letters, it is hoped, afford many useful lessons to the gay part of mankind, against that misuse of wit and youth, of rank and fortune, and of every outward accomplishment, which turns them into a curse to the miserable possessor, as well as to all around him.

10 Hester Piozzi

FROM *Anecdotes of the Late Samuel Johnson, L.L.D.,* 1786[1]

And when he talked of authors, his praise went spontaneously to such passages as are sure in his own phrase to leave something behind them useful on common occasions, or observant of common manners. For example, it was not the two *last,* but the two *first,* volumes of Clarissa that he prized; 'For give me a sick bed, and a dying lady (said he), and I'll be pathetic myself: but Richardson had picked the kernel of life (he said), while Fielding was contented with the husk.'

1. Reprinted from George Birkbeck Hill, ed., *Johnsonian Miscellanies,* New York: Harper Brothers, 1897, vol. II, p. 282.

11 *William Hazlitt*

FROM "Lectures on the English Poets"[1]

It has been made a question whether Richardson's romances are poetry; and the answer perhaps is, that they are not poetry, because they are not romance. The interest is worked up to an inconceivable height; but it is by an infinite number of little things, by incessant labour and calls upon the attention, by a repetition of blows that have no rebound in them. The sympathy excited is not a voluntary contribution, but a tax. Nothing is unforced and spontaneous. There is a want of elasticity and motion. The story does not 'give an echo to the seat where love is throned.' The heart does not answer of itself like a chord in music. The fancy does not run on before the writer with breathless expectation, but is dragged along with an infinite number of pins and wheels, like those with which the Lilliputians dragged Gulliver pinioned to the royal palace. . . . Clarissa, the divine Clarissa, is too interesting by half. She is interesting in her ruffles, in her gloves, her samplers, her aunts and uncles—she is interesting in all that is uninteresting. Such things, however intensely they may be brought home to us, are not conductors to the imagination.

FROM "Standard Novels and Romances"[2]

It is not, in our opinion, a very difficult attempt to class Fielding or Smollett;—the one as an observer of the characters of human life, the other as a describer of its various eccentricities. But it is by no means so easy to dispose of Richardson, who was neither an observer of the one, nor a describer of the other; but who seemed

1. Reprinted by permission of the publisher, from P. P. Howe, ed., from *The Complete Works of William Hazlitt,* London: J. M. Dent & Sons, 1930–34, vol. V, pp. 14–15.
2. Reprinted by permission of the publisher, from P. P. Howe, ed., from *The Complete Works of William Hazlitt,* London: J. M. Dent & Sons, 1930–34, vol. XVI, pp. 15–18.

to spin his materials entirely out of his own brain, as if there had been nothing existing in the world beyond the little shop in which he sat writing. There is an artificial reality about his works, which is nowhere [else] to be met with. They have the romantic air of a pure fiction, with the literal minuteness of a common diary. The author had the strangest matter-of-fact imagination that ever existed, and wrote the oddest mixture of poetry and prose. He does not appear to have taken advantage of any thing in actual nature, from one end of his works to the other: and yet, throughout all his works (voluminous as they are—and this, to be sure, is one reason why they are so), he sets about describing every object and transaction, as if the whole had been given in on evidence by an eyewitness. This kind of high finishing from imagination is an anomaly in the history of human genius; and certainly nothing so fine was ever produced by the same accumulation of minute parts. There is not the least distraction, the least forgetfulness of the end: every circumstance is made to tell. We cannot agree that this exactness of detail produces heaviness; on the contrary, it gives an appearance of truth, and a positive interest to the story; and we listen with the same attention as we should to the particulars of a confidential communication.

. . . Richardson's nature is always the nature of sentiment and reflection, not of impulse or situation. He furnishes his characters, on every occasion, with the presence of mind of the author. He makes them act, not as they would from the impulse of the moment, but as they might upon reflection, and upon a careful review of every motive and circumstance in their situation. They regularly sit down to write letters: and if the business of life consisted in letter-writing, and was carried on by the post (like a Spanish game at chess), human nature would be what Richardson represents it. All actual objects and feelings are blunted and deadened by being presented through a medium which may be true to reason, but is false in nature. He confounds his own point of view with that of the immediate actors in the scene; and hence presents you with a conventional and factitious nature, instead of that which is real. Dr. Johnson seems to have preferred this truth of reflection to the truth of nature, when he said that there was more knowledge of the human heart in a page of Richardson than in all Fielding. Fielding, however, saw more of the practical results, and understood the principles as well; but he had not the same power of speculating upon their possible results, and combining them in certain ideal forms of passion and imagination, which was Richardson's real excellence.

It must be observed, however, that it is this mutual good understanding, and comparing of notes between the author and the persons he describes; his infinite circumspection, his exact process of ratiocination and calculation, which gives such an appearance of coldness and formality to most of his characters,—which makes prudes of his women, and coxcombs of his men. Every thing is too conscious in his works. Every thing is distinctly brought home to the mind of the actors in the scene, which is a fault undoubtedly: but then, it must be confessed, every thing is brought home in its full force to the mind of the reader also; and we feel the same interest in the story as if it were our own. . . . Clarissa is, however, his masterpiece, if we except Lovelace. If she is fine in herself, she is still finer in his account of her. With that foil, her purity is dazzling indeed: and she who could triumph by her virtue, and the force of her love, over the regality of Lovelace's mind, his wit, his person, his accomplishments and his spirit, conquers all hearts. We should suppose that never sympathy more deep or sincere was excited than by the heroine of Richardson's romance, except by the calamities of real life. The links in this wonderful chain of interest are not more finely wrought, than their whole weight is overwhelming and irresistible. Who can forget the exquisite gradations of her long dying scene, or the closing of the coffin-lid, when Miss Howe comes to take her last leave of her friend; or the heart-breaking reflection that Clarissa makes on what was to have been her wedding-day? Well does a modern writer exclaim—

> 'Books are a real world, both pure and good,
> Round which, with tendrils strong as flesh and blood,
> Our pastime and our happiness may grow!'

Richardson's wit was unlike that of any other writer;—his humour was so too. Both were the effect of intense activity of mind;— laboured, and yet completely effectual. We might refer to Lovelace's reception and description of Hickman, when he calls out Death in his ear, as the name of the person with whom Clarissa had fallen in love; and to the scene at the glove shop. What can be more magnificent than his enumeration of his companions—'Belton so pert and so pimply—Tourville so fair and so foppish,' &c.? In casuistry, he is quite at home; and, with a boldness greater even than his puritanical severity, has exhausted every topic on virtue and vice. There is another peculiarity in Richardson, not perhaps so uncommon, which is, his systematically preferring his most insipid characters to his finest, though both were equally his own invention, and he must be supposed to have understood something of their qualities.

Laurence Sterne
Tristram Shandy
1767

1 *Samuel Johnson*

Nothing odd will do long. "Tristram Shandy" did not last.

2 *Thomas Jefferson*

FROM A Letter to Peter Carr, August 10, 1787

The writings of Sterne particularly form the best course of morality that ever was written.

3 *Samuel Johnson*

I was but once in Sterne's company, and then his only attempt at merriment consisted in his display of a drawing too indecently gross to have delighted even in a brothel.

4 *Horace Walpole*

FROM A Letter to Dalrymple, April 4, 1760[1]

At present nothing is talked of, nothing admired, but what I cannot help calling a very insipid and tedious performance: it is a kind of novel called, *The Life and Opinions of Tristram Shandy*, the great humour of which consists in the whole narration always going backwards. I can conceive a man saying that it would be droll to write a book in that manner, but have no notion of his persevering in executing it. It makes one smile two or three times at the beginning, but in recompense makes one yawn for two hours. The characters are tolerably kept up; but the humour is forever attempted and missed. The best thing in it is a sermon—oddly coupled with a good deal of bawdy, and both the composition of a clergyman.

5 *Samuel Richardson*

FROM A Letter to the Reverend Mr. Hildesley, 1761[2]

Who is this Yorick? you are pleased to ask me. You cannot, I imagine have looked into his books: execrable I cannot but call them; for I am told that the third and fourth volumes are worse, if possible, than the two first; which, only, I have had the patience to run through. One extenuating circumstance attends his works, that they are too gross to be inflaming.

My daughter shall transcribe for me the sentiments of a young lady, as written to another lady, her friend in the country, on the publication of the two first volumes only.

1. Reprinted by permission of the publisher from W. S. Lewis, ed., *The Yale Edition of Horace Walpole's Correspondence*, New Haven: Yale University Press, 1951, vol. XV, p. 66.
2. Reprinted from Anna L. Barbauld, ed., *The Correspondence of Samuel Richardson*, London: R. Phillips, 1804, vol. V, pp. 146–149.

"Happy are you in your retirement, where you read what books you choose, either for instruction or entertainment; but in this foolish town, we are obliged to read every foolish book that fashion renders prevalent in conversation; and I am horribly out of humour with the present taste, which makes people ashamed to own they have not read, what if fashion did not authorise, they would with more reason blush to say they had read! Perhaps some polite person from London, may have forced this piece into your hands, but give it not a place in your library; let not Tristram Shandy be ranked among the well chosen authors there. It is, indeed, a little book, and little is its merit, though great has been the writer's reward! Unaccountable wildness; whimsical digressions; comical incoherencies; uncommon indecencies; all with an air of novelty, has catched the reader's attention, and applause has flown from one to another, till it is almost singular to disapprove: even the bishops admire, and recompense his wit, though his own character as a clergyman seems much impeached by printing such gross and vulgar tales, as no decent mind can endure without extreme disgust! Yet I will do him justice; and, if forced by friends, or led by curiosity, you have read, and laughed, and almost cried at Tristram, I will agree with you that there is subject for mirth, and some affecting strokes; Yorick, Uncle Toby, and Trim are admirably characterised, and very interesting, and an excellent sermon of a peculiar kind, on conscience, is introduced; and I most admire the author for his judgment in seeing the town's folly in the extravagant praises and favours heaped on him; for he says, he passed unnoticed by the world till he put on a fool's coat, and since that every body admires him!

But mark my prophecy, that by another season, this performance will be as much decryed, as it is now extolled; for it has not intrinsic merit sufficient to prevent its sinking, when no longer upheld by the short-lived breath of fashion: and yet another prophecy I utter, that this ridiculous compound will be the cause of many more productions, witless and humourless, perhaps, but indecent and absurd; till the town will be punished for undue encouragement, by being poisoned with disgustful nonsense."

6 Laurence Sterne

FROM "Sterne's Letter Book"[1]

FROM A letter to an unidentified recipient
January 1, 1760

I have rec^d y^r Letter of Counsil which contrary to my natural humour, has set me half a day upon looking a little gravely and upon thinking a little gravely too. Sometimes I concluded you had not spoke out, but had stronger grounds for some discourageing Hints upon Tristram Shandy, than what your good nature knew well how to tell me——particularly with regard to the point of prudence as a Divine &c——and that you really thought in your heart the vein of humour too light for the colour of my Cassock——a Meditation upon the four last things had suited it better—I own—but then it must not have been wrote by me. . . .

——I deny it——I have not gone as far as Swift—He keeps due distance from Rabelais——& I from him. Swift sais 500 things, I dare not say,——unless I was Dean of Saint Patricks.

As for the ambitiosa Ornamenta you hint at,—Upon revising my book, I will shrift my conscience as I go along upon that sin—and whatever ornaments it confesses to, of that kind, shall be defaced without mercy—they are vices of my constitution more than a Love of finery & Parade when I fall into them—and tho' I have a terrible dread of writing like a dutch Commentator—yet these luxuriant Shoots, as far as I am a Judge, shall be pruned, if not entirely cut away for the tree's good.

* * *

1. Reprinted by permission of the publisher from Wilbur Lucius Cross, *The Life and Times of Laurence Sterne*, 3rd Edition, with alterations and additions [1929], New York: Russell & Russell, 1967, pp. 560–561, 564–567, 572–574, 585.

A letter from Mr. Brown to Hall-Stevenson
July 25, 1760[1]

————Tristram Shandy has at last made his way here. never did I read any thing with more delectation. What a comical Fellow the author must be! & I may add also what a Connoisseur in Mankind! Perhaps if the Book has any fault at all, it is, that some of his touches are too refined to be perceived in their full force & extent by every Reader. We have been told here he is a Brother of the cloath; pray is it really so? or in what part of the Vineyard does he labour? I'd ride fifty miles to smoak a pipe with him, for I could lay any wager that so much humour has not been hatch'd or concocted in his pericrainium without the genial fumes of celestial Tobacco: but perhaps like one of the same Trade, tho' his Letters be strong and powerful, his speech is mean and his bodily presence contemptible—
—Yet I can hardly think it. He must be a queer dog, if not sooner, at least after supper; I would lay too, that he is no stranger to Montaigne; nay that he is full as well acquainted with him, as with the book of common prayer, or the Bishop of London's pastoral Letters; tho at the same time I would be far from insinuating, either on one hand, that his Reverence is not as good a Tradesman in his way as any of his neighbours,—or on the other, That this celebrated Performance of his, is not perfectly an Original. The Character of Uncle Toby, his conversations with his Brother, who is also a very drole and excellent personage, & I protest such Characters I have known—his Acc^{ts} of the Campaign &c &c are inimitable. I have been much diverted wth some people here who have read it. they torture their brains to find out some hidden meaning in it, & will per force have all the Starts—Digressions—& Ecarts which the Author runs out into, & which are surely the Excellencies of his Piece, to be the constituent Members of a close connected Story. is it not provoking to meet with such wise acres who, tho' there be

1. "Mr. Brown was a clergyman living in Geneva, where Hall-Stevenson became acquainted with him. On receiving the enquiry about the author of *Tristram Shandy*, the master of Skelton sent the letter over to Coxwold. Sterne made a copy of it and doubtless returned the original to Hall-Stevenson." —Cross's note.

no trace of any consistent plan in the whole of their insipid Life, & tho their Conversation if continued for half a quarter of an hour has neither head or tail, yet will pretend to seek for connection in a Work of this Nature.

* * *

FROM Sterne's reply to Mr. Brown
September 9, 1760

My good friend Mr Hall knowing how happy it would make me, to hear that Tristram Shandy had found his way to Geneva, and had met with so kind a reception from a person of your Character, was so obliging as to send me y^r letter to him. I return you Sir, all due thanks and desire you will suffer me to place the many civilities done to this ungracious whelp of mine, to my own account, and accept of my best acknowledgements thereupon.

You are absolutely right in most of your conjectures about me (unless what are excessively panygerical)—1st That I am "a queer dog"—, only that you must not wait for my being so, till supper, much less till an hour after—for I am so before I breakfast. 2^d "for my conning Montaigne as much as my pray'r book"—there you are right again,—but mark, a 2^d time, I have not said I admire him as much;—tho' had he been alive, I would certainly have gone twice as far to have smoakd a pipe with him, as with Arch-Bishop Laud or his Chaplains, (tho' one of 'em by the bye, was my grandfather). As for the meaness of my speech, and contemptibility of my bodily presence,—I'm the worst Judge in the world of 'em—Hall is ten times better acquainted with those particulars of me, & will write you word. In y^r Conjecture of smoaking Tobacco——there you are sadly out—not that the conjecture was bad but that my brain is so—it will not bear Tobacco, inasmuch as the fumes thereof do concoct my conceits too fast so that they would be all done to rags before they could be well served up—the heat however at 2^d hand, does very well with them, so that you may rely upon it, that for every mile you go to meet me for this end, I will go twain; and tho I can not smoak wth you, yet to shew you, I am in full harmony with you, I'll fiddle you a grave movement whilst you pipe it in your way & Hall shall dance a Saraband to us with a pair of bellows & Tongs, in which accompanyment You must know, he has done wonders since he left Geneva.

The Wise heads I see on the continent are made up of the same materials, & cast in the same Moulds, with the Wise heads of this Island,—they philosophize upon Tristram Shandy alike to a T——— they all look to high—tis ever the fate of low minds. . . .

* * *

A letter to Mrs. F———[1]
Spring, 1765

To M^rs F———

—and pray what occasion, (either real or ideal) have You Madam, to write a Letter from Bath to Town, to enquire whether Tristram Shandy is a married Man or no?—and You may ask in Your turn, if you please, What occasion has Tristram Shandy gentleman to sit down and answer it?

for the first, dear Lady (for we are beginning to be a little acquainted) You must answer to your own conscience—as I shall the 2^d, to mine; for from an honest attention to my internal workings in that part where the Conscience of a gallant man resides, I perceive plainly, that such fair advances from so fair a Princess— (freer & freer still) are not to be withstood by one of Tristram Shandy's make and complexion—Why my dear Creature (—we shall soon be got up to the very climax of familiarity)—If T. Shandy had but one single spark of galanty-fire in any one apartment of his whole Tenement, so kind a tap at the dore would have call'd it all forth to have enquired What gentle Dame it was that stood without—good God! is it You M^rs F — — — —! What a fire have you lighted up! tis enough to set the whole house in a flame

1. Cross does not feel the recipient can be positively identified.

"If Tristram Shandy was a single Man"—(o dear!)— "from
the Attacks of Jack Dick and Peter I am quite secure—(this by the
by Madam, requires proof)—But my dear Tristram! *If* thou wast a
single man—bless me, Mad^m, this is downright wishing for I swear
it is in the *optative Mood* & no other—well! but my dear T. Shandy
wast thou a single Man, I should not know what to say—& may I be
Tristram'd to death, if I should know what to do——

do You know my dear Angle (for you may feel I am creeping still
closer to you and before I get to the end of my letter I forsee the
freedome betwixt us will be kept within no decent bounds)—do You
know I say to what a devil of a shadow of a tantalizing Help mate
you must have fallen a victime on that supposision—why my most
adorable! except that I am tolerably strait made, and near six feet
high, and that my Nose, (whatever as an historian I say to the
contrary), is an inch at least longer that most of my neighbours—
except that—That I am a two footed animal without one Lineament
of Hair of the beast upon me, totally spiritualized out of all form
for conubial purposes——let me whisper, I am now 44—and shall this
time twelve-month be 45^1——That I am moreover of a thin, dry
hectic, unperspirable habit of Body—so sublimated and rarified in all
my parts That a Lady of y^r Wit would not give a brass farthing for a
dozen such: next May when I am at my best, You shall try me—tho
I tell You before hand I have not an ounce & a half of carnality
about me—& what is that for so long a journey?

In such a Land of scarsity, I well know, That Wit profiteth nothing—all I have to say is, That as I sh^d have little else to give, what
I had, should be most plenteously shed upon you.—but then, the
devil an' all is, You are a Wit Y^rself, and tho' there might be abundance of peace so long as the *Moon* endured—Yet when that luscious
period was run out, I fear we sh^d never agree one day to an end;
there would be such Satyre & sarcasm—scoffing & flouting—rallying
& reparteeing of it,—thrusting & parrying in one dark corner or
another, There w^d be nothing but mischief—but then—as we sh^d be
two people of excellent Sense, we sh^d make up matters as fast as they
went wrong—What tender reconciliations!—by heaven! it would be
a Land of promise—milk & Honey!

1. Actually Sterne was fifty-two.

—Honey! aye there's the rub—
—I once got a surfeit of it

> I have the honour to be with the utmost
> regard
> > Mad^m Y^r most obed^t humble Servt
> > > T. Shandy.

* * *

A letter to David Garrick
January 1, 1760[1]

S^r

I dare say You will wonder to receive an Epistle from me, and the Subject of it will surprise You still more, because it is to tell You something about Books.

There are two Volumes just published here which have made a great noise, & have had a prodigious Run; for in 2 Days after they came out, the Bookseller sold two hundred—& continues selling them very fast. It is, The Life & Opinions of Tristram Shandy, which the Author told me last night at our Concert, he had sent up to London, so perhaps you have seen it; if you have not seen it, pray get it & read it, because it has a great Character as a witty smart Book, and if You think it is so, your good word in Town will do the Author, I am sure great Service; You must understand, He is a kind & generous friend of mine whom Providence has attach'd to me in this part of the world where I came a stranger—& I could not think how I could make a better return than by endeavouring to make you a friend to him & his Performance.—this is all my Excuse for this Liberty, which I hope you will excuse. His name is Sterne, a gentleman of great Preferment & a Prebendary of the Church of York, & has a great Character in these Parts as a man of Learning & wit,—the Graver People however say, tis not fit for young Ladies to read

---

1. This letter written by Sterne himself was copied out at Sterne's request by Miss Catherine Fourmantelle and sent to David Garrick over her signature in the hope that he would use his influence in recommending *Tristram Shandy* to his friends. Volumes I and II of *Tristram Shandy* first appeared in December, 1759.

his Book. so perhaps you'l think it not fit for a young Lady to recommend it. however the Nobility, & great Folks stand up mightily for it, & say tis a good Book tho' a little tawdry in some places,—

I am dear Sir

Y^r most Obd^t &

humble Servant

FROM A Letter to Doctor [Noah Thomas?], January 30, 1760[1]

[In the opening paragraphs Sterne defends his right to satirize and caricature specific figures no longer alive to defend themselves, in particular with respect to his character, Kunastrokius.]

—The consolation you give me, "That my book, however, will be read enough to answer my design of raising a tax upon the public"—is very unconsolatory—to say nothing how very mortifying! By h——n! an author is worse treated than a common ***** at this rate—"*You will get a penny by your sins, and that's enough.*"—Upon this chapter let me comment.—That I proposed laying the world under contribution when I set pen to paper—is what I own, and I suppose I may be allow'd to have that view in my head in common with every other writer, to make my labour of advantage to myself.

Do you not do the same? but I beg I may add, that whatever views I had of that kind, I had other views—the first of which was, the hopes of doing the world good, by ridiculing what I thought deserving of it—or of disservice to sound learning, &c.——how I have succeeded, my book must show—and this I leave entirely to the world—but not to that little world *of your acquaintance,* whose opinion and sentiments you call the general opinion of the best judges *without exception,* who all affirm (you say) that my book cannot be put into the hands of any woman of *character.* (I hope you except widows, doctor—for they are not *all* so squeamish, but I am told they are all really of my party, in return for some good offices done their interests in the 176th page of my

---

1. Reprinted from *The Works and Life of Laurence Sterne,* (York Edition), New York: J. F. Taylor & Co., 1904, vol. III, pp. 135–137.

second volume). But for the chaste married, and chaste unmarried part of the sex—they must not read my book! Heaven forbid the stock of chastity should be lessen'd by the Life and Opinions of Tristram Shandy—yes, his Opinions—it would certainly debauch 'em! God take them under his protection in this fiery trial, and send us plenty of Duennas to watch the workings of their humours, till they have safely got through the whole work.—

A Letter to Doctor Eustace, February 9, 1768[1]

SIR,—I this moment received your obliging letter and Shandean piece of scuplture along with it, of both which testimonies of your regard I have the justest sense, and return you, dear Sir, my best thanks and acknowledgment. Your walking stick is in no sense more Shandaic than in that of its having more handles than one; the parallel breaks only in this, that in using the stick, every one will take the handle which suits his convenience. In Tristram Shandy the handle is taken which suits the passions, their ignorance, or their sensibility. There is so little true feeling in the herd of the world, that I wish I could have got an act of parliament, when the books first appeared, that none but wise men should look into them. It is too much to write books and find heads to understand them; the world, however, seems to come into a better temper about them, the people of genius here, being to a man on its side; and the reception it has met with in France, Italy, and Germany, has engaged one part of the world to give it a second reading. The other, in order to be on the strongest side, has at length agreed to speak well of it too. A few hypocrites and tartuffes, whose approbation could do it nothing but dishonour, remain unconverted.

I am very proud, Sir, to have had a man like you on my side from the beginning; but it is not in the power of every one to taste humour, however he may wish it; it is the gift of God: and, besides, a true feeler always brings half the entertainment along with him; his own ideas are only called forth by what he reads, and the vibra-

---

1. Reprinted from *The Works and Life of Laurence Sterne,* (York Edition), New York: J. F. Taylor & Co., 1904, vol. IV, pp. 215–216.

tions within him intirely correspond with those excited.—'Tis like reading himself——and not the book.

In a week's time I shall be delivered of two volumes of the Sentimental Travels of Mr. Yorick through France and Italy; but, alas! the ship sails three days too soon, and I have but to lament it deprives me of the pleasure of presenting them to you.

Believe me, dear Sir, with great thanks for the honour you have done me, with true esteem, your obliged humble servant,

7

FROM A Review of Volumes III and IV of *Tristram Shandy, Monthly Review,* February, 1761[1]

In our Review of the first two volumes of this whimsical and extravagant work, we ventured to recommend Mr. Tristram Shandy as a Writer infinitely more ingenious and entertaining than any other of the present race of Novelists: and, indeed, amidst all the things of that kind, which we are condemned to peruse, we were glad to find one which merited distinction. His characters, as we took notice, were striking and *singular,* his observations shrewd and pertinent; and, *allowing a few exceptions,* his humour easy and genuine. As the work had confessedly, merit upon the whole, we forbore any strictures on the indelicacies with which it was interspersed, and which we attributed to the warm imagination of some *young Genius* in Romance.

Little did we imagine, that the diminutive volumes then before us, would swell into such importance with the public: much less could we suppose, that a work of so light a nature, could be the production of a Dignitary of the Church of England, had not the wanton brat been publicly owned by its reverend Parent.

It is true, that in some degree, it is our duty, as Reviewers, to

1. Vol. XXIV, pp. 101–106, 109, 111, 116.

examine books, abstracted from any regard to their Author. But this rule is not without exception: for where a Writer is publicly known, by his own acknowlegement, it then becomes a part of our duty, to animadvert on any flagrant impropriety of character. What would be venial in the farcical Author of the *Minor*, would be highly reprehensible from the pen of a Divine. In short, there is a certain faculty called *Discretion,* which reasonable men will ever esteem; tho' you, the arch *Prebend* Mr. *Yorick,* alias *Tristram Shandy,* have done all in your power to laugh it out of fashion.

. . . Hast not thou, O Tristram! run over things holy, profane, clean, obscene, grave, and light, without regard to time, place, thy *own person,* or the persons of *thy Readers?* Hast thou not written thy extravagant and pleasant Fancies about unclean things, about *Forceps, Tire Tete,* and *Squirts,* which became none but an Anatomist, a Physician, or the obstetrical Doctor Slop? Hast thou not tumbled into the dirt, and after being worse beluted and bemired than the aforesaid squab Doctor, hast thou not indecently presented thyself before good, nay before the best company? Hast thou not played with sounds, and equivocal significations of words, ay, and with *Stars* and *Dashes,* before those whom thou oughtest to reverence— for whom should'st thou reverence more than the *Public?* Will not these things be accounted unto thee as *Folly?* Do they not most manifestly prove, what the Philosopher has most justly concluded, that *Fancy without Judgment,* is *not Wit.*

But your Indiscretion, good Mr. Tristram, is not all we complain of in the volumes now before us. We must tax you with what you will dread above the most terrible of all imputations—nothing less than DULLNESS. Yes, indeed, Mr. Tristram, your are dull, *very dull.* Your jaded Fancy seems to have been exhausted by two pigmy octavos, which scarce contained the substance of a twelve-penny pamphlet; and we now find nothing new to entertain us.

Your characters are no longer striking and singular. We are sick of your uncle Toby's wound in his groin; we have had enough of his ravelines and breastworks: in short, we are quite tired with his *hobby horses*; and we can no longer bear with Corporal Trim's insipidity: and as to your wise father, his passion for Trismegistus, and all his whimsical notions, are worn threadbare. The novelty and extravagance of your manner, pleased at first; but discretion, Shandy, would have taught you, that a continued affectation of extravagance, soon becomes insipid. What we prophesied in our Review of the first two volumes, will be soon accomplished to your cost and confusion. We there told you, that—"If you did not pay a little more regard to going strait forward, the generality of your Readers, despairing of ever seeing the end of their journey, would tire, and leave you to jog on by yourself." In short, *Polly Honeycomb,* or any of Mr. *Noble's* fair Customers, would have told you, that novelty is the very soul of Romance; and when you are continually chiming on one set of ideas, let them be ever so extravagant and luscious, they soon become stupid and unaffecting.

But you will tells us, that you have introduced a new character. Who is he? What! the Stranger from the Promontary, with his great nose, and his fringed————? No, absolutely we will not stain our paper with so gross an epithet.—It would ill become us to transcribe what you, Mr. Shandy, do not blush to write at full length. But after all, what does this Stranger do or say? Why he brandishes his naked scymetar, swears no body shall touch his nose, sighs for his Julia, and then leaves us in the lurch.

There may be some ingenious or deep allusion in this nasonic Rhodomontade; but we confess, that we have not capacity enough to fathom it. Whether it is religious, political, or lascivious, is difficult to determine; and, in truth, not worth a scrutiny. Much may be said on all sides, but on which side soever the allusion lies, we will venture to observe, it is so far fetched, that it loses its zest before it comes home.

We hope that Mr. Shandy will not be offended at our freedom; for, in truth, we set down nought in malice. Nevertheless, we wish, and that without any degree of malevolence, that we could rumple the *lining of his jerkin,* as it is the best expedient we know of, to make the owner ashamed of exposing it: for though he assures us, that it is not yet frayed, yet all the world may see that it is in a filthy pickle.

Our former animadversions on the Reverend *Yorick,* were intended as a warning to Mr. *Shandy,* to hide his dirty lining: but though our counsel was lost on a giddy mortal, who has no sense of decency, yet we cannot but admire the good humour with which he received it. It will be necessary to transcribe his own words, that our Readers may understand this *jerkin* gibberish.

[The reviewer then quotes Chapter 4, Volume III of *Tristram Shandy* in full.]

Very right, Mr. Shandy! the world to be sure is wide enough to hold us all. Yet was it ten times as wide as it is, we should never walk without interruption, when we deviate from the paths of Discretion. When once we leave that track, we shall infallibly meet with some indignant spirits, who will think it meritorious to jostle us.

But after all, if this gumtaffeta jerkin has been a kind of heir-loom in the Shandean family, yet only imagine to yourself, what an antic figure it must cut upon a prunella gown and cassock! As well might a grave Judge wear a Jockey's cap on his full-bottomed periwig, or a right reverend Bishop clap a grenadier's cap over his mitre. Do, for shame, Mr. Shandy, hide your jerkin, or, at least, send the lining to the Scowerer's. Believe us, when it is once thoroughly cleaned, you will find it as apt to fray and fret as other people's, but at present it is covered with such a thick scale of nastiness, that there is no coming at a single thread of it.

We know that you hate gravity, but you must pardon us one dull reflection. If, to drop your whimsical metaphor, your mind is really as callous as you describe it, you should have kept the secret to yourself. For we will not scruple to affirm, that where sensibility is wanting, every virtue is deficient. . . .

In this volume, however, our Hero is brought into the world; but we are told, that the Doctor, with his vile instruments, crushed poor Tristram's nose as flat as a pancake. This disaster makes room for a great deal of humour on the subject of noses. The elder Shandy, among other particulars, had a great aversion to short noses, and would often declare, that he did not see how the greatest family in England could stand it out against an uninterrupted succession of six or seven short noses.

This topic, as might be supposed, affords the wanton Tristram an opportunity of indulging his prurient humour, in a variety of indelicate and sensual allusions. But had he been master of true wit, he might have been entertaining without having recourse to obscenity. Wit thus prostituted, may be compared to the spices which embalm a putrid carcase. . . .

The remainder of this volume, and above a third part of the fourth, is taken up with a tedious dissertation on noses, in which there is not a glimmering of true wit or humour. The tale of Slawkenbergius is interspersed with ribaldry and double entendre: and in the *Intricacies* of Diego and Julia, he gives a palpable description of two Lovers in the paroxysm of ————. In short, all Mr. Shandy's ideas center *circa cingulum*. . . .

Having thus endeavoured to give our Readers a general idea of this whimsical romance, we will add, that we have done Mr. Shandy the justice to select the most curious and entertaining parts of these little volumes, which, *upon the whole* are not only scandalously indecent, but absolutely DULL. So far from being a remedy against the spleen, as he vainly presumes, the work is rather a dose of *diacodium,* which would lull us to sleep, was it not seasonably dashed with a little tincture of *canthar*—In short, if the Author cannot infuse more spirit, and preserve more decency in the *continuation,* we advise him to remain where he is, in his *swadling cloaths,* without insulting the public any farther. We hope he will take our friendly admonitions in good part, for if he goes on at the rate of the two volumes before us, he will unavoidably sink into that contempt, which, sooner or later, ever attends the misapplication of talents.

FROM A Review of Volumes III and IV of *Tristram Shandy, Critical Review,* April, 1761[1]

A man who possesses the faculty of exciting mirth, without exposing himself as the subject of it, is said to have humour, and this humour appears in a thousand different forms, according to the variety of attitudes in which folly is exhibited; but all these attitudes must be in themselves ridiculous: for humour is no more than the power of holding up and displaying the ridiculous side of every object with which it is concerned. Every body has heard of the

1. Vol. XI, pp. 314–317.

different species of humour; grave humour and gay humour, genteel humour and low humour, natural humour and extravagant humour, grotesque and buffoonery. Perhaps these two last may be more properly stiled the bastards of humour than the power itself, although they have been acknowledged and adopted by the two arch priests of laughter *Lucian* and *Rabelais.* They deserve to be held illegitimate, because they either desert nature altogether, in their exhibitions, or represent her in a state of distortion. Lucian and Rabelais, in some of their writings, seem to have no moral purpose in view, unless the design of raising laughter may in some cases be thought a moral aim. It must be owned, that there is abundance of just satire in both; but at the same time they abound with extravagances, which have no foundation in nature, or in reason. . . . We the rather take notice of Rabelais on this occasion, as we are persuaded that he is the pattern and prototype of Tristram Shandy, notwithstanding the declaration of our modern author, when he exclaims in a transport, 'My dear Rabelais, and my dearer Cervantes!' There is no more resemblance between his manner and that of Cervantes, than there is between the solemnity of a Foppington and the grimace of a Jack Pudding. On the other hand, we see in Tristram Shandy the most evident traces of Rabelais, in the address, the manner, and colouring, tho' he has generally rejected the extravagancies of his plan. We find in both the same sort of apostrophes to the reader, breaking in upon the narrative, not unfrequently with an air of petulant impertinence; the same *sales Plautini;* the *immunda— ignominiosaq; dicta;* the same whimsical digressions; and the same parade of learning. . . . Perhaps it would be no difficult matter to point out a much closer affinity between the works of the French and English author; but we have not leisure to be more particular. Nor will it be necessary to explain the conduct of the performance now before us, as it is no more than a continuation of the first two volumes, which were published last year, and received with such avidity by the public, as boded no good to the sequel; for that avidity was not a natural appetite, but a sort of *fames canina,* that must have ended in *nausea* and *indigestion.* Accordingly all novel readers, from the stale maiden of quality to the snuff-taking chambermaid, devoured the first part with a most voracious swallow, and rejected the last with marks of loathing and aversion. We must not look for the reason of this difference in the medicine, but in the patient to which it was administered. While the two first volumes of Tristram Shandy lay half-buried in obscurity, we, the Critical Reviewers, recommended it to the public as a work of humour and ingenuity, and, in return, were publickly reviled with the most dull and indelicate abuse: but neither that ungrateful insult, nor the maukish disgust so generally manifested towards the second part of Tristram Shandy, shall warp our judgment or integrity so far, as to join the cry in condemning it as unworthy of the first. One had merit, but was extolled above its value; the other has defects, but is too severely decried. The reader will not expect that we should pretend to give a detail of a work, which seems to have been written without any plan, or any other design than that of shewing the author's wit, humour, and learning, in an unconnected effusion of sentiments and remarks, thrown out indiscriminately as they rose in his imagination. Nevertheless, incoherent and digressive as it is, the book certainly abounds with pertinent observations on life and characters, humourous incidents, poignant ridicule, and marks of taste and erudition. We will venture also to say, that the characters of the father and uncle are interesting and well sustained, and that corporal Trim is an amiable picture of low life.

In the third volume we find the form of an excommunication in Latin, said to be procured out of the leger-book of the church of Rochester, writ by Ernulphus the bishop of that diocese; and so far as we are able to judge, it bears the marks of authenticity.

The last volume is enriched with a tale in the same language, said to be extracted from the decads of *Hafen Slakenbergius;* of which tale it would not be easy to point out the scope and intention, unless we suppose it was an expedient to shew that our author could write good Latin; for, in fact, the pretended Slakenbergius is he himself; and all the merit we can allow the tale is, that the part of it which we have in Latin is written with elegance and propriety.

Having pointed out the beauties of this performance, we cannot, in justice to the public, but take some notice also of its defects. We frequently see the author failing in his endeavours to make the reader laugh; a circumstance which throws him into a very aukward attitude, so as even to excite contempt, like an unfortunate *relator,* who says, "O! I'll tell you a merry story, gentlemen, that will make you burst your sides with laughing;" and begins with a ha! ha! ha! to recite a very dull narrative, which ends in a general groan of the audience. Most of his apostrophes and digressions are mere tittle-tattle, that species which the French distinguish by the word *caqueter*, fitter for the nursery than the closet. A spirit of petulance, an air of self-conceit, and an affectation of learning, are diffused through the whole performance, which is likewise blameable for some gross expressions, impure ideas, and a general want of decorum. If we thought our opinion could have any weight with a gentleman who seems to stand so high in his own opinion, we would advise him to postpone the history of Tristram's childhood and youth, until the world shall have forgot the misfortune he received in his birth: by that time he may pass for a new man, and once more enjoy that advantage which novelty never fails to have with the public.

FROM A Review of Volumes V and VI of *Tristram Shandy, Critical Review,* January, 1762[1]

Mr. S—— might have saved himself the trouble of signing his name to each volume of this performance; a precaution first used (if we mistake not) by the ingenious Mrs. Constantia Philips, as it would be impossible for any reader, even of the least discernment, not to see in the perusal of half a page, that these volumes can be the production of no other than the original author of Tristram Shandy. Here we find the same unconnected rhapsody, the same rambling digression, the eccentric humour, the peculiar wit, petulance, pruriency and ostentation of learning by which the former part was so happily distinguished. With respect to the moral tendency of the work, and the decency of the execution, we shall refer the reader to the observations of other critics, who have taken the trouble to discuss these particulars: our business shall be to consider how far the performance conduces to the entertainment or information of the reader. Common justice obliges us to own that it contains much good satire on the follies of life; many perti-

1. Vol. XIII, pp. 66–69.

nent remarks on characters and things; and some pathetic touches of nature, which compels us to wish the author had never stooped to the exhibition of buffoonery. The incidents upon which these two volumes turn, are these: a ridiculous disaster which happened to Tristram Shandy in his infancy, and which we think rather too impure to be repeated; the death of lieutenant Le Fever; and the memoirs of uncle Toby. All these incidents, however, are comprehended in a very few pages. The rest of the book is filled with fine things to make the reader laugh and stare, and wonder with a foolish face of praise, at the witty conceits and immense erudition of the author. But the author of Tristram Shandy, with all his merit, is not so much of an original as he is commonly imagined. Rabelais dealt in the same kind of haberdashery. His wit was as bright, his satire as keen, and his humour as powerful as any we have yet seen in Tristram Shandy. He had his extravagant rhapsodies, his abrupt transitions, his flux of matter, his familiar apostrophes, his disquisitions on arts and sciences, theology and ethics; his Hebrew, Greek, Latin, Italian, Spanish, High Dutch, Low Dutch, Lanternois, &c. his decent allusions to the work of generation, and the parts that distinguish the sexes; and his cleanly comments upon intestinal exoneration. Every body has heard of his *Torche-cul,* his *Rondeau,* beginning *En chiant, &c.* his *Emerald que avoit une vertu erective & confortative du membre naturel;* and his dispute *de ventre inspiciendo.* But, we are forced to acknowledge there are some strokes of humour in Tristram Shandy, which far transcend any thing in the French author. For example, can any thing be more witty than page 147, Vol. II. which is left blank for the entertainment of the reader? This is to elevate and surprize—and what can be more sagacious or satirical than the remark upon this blank page. "Thrice happy book! thou wilt have one page at least, within thy covers, which malice will not blacken, and which ignorance cannot misrepresent." *A fortiori,* had all the leaves been blank, the author would have been still more exempt from the arrows of censure. In that case we could only have said, that he sold his memorandum-books too dear. This conceit of leaving a blank leaf in order to disappoint the critic, puts us in mind of a puritan who slept all Sunday that he might not break the Sabbath, and then boasted of his having committed no sin on the seventh day, though he had cheated all the other six. For our parts, we give Tristram credit for his blank leaf, as likewise for the asterisks, dashes, hiatuses, and indented lines which help to fill up the volume, and throw the reader into an agreeable maze of perplexity and conjecture. . . .

Of a very different stile are some touches of character relating to Toby and to Trim, that we meet with in this volume, by which it appears, that if our author has sometimes lost sight of Rabelais, he has directed his eye to a still greater original, even nature herself. The episode of Le Fever is beautifully pathetic, and exhibits the character of Toby and his corporal in such a point of view, as must endear them to every reader of sensibility. The author has contrived to make us laugh at the ludicrous peculiarity of Toby, even while we are weeping with tender approbation at his goodness of heart. . . .

We know not whether most to censure the impertinence, or commend the excellencies of this strange, incongruous, whimsical performance.

FROM A Review of Volume IX of *Tristram Shandy, Monthly Review,* February, 1767[1]

Several have compared Mr. Sterne, in his humorous capacity, to Cervantes; and others, with more propriety, to Rabelais; but they are all mistaken. The Reviewers have, at length, discovered his *real* prototype,—HARLEQUIN. Do you see the resemblance, Reader? if you do not, with a single glance of the mind's eye, perceive it, it would be an idle attempt for us to set about *making it out;*—you would, mean while, have a dull time of it: and we might lose our labour at last. To *us,* however, it is a clear case, that the *Reverend Tristram,* does not sound half so well as *Harlequin-Shandy;* and that, after all the scholia, commentaries and glossaries that have appeared, in order to explain the nature and design of these whimsical volumes, and to ascertain the class and order of literary composition to which they belong, we scruple not to affirm, that so

1. Vol. XXXVI, p. 93–94, 101–102.

55809

motley a performance, taking the whole together, as far as the publication hath hitherto proceeded, can only be denominated the PANTOMIME OF LITERATURE.

Uncle Toby's amours are proposed as the main subject of this ninth volume; but what is *proposed,* and what is *done,* are, with this Author, points as little connected as the south pole is with the North; or the dispute between Hume and Rousseau with the Dissentions among the Genoese and the Corsicans.

The volume opens with a *dedication,* to a great man:—and a *great man* he must be, indeed, who finds out the wit or the humour of this preliminary scrap. But, with this Merry-Andrew of a writer, the jest oftentimes consists only in his setting dull readers to work, in order to *find the jest out:* while he stands by, grinning like a satyr, and enjoying the fun of seeing them busily employed, like the wise men of Gotham, in dragging the fish-pond to get out the moon.

. . . Let us see,—where are we now? Do we *advance* forward or backward?—What is there in chap. xxi? Nothing but nonsense (your pardon, Mr. Yorick!) about *Slawkenbergius,* and a string of asses: fye on all such idle trumpery!—'Gentle spirit of sweetest humour,' would the chaste pen of thy 'beloved Cervantes' ever have given us such ribaldry?—But is chap. xxii. any better? not much: nor xxiii. nor xxiv.—In xxv. we have an apology for the Author's conceit of the two blank chapters, which we do not think altogether inadmissible; viz. 'That whatever resemblance it may bear to half the chapters which are written in the world, or, for aught I know, may be now writing in it—that it was as casual as the foam of Zeuxis his horse: besides, says he, I look upon a chapter which has, *only nothing in it,* with respect; and considering what worse things there are in the world——'

Very true! there are millions of folios, quartos, octavos, and duodecimos in the world, which are a thousand times worse than these thy inoffensive spotless pages: and well would it have been for thy reputation S——! had some scores of *thine* too, which are *not* blank, been left in the like state of primæval innocence!

Chap. xxvi. has already contributed toward the entertainment of our Readers.

Chap. xxvii. of two lines only, cannot possibly contribute any thing toward the entertainment of any Readers, whatever. . . .

The remainder of the volume affords nothing to blame, and almost as little to commend; if we except the story of the parish bull, in the last chapter,—which is dull, gross, and vulgar.——O what pity that Nature should thus capriciously have embroidered the choicest flowers of genius, on a paultry groundwork of buffoonry!

8 William Hazlitt

"Lectures on the Comic Writers"[1]

It remains to speak of Sterne; and I shall do it in few words. There is more of *mannerism* and affectation in him, and a more immediate reference to preceding authors; but his excellences, where he is excellent, are of the first order. His characters are intellectual and inventive, like Richardson's; but totally opposite in the execution. The one are made out by continuity, and patient repetition of touches: the others, by glancing transitions and graceful apposition. His style is equally different from Richardson's: it is at times the most rapid, the most happy, the most idiomatic of any that is to be found. It is the pure essence of English conversational style. His works consist only of *morceaux*—of brilliant passages. I wonder that Goldsmith, who ought to have known better, should call him 'a dull fellow.' His wit is poignant, though artificial; and his characters (though the groundwork of some of them had been laid before) have yet invaluable original differences; and the spirit of the execution, the master-strokes constantly thrown into them, are not to be surpassed. It is sufficient to name them;—Yorick, Dr. Slop, Mr. Shandy, My Uncle Toby, Trim, Susanna, and the Widow Wadman. In these he has contrived to oppose, with equal felicity and originality, two characters, one of pure intellect, and the other of pure good nature, in My Father and My Uncle Toby. There appears to

1. Reprinted by permission of the publisher, from P. P. Howe, ed., from *The Complete Works of William Hazlitt*, London: J. M. Dent & Sons, 1930–1934, vol. VI, pp. 120–121.

have been in Sterne a vein of dry, sarcastic humour, and of extreme tenderness of feeling; the latter sometimes carried to affectation, as in the tale of Maria, and the apostrophe to the recording angel: but at other times pure, and without blemish. The story of Le Fevre is perhaps the finest in the English language. My Father's restlessness, both of body and mind, is inimitable. It is the model from which all those despicable performances against modern philosophy ought to have been copied, if their authors had known any thing of the subject they were writing about. My Uncle Toby is one of the finest compliments ever paid to human nature. He is the most unoffending of God's creatures; or, as the French express it, *un tel petit bon homme!* Of his bowling-green, his sieges, and his amours, who would say or think any thing amiss!

9 Samuel Taylor Coleridge

FROM "Recollections of Another of Mr. Coleridge's Lectures," *Tatler,* May 24, 1831[1]

(1818[2])

The origin of the word humour may be traced to the science of Pathology. The ancients were unacquainted with its present meaning. They considered the human body as the repository of four humours, viz., blood, phlegm, bile or gall, and the black bile, and according to the predominance of either of these they believed the character to be sanguine, phlegmatic, choleric, or melancholy. When these distinctions ceased to be regarded, the word was still retained, and one of its applications was to persons engaged in pursuits of no

1. Reprinted by permission of the editor, from Thomas Middleton Raysor, ed., from *Coleridge's Miscellaneous Criticism,* London: Constable 1936, pp. 112–113, 116–117.

2. This lecture was part of a series of public lectures Coleridge delivered in 1818. The syllabus for Lecture IX read as follows: "On Rabelais, Swift, and Sterne: on the Nature and Constituents of genuine Humour, and on the Distinctions of the Humourous from the Witty, the Fanciful, the Droll, the Odd, &c."

abstract utility, but which had the limited effect of making happy those engaged in them. Sterne's Uncle Toby is of this kind. The fortifications on which he employed himself in his garden are represented as a source of unceasing delight to him, totally abstracted from the remotest idea of utility. Humour is also displayed in the comparison of finite things with those which our imaginations cannot bound; such as make our great appear little and our little great; or, rather, which reduces to a common littleness both the great and the little, when compared with infinity. . . .

Humour and pathos are generally found together. In Sterne, they are admirably blended, so as to serve as reliefs to each other. . . .

He [Coleridge] next passed to the faults of Sterne, whom he severely censured for his indecency, his degradation of the passion of Love, and his affected sensibility. In conclusion, he expressed his opinion that the works of Sterne had been productive of much more evil than good.

FROM Coleridge's Manuscript Notes for Lecture IX[1]

EXCELLENCES

1. The bringing forward into distinct consciousness those minutiae of thought and feeling which appear trifles, have an importance [only] for the moment, and yet almost every man feels in one way or other. Thus it has the novelty of an individual peculiarity, and yet the interest of a something that belongs to our common nature. In short, to seize happily on those points in which every man is more or less a *humorist*. And the propensity to notice these things does itself constitute a humorist, and the superadded power of so presenting them to men in general gives us the man of humor. Hence the difference of the man of humor, the effect of whose portraits does not depend on the felt presence of himself as a humorist, as Cervantes and Shakespeare, nay, Rabelais—and those in whom the effect is in the humorist's own oddity—Sterne (and *Swift?*).

1. Raysor, ed., pp. 123–126. Reprinted by permission of the editor.

2. Traits of *human* nature, which so easily assume a particular cast and color from individual character. Hence this, and the pathos connected with it, quickly passes into *humor*, and forms the ground of it—[as in] the story of the Fly. Character [is created] by a delicacy and higher degree of a good quality.

> [Go,—says he, one day at dinner, to an overgrown one which had buzzed about his nose, and tormented him cruelly all dinner-time,—and which after infinite attempts, he had caught at last, as it flew by him;—I'll not hurt thee, says my Uncle *Toby*, rising from his chair, and going across the room, with the fly in his hand,—I'll not hurt a hair of thy head:—Go, says he, lifting up the sash, and opening his hand as he spoke, to let it escape;—go, poor devil, get thee gone, why should I hurt thee?—This world surely is wide enough to hold both thee and me. Book II, ch. xii.]

3. In Mr. Shandy's character, as of all Mr. Shandys, a craving for sympathy in exact proportion to the oddity and unsympathizability; next to this, [craving] to be at least disputed with, or rather both in one, [to] dispute and yet agree; but [holding] worst of all, to acquiesce without either resistance or sympathy—[all this is] most happily conceived.

Contrasts sometimes increasing the love between the brothers—and always either balanced or remedied.

Drollery in Obadiah.

4. No writer so happy as Sterne in the unexaggerated and truly natural representation of that species of slander which consists in gossiping about our neighbours, as *whetstones* of our moral discrimination—as if they were conscience-blocks which we used in our apprenticeship, not to waste such precious materials as our own consciences in the trimming and shaping by self-examination.

> [Alas o'day;—had Mrs. *Shandy*, poor gentlewoman! had but her wish in going up to town just to lye-in and come down again;—which, they say, she begged and prayed for upon her bare knees,—and which, in my opinion, considering the fortune which Mr. *Shandy* got with her,—was no such mighty matter to have complied with, the lady and her babe might both of them have been alive at this hour. Book I, ch. xviii.]

6. The physiognomic tact common, in very different degrees in-

deed, to us all, [is] gratified in Dr. Slop. And in general, [note] all that happiest use of drapery and attitude, which at once gives the *reality* by individualizing, and the vividness by unusual, yet probable combinations.

> [Imagine to yourself a little squat, uncourtly figure of a Doctor *Slop*, of about four feet and a half perpendicular height, with a breadth of back, and a sesquipedality of belly, which might have done honour to a serjeant in the horse-guards. . . .
>
> .   .   .   .   .   .
>
> Imagine such a one,—for such, I say, were the outlines of Dr. *Slop's* figure, coming slowly along, foot by foot, waddling thro' the dirt upon the vertebrae of a little diminutive pony, of a pretty colour—but of strength,—alack!—scarce able to have made an amble of it, under such a fardel, had the roads been in an ambling condition.—They were not.—Imagine to yourself, *Obadiah* mounted upon a strong monster of a coach-horse, pricked into a full gallop, and making all practicable speed the adverse way.   Book II, ch. ix.]

7. More humor in the single remark, "Learned men, Brother Toby, do not write dialogues on long noses for nothing," than in the whole Slawkenburghian tale that follows, which is oddity interspersed with drollery.

8. The moral *good* of Sterne in the characters of Trim, etc., as contrasted with Jacobinism. [Book V, ch. vii. Trim mourning the death of his young master, Bobby.]

9. Each part by right of humoristic universality, a whole. Hence the digressive spirit [is] not wantonness, but the *very form* of his genius. The connection is given by the continuity of the characters.

FROM "Table Talk," August 18, 1833[1]

I think highly of Sterne—that is, of the first part of Tristram Shandy: for as to the latter part about the widow Wadman, it is stupid and disgusting; and the Sentimental Journey is poor sickly stuff. There is a great deal of affectation in Sterne, to be sure; but still the characters of Trim and the two Shandies are most individual and delightful. Sterne's morals are bad, but I don't think they can

---

1. Raysor, ed., pp. 426–427. Reprinted by the permission of the editor.

do much harm to any one whom they would not find bad enough before. Besides, the oddity and erudite grimaces under which much of his dirt is hidden take away the effect for the most part; although, to be sure, the book is scarcely readable by women.

FROM "Wit and Humor"[1]

IV. In the simply laughable there is a mere disproportion between a definite act and a definite purpose or end, or a disproportion of the end itself to the rank or circumstances of the definite person; but humour is of more difficult description. I must try to define it in the first place by its points of diversity from the former species. Humour does not, like the different kinds of wit, which is impersonal, consist wholly in the understanding and the senses. No combination of thoughts, words, or images will of itself constitute humour, unless some peculiarity of individual temperament and character be indicated thereby, as the cause of the same. Compare the comedies of Congreve with the Falstaff in Henry IV, or with Sterne's Corporal Trim, Uncle Toby, and Mr. Shandy, or with some of Steele's charming papers in the Tatler, and you will feel the difference better than I can express it. Thus again, (to take an instance from the different works of the same writer), in Smollett's Strap, his Lieutenant Bowling, his Morgan the honest Welshman, and his Matthew Bramble, we have exquisite humour,—while in his Peregrine Pickle we find an abundance of drollery, which too often degenerates into mere oddity; in short, we feel that a number of things are put together to counterfeit humour, but that there is no growth from within. And this indeed is the origin of the word, derived from the humoral pathology, and excellently described by Ben Jonson:

> So in every human body,
> The choler, melancholy, phlegm, and blood,
> By reason that they flow continually
> In some one part, and are not continent,

1. *Ibid.* 442–444. Students should consult Raysor's extensive notes to this section concerning the reliability of this text and of H. N. Coleridge's editing. It first appeared in *Literary Remains,* edited by Henry Nelson Coleridge.

Receive the name of humours. Now thus far
It may, by metaphor, apply itself
Unto the general disposition:
As when some one peculiar quality
Doth so possess a man, that it doth draw
All his effects, his spirits, and his powers,
In their confluctions, all to run one way,
This may be truly said to be a humour.

Hence we may explain the congeniality of humour with pathos, so exquisite in Sterne and Smollett, and hence also the tender feeling which we always have for, and associate with, the humours or hobby-horses of a man. First, we respect a humourist, because absence of interested motive is the ground-work of the character, although the imagination of an interest may exist in the individual himself, as if a remarkably simple-hearted man should pride himself on his knowledge of the world, and how well he can manage it:— and secondly, there always is in a genuine humour an acknowledgment of the hollowness and farce of the world, and its disproportion to the godlike within us. And it follows immediately from this, that whenever particular acts have reference to particular selfish motives, the humourous bursts into the indignant and abhorring; whilst all follies not selfish are pardoned or palliated. The danger of this habit, in respect of pure morality, is strongly exemplified in Sterne.

10 Walter Bagehot

FROM "Sterne and Thackeray," 1864[1]

Sterne went to Cambridge, and though he did not acquire elaborate learning, he thoroughly learned a gentlemanly stock of elementary knowledge. There is even something scholarlike about his style. It bears the indefinable traces which an exact study of words will always leave upon the use of words. He was accused of stealing

1. Reprinted from Richard Holt Hutton, ed., *Literary Studies by the late Walter Bagehot,* London: Longmans, Green, and Co., 1884, vol. II, pp. 109–111, 116–127.

learning, and it is likely enough that a great many needless quotations which were stuck into *Tristram Shandy* were abstracted from secondhand storehouses where such things are to be found. But what he stole was worth very little, and his theft may now at least be pardoned, for it injures the popularity of his works. Our present novel-readers do not at all care for an elaborate caricature of the scholastic learning; it is so obsolete that we do not care to have it mimicked. Much of *Tristram Shandy* is a sort of antediluvian fun, in which uncouth Saurian jokes play idly in an unintelligible world.

When he left college, Sterne had a piece of good fortune which in fact ruined him. He had an uncle with much influence in the Church, and he was thereby induced to enter the Church. There could not have been a greater error. He had no special vice; he was notorious for no wild dissipation or unpardonable folly; he had done nothing which even in this more discreet age would be considered imprudent. He had even a refinement which must have saved him from gross vice, and a nicety of nature which must have saved him from coarse associations. But for all that he was as little fit for a Christian priest as if he had been a drunkard and a profligate. Perhaps he was less fit.

There are certain persons whom taste guides, much as morality and conscience guide ordinary persons. They are 'gentlemen.' They revolt from what is coarse; are sickened by that which is gross; hate what is ugly. They have no temptation to what we may call ordinary vices; they have no inclination for such raw food; on the contrary, they are repelled by it, and loathe it. The law in their members does *not* war against the law of their mind; on the contrary, the *taste* of their bodily nature is mainly in harmony with what conscience would prescribe or religion direct. They may not have heard the saying that the 'beautiful is higher than the good, for it includes the good.' But when they do hear it, it comes upon them as a revelation of their instinctive creed, of the guidance under which they have been living all their lives. They are pure because it is ugly to be impure; innocent because it is out of taste to be otherwise; they live within the hedge-rows of polished society; they do not wish to go beyond them into the great deep of human life; they have a horror of that 'impious ocean,' yet not of the impiety, but of the miscellaneous noise, the disordered confusion of the whole. These are the men whom it is hardest to make Christian,—for the simplest reason; paganism is sufficient for them. Their pride of the eye is a good pride; their love of the flesh is a delicate and directing love. They keep 'within the pathways' because they dislike the gross, the uncultured, and the untrodden. Thus they reject the primitive precept which comes before Christianity. Repent! repent! says a voice in the wilderness; but the delicate pagan feels superior to the voice in the wilderness. Why should he attend to this uncouth person? He has nice clothes and well-chosen food, the treasures of exact knowledge, the delicate results of the highest civilisation. Is he to be directed by a person of savage habits, with a distorted countenance, who lives on wild honey, who does not wear decent clothes? To the pure worshipper of beauty, to the naturally refined pagan, conscience and the religion of conscience are not merely intruders, but barbarous intruders. At least so it is in youth, when life is simple and temptations if strong are distinct. Years afterwards, probably, the purest pagan will be taught by a constant accession of indistinct temptations, and by a gradual declension of his nature, that taste at the best, and sentiment of the very purest, are insufficient guides in the perplexing labyrinth of the world.

Sterne was a pagan. He went into the Church; but Mr. Thackeray, no bad judge, said most justly that his sermons 'have not a single Christian sentiment.' They are well expressed, vigorous, moral essays; but they are no more. Much more was not expected by many congregations in the last age. The secular feeling of the English people, though always strong,—though strong in Chaucer's time, and though strong now,—was never so all-powerful as in the last century. It was in those days that the poet Crabbe was remonstrated with for introducing heaven and hell into his sermons; such extravagances, he was told, were very well for the Methodists, but a *clergyman* should confine himself to sober matters of this world, and show the prudence and the reasonableness of virtue during this life. There is not much of heaven and hell in Sterne's sermons, and what there is seems a rhetorical emphasis which is not essential to the argument, and which might perhaps as well be left out. Auguste Comte might have admitted most of these sermons; they are healthy statements of earthly truths, but they would be just as true if there was no religion at all. Religion helps the argument, because foolish people might be perplexed with this world, and they yield readily to another; religion enables you—such is the real doctrine of these divines, when you examine it—to coax and persuade those whom you cannot rationally convince; but it does not alter the matter in hand —it does not affect that of which you wish to persuade men, for you are but inculcating a course of conduct *in this life*. Sterne's sermons would be just as true if the secularists should succeed in their argument, and the 'valuable illusion' of a deity were omitted from the belief of mankind.

. . . We do not know with great accuracy what Sterne's temptations were; but there was one, which we can trace with some degree of precision, which has left ineffaceable traces on his works,—which probably left some traces upon his character and conduct. There was in that part of Yorkshire a certain John Hall Stevenson, a country gentleman of some fortune, and possessed of a castle, which he called Crazy Castle. . . . Exactly what sort of life they led at Crazy Castle we do not know; but vaguely we do know, and we may be sure *Mrs.* Sterne was against it.

One part of Crazy Castle has had effects which will last as long as English literature. It had a library richly stored in old folio learning, and also in the amatory reading of other days. Every page of *Tristram Shandy* bears traces of both elements. Sterne, when he wrote it, had filled his head and his mind, not with the literature of his own age, but with the literature of past ages. He was thinking of Rabelais rather than of Fielding; of forgotten romances rather than of Richardson. He wrote, indeed, of his own times and of men he had seen, because his sensitive vivid nature would only endure to write of present things. But the *mode* in which he wrote was largely coloured by literary habits and literary fashions that had long passed away. The oddity of the book was a kind of advertisement to its genius, and that oddity consisted in the use of old manners upon new things. No analysis or account of *Tristram Shandy* could be given which would suit the present generation; being, indeed, a book without plan or order, it is in every generation unfit for analysis. This age would not endure a statement of the most telling points, as the writer thought them, and no age would

like an elaborate plan of a book in which there is no plan, in which
the detached remarks and separate scenes were really meant to be
the whole. The notion that 'a plot was to hang plums upon' was
Sterne's notion exactly.

The real excellence of Sterne is single and simple; the defects
are numberless and complicated. He excels, perhaps, all other
writers in mere simple description of common sensitive human action.
He places before you in their simplest form the elemental facts of
human life; he does not view them through the intellect, he scarcely
views them through the imagination; he does but reflect the unimpaired impression that the facts of life, which do not change from
age to age, make on the deep basis of human feeling, which changes
as little though years go on. . . . Sterne's feeling in his higher moments so much overpowered his intellect, and so directed his imagination, that no intrusive thought blemishes, no distorting fancy
mars, the perfection of the representation. The disenchanting facts
which deface, the low circumstances which debase the simpler feelings oftener than any other feelings, his art excludes. The feeling
which would probably be coarse in the reality is refined in the picture. The unconscious tact of the nice artist heightens and chastens
reality, but yet it is reality still. His mind was like a pure lake of
delicate water: it reflects the ordinary landscape, the rugged hills,
the loose pebbles, the knotted and the distorted firs perfectly and as
they are, yet with a charm and fascination that they have not in
themselves. This is the highest attainment of art, to be at the same
time nature and something more than nature.

But here the great excellence of Sterne ends as well as begins.
In *Tristram Shandy* especially there are several defects which, while
we are reading it, tease and disgust so much that we are scarcely
willing even to admire as we ought to admire the refined pictures of
human emotion. The first of these, and perhaps the worst, is the
fantastic disorder of the form. It is an imperative law of the writ-
ing-art, that a book should go straight on. A great writer should
be able to tell a great meaning as coherently as a small writer tells
a small meaning. The magnitude of the thought to be conveyed,
the delicacy of the emotion to be painted, render the introductory
touches of consummate art not of less importance, but of more importance. A great writer should train the mind of the reader for

his greatest things; that is, by first strokes and fitting preliminaries he should form and prepare his mind for the due appreciation and the perfect enjoyment of high creations. He should not blunder upon a beauty, nor, after a great imaginative creation, should he at once fall back to bare prose. The high-wrought feeling which a poet excites should not be turned out at once and without warning into the discomposing world. It is one of the greatest merits of the greatest living writer of fiction,—of the authoress of *Adam Bede*,[1]—that she never brings you to anything without preparing you for it; she has no loose lumps of beauty; she puts in nothing at random; after her greatest scenes, too, a natural sequence of subordinate realities again tones down the mind to this sublunary world. Her logical style —the most logical, probably, which a woman ever wrote—aids in this matter her natural sense of due proportion. There is not a space of incoherency—not a gap. It is not natural to begin with the point of a story, and she does not begin with it. When some great marvel has been told, we all wish to know what came of it, and she tells us. Her natural way, as it seems to those who do not know its rarity, of telling what happened produces the consummate effect of gradual enchantment and as gradual disenchantment. But Sterne's style is *un*natural. He never begins at the beginning and goes straight through to the end. He shies-in a beauty suddenly; and just when you are affected he turns round and grins at it. 'Ah,' he says, 'is it not fine?' And then he makes jokes which at that place and that time are out of place, or passes away into scholastic or other irrelevant matter, which simply disgusts and disheartens those whom he has just delighted. People excuse all this irregularity of form by saying that it was imitated from Rabelais. But this is nonsense. Rabelais, perhaps, could not in his day venture to tell his meaning straight out; at any rate, he did not tell it. Sterne should not have chosen a model so monstrous. Incoherency is not less a defect because an imperfect foreign writer once made use of it. 'You may have, sir, a reason,' said Dr. Johnson, 'for saying that two and two make five, but they will still make four.' Just so, a writer may have a reason for selecting the defect of incoherency, but it is a defect still. Sterne's best things read best out of his books,—in Enfield's

1. George Eliot.

Speaker and other places,—and you can say no worse of any one as a continuous artist.

Another most palpable defect—especially palpable nowadays— in *Tristram Shandy* is its indecency. It is quite true that the customary conventions of writing are much altered during the last century, and much which would formerly have been deemed blameless would now be censured and disliked. The audience has changed; and decency is of course in part dependent on who is within hearing. A divorce case may be talked over across a club-table with a plainness of speech and development of expression which would be indecent in a mixed party, and scandalous before young ladies. Now, a large part of old novels may very fairly be called club-books; they speak out plainly and simply the notorious facts of the world, as men speak of them to men. Much excellent and proper masculine conversation is wholly unfit for repetition to young girls; and just in the same way, books written—as was almost all old literature,— for men only, or nearly only, seem coarse enough when contrasted with novels written by young ladies upon the subjects and in the tone of the drawing-room. The change is inevitable; as soon as works of fiction are addressed to boys and girls, they must be fit for boys and girls; they must deal with a life which is real so far as it goes, but which is yet most limited; which deals with the most passionate part of life, and yet omits the errors of the passions; which aims at describing men in their relations to women, and yet omits an all but universal influence which more or less distorts and modifies all these relations.

As we have said, the change cannot be helped. A young ladies' literature must be a limited and truncated literature. The indiscriminate study of human life is not desirable for them, either in fiction or in reality. But the habitual formation of a scheme of thought and a code of morality upon incomplete materials is a very serious evil. The readers for whose sake the omissions are made cannot fancy what is left out. Many a girl of the present day reads novels, and nothing but novels; she forms her mind by them, as far as she forms it by reading at all; even if she reads a few dull books, she soon forgets all about them, and remembers the novels only; she is more influenced by them than by sermons. They form her idea of the world, they define her taste, and modify her morality; not so much in explicit thought and direct act, as unconsciously and in her floating fancy. How is it possible to convince such a girl, especially if she is clever, that on most points she is all wrong? She has been reading most excellent descriptions of mere society; she comprehends those descriptions perfectly, for her own experience elucidates and confirms them. She has a vivid picture of a *patch* of life. Even if she admits in words that there is something beyond, something of which she has no idea, she will not admit it really and in practice. What she has mastered and realised will incurably and inevitably overpower the unknown something of which she knows nothing, can imagine nothing, and can make nothing. 'I am not sure,' said an old lady, 'but I think it's the novels that make my girls so *heady*.' It is the novels. A very intelligent acquaintance with limited life makes them think that the world is far simpler than it is, that men are easy to understand, 'that mamma is *so* foolish.'

The novels of the last age have certainly not this fault. They do not err on the side of reticence. A girl may learn from them more than it is desirable for her to know. But, as we have explained, they were meant for men and not for girls; and if *Tristram Shandy* had simply given a plain exposition of necessary facts—necessary, that is, to the development of the writer's view of the world, and to the telling of the story in hand,—we should not have complained; we should have regarded it as the natural product of a now extinct society. But there are most unmistakable traces of 'Crazy Castle' in *Tristram Shandy*. There is indecency for indecency's sake. It is made a sort of recurring and even permeating joke to mention things which are not generally mentioned. Sterne himself made a sort of defence, or rather denial, of this. He once asked a lady if she had read *Tristram*. 'I have not, Mr. Sterne,' was the answer; 'and, to be plain with you, I am informed it is not proper for female perusal.' 'My dear good lady,' said Sterne, 'do not be gulled by such stories; the book is like your young heir there' (pointing to a child of three years old who was rolling on the carpet in white tunics): 'he shows at times a good deal that is usually concealed, but it is all in perfect innocence.' But a perusal of *Tristram* would not make good the plea. The unusual publicity of what is ordinarily imperceptible is not the thoughtless accident of amusing play; it is deliberately sought after as a nice joke; it is treated as a good in itself.

The indecency of *Tristram Shandy*—at least of the early part, which was written before Sterne had been to France—is especially an offence against taste, because of its ugliness. *Moral* indecency is always disgusting. There certainly is a sort of writing which cannot be called decent, and which describes a society to the core immoral, which nevertheless is no offence against art; it violates a higher code than that of taste, but it does not violate the code of taste. . . .

But *Tristram Shandy's* indecency is the very opposite to this refined sort. It consists in allusions to certain inseparable accompaniments of actual life which are not beautiful, which can never be made interesting, which would, *if* they were decent, be dull and uninteresting. There is, it appears, a certain excitement in putting such matters into a book: there is a minor exhilaration even in petty crime. At first such things look so odd in print that you go on reading them to see what they look like; but you soon give up. What is disenchanting or even disgusting in reality does not become enchanting or endurable in delineation. You are more angry at it in literature than in life; there is much which is barbarous and animal in reality that we could wish away; we endure it because we cannot help it, because we did not make it and cannot alter it, because it is an inseparable part of this inexplicable world. But why we should put this coarse alloy, this dross of life, into the *optional* world of literature, which we can make as we please, it is impossible to say. The needless introduction of accessory ugliness is always a sin in art, and is not at all less so when such ugliness is disgusting and improper. *Tristram Shandy* is incurably tainted with a pervading vice; it dwells at length on, it seeks after, it returns to, it gloats over, the most unattractive part of the world.

There is another defect in *Tristram Shandy* which would of itself remove it from the list of first-rate books, even if those which we have mentioned did not do so. It contains eccentric characters only. . . . Much of the delineation is of the highest merit. Sterne knew how to describe eccentricity, for he showed its relation to our common human nature: he showed how we were related to it, how in some sort and in some circumstances we might ourselves become it. He reduced the abnormal formation to the normal rules. Except upon this condition, eccentricity is no fit subject for literary art. Every one must have known characters which, if they were put down in books, barely and as he sees them, would seem monstrous and disproportioned,—which would disgust all readers,—which every critic would term unnatural. While characters are monstrous, they should be kept out of books; they are ugly unintelligibilities, foreign to the realm of true art. But as soon as they can be explained to us, as soon as they are shown in their union with, in their outgrowth from common human nature, they are the best subjects for great art—for they are new subjects. They teach us, not the old lesson which our fathers knew, but a new lesson which will please us and make us better than they. Hamlet is an eccentric character, one of the most eccentric in literature; but because, by the art of the poet, we are made to understand that he is a possible, a *vividly* possible man, he enlarges our conceptions of human nature; he takes us out of the bounds of commonplace. He 'instructs us by means of delight.' Sterne does this too. Mr. Shandy, Uncle Toby, Corporal Trim, Mrs. Shandy,—for in strictness she too is eccentric from her abnormal commonplaceness,—are beings of which the possibility is brought home to us, which we feel we could under circumstances and by influences become; which, though contorted and twisted, are yet spun out of the same elementary nature, the same thread as we are. Considering how odd these characters are, the success of Sterne is marvellous, and his art in this respect consummate. But yet on a point most nearly allied it is very faulty. Though each individual character is shaded off into human nature, the whole is not shaded off into the world. This society of originals and oddities is left to stand by itself, as if it were a natural and ordinary society,—a society easily conceivable and needing no explanation. Such is not the manner of the great masters; in their best works a constant atmosphere of half commonplace personages surrounds and shades off, illustrates and explains every central group of singular persons.

On the whole, therefore, the judgment of criticism on *Tristram Shandy* is concise and easy. It is immortal because of certain scenes suggested by Sterne's curious experience, detected by his singular sensibility, and heightened by his delineative and discriminative imagination. It is defective because its style is fantastic, its method illogical and provoking; because its indecency is of the worst sort, as far as in such matters an artistic judgment can speak of worst and best; because its world of characters forms an incongruous group of singular persons utterly dissimilar to, and irreconcilable with the world in which we live. It is a great work of art, but of barbarous art. Its mirth is boisterous. It is *provincial*. It is redolent of an inferior society; of those who think crude animal spirits in themselves delightful; who do not know that, without wit to point them, or humour to convey them, they are disagreeable to others; who like disturbing transitions, blank pages, and tricks of style; who do not know that a simple and logical form of expression is the most effective, if not the easiest—the least laborious to readers, if not always the most easily attained by writers.

The oddity of *Tristram Shandy* was, however, a great aid to its immediate popularity. If an author were to stand on his head now and then in Cheapside, his eccentricity would bring him into contact with the police, but it would advertise his writings; they would sell better: people would like to see what was said by a great author who was so odd as to stand so. Sterne put his eccentricity into his writings, and therefore came into collision with the critics; but he attained the same end. His book sold capitally. As with all popular authors, he went to London; he was fêted. 'The *man* Sterne,' growled Dr. Johnson, 'has dinner engagements for three months.' The upper world—ever desirous of novelty, ever tired of itself, ever anxious to be amused—was in hopes of a new wit. It naturally hoped that the author of *Tristram Shandy* would talk well, and it sent for him to talk.

He did talk well, it appears, though not always very correctly, and never very clerically. His appearance was curious, but yet refined. Eager eyes, a wild look, a long lean frame, and what he called a cadaverous bale of goods for a body, made up an odd exterior, which attracted notice, and did not repel liking. He looked like a scarecrow with bright eyes. With a random manner, but not without a nice calculation, he discharged witticisms at London parties. His keen nerves told him which were fit witticisms; *they* took, and *he* was applauded.

Jane Austen
Emma
1815

※ *1*

FROM "Monthly Catalogue, Novels," *Monthly Review,* July, 1816[1]

Emma. By the Author of "Pride and Prejudice," &c.
    12mo. 3 Vols. 1l. 1s. Boards. Murray. 1816.
If this novel can scarcely be termed a composition, because it contains but one ingredient, *that one* is, however, of sterling worth; being a strain of genuine natural humour, such as is seldom found conjointly with the complete purity of images and ideas which is here conspicuous. The character of Mr. Woodhouse, with his 'habits of gentle selfishness,' is admirably drawn, and the dialogue is easy and lively. The fair reader may also glean by the way some useful hints against forming romantic schemes, or indulging a spirit of patronage in defiance of sober reason; and the work will probably become a favourite with all those who seek for harmless amusement, rather than deep pathos or appalling horrors, in works of fiction.

1. Vol. LXXX, p. 320.

FROM "Review of New Publications," *Gentleman's Magazine,* September, 1816[1]

Emma: *A Novel. By the Author of "Pride and Prejudice."* 12mo. Murray.

DULCE est desipere in loco; and a good Novel is now and then an agreeable relaxation from severer studies. Of this description was "Pride and Prejudice;" and from the entertainment which those volumes afforded us, we were desirous to peruse the present work; nor have our expectations been disappointed. If "Emma" has not the highly-drawn characters in superior life which are so interesting in 'Pride and Prejudice;' it delineates with great accuracy the habits and the manners of a middle class of gentry; and of the inhabitants of a country village at one degree of rank and gentility beneath them. Every character throughout the work, from the heroine to the most subordinate, is a portrait which comes home to the heart and feelings of the Reader; who becomes familiarly acquainted with each of them, nor loses sight of a single individual till the completion of the work. The unities of time and place are well preserved; the language is chaste and correct; and if 'Emma' be not allowed to rank in the very highest class of modern Novels, it certainly may claim at least a distinguished degree of eminence in that species of composition. It is amusing, if not instructive; and has no tendency to deteriorate the heart.

2 [*Sir Walter Scott*]

FROM A Review of *Emma, Quarterly Review,* October, 1815[2]

There are some vices in civilized society so common that they are hardly acknowledged as stains upon the moral character, the

1. Vol. LXXXVI, pp. 248–249.
2. Vol. XIV, pp. 188–194, 197, 199–201.

propensity to which is nevertheless carefully concealed, even by those who most frequently give way to them; since no man of pleasure would willingly assume the gross epithet of a debauchee or a drunkard. One would almost think that novel-reading fell under this class of frailties, since among the crowds who read little else, it is not common to find an individual of hardihood sufficient to avow his taste for these frivolous studies. A novel, therefore, is frequently 'bread eaten in secret;' and it is not upon Lydia Languish's toilet alone that Tom Jones and Peregrine Pickle are to be found ambushed behind works of a more grave and instructive character. And hence it has happened, that in no branch of composition, not even in poetry itself, have so many writers, and of such varied talents, exerted their powers. It may perhaps be added, that although the composition of these works admits of being exalted and decorated by the higher exertions of genius; yet such is the universal charm of narrative, that the worst novel ever written will find some gentle reader content to yawn over it, rather than to open the page of the historian, moralist, or poet. We have heard, indeed, of one work of fiction so unutterably stupid, that the proprietor, diverted by the rarity of the incident, offered the book, which consisted of two volumes in duodecimo, handsomely bound, to any person who would declare, upon his honour, that he had read the whole from beginning to end. But although this offer was made to the passengers on board an Indiaman, during a tedious outward-bound voyage, the 'Memoirs of Clegg the Clergyman,' (such was the title of this unhappy composition,) completely baffled the most dull and determined student on board, and bid fair for an exception to the general rule abovementioned,—when the love of glory prevailed with the boatswain, a man of strong and solid parts, to hazard the attempt, and he actually conquered and carried off the prize!

The judicious reader will see at once that we have been pleading our own cause while stating the universal practice, and preparing him for a display of more general acquaintance with this fascinating department of literature, than at first sight may seem consistent with the graver studies to which we are compelled by duty: but in truth, when we consider how many hours of languor and anxiety, of deserted age and solitary celibacy, of pain even and poverty, are beguiled by the perusal of these light volumes, we cannot austerely condemn the source from which is drawn the alleviation of such a portion of human misery, or consider the regulation of this department as beneath the sober consideration of the critic.

If such apologies may be admitted in judging the labours of ordinary novelists, it becomes doubly the duty of the critic to treat with kindness as well as candour works which, like this before us, proclaim a knowledge of the human heart, with the power and resolution to bring that knowledge to the service of honour and virtue. The author is already known to the public by the two novels announced in her title-page, and both, the last especially, attracted, with justice, an attention from the public far superior to what is granted to the ephemeral productions which supply the regular demand of watering-places and circulating libraries. They belong to a class of fictions which has arisen almost in our own times, and which draws the characters and incidents introduced more immediately from the current of ordinary life than was permitted by the former rules of the novel.

In its first appearance, the novel was the legitimate child of the romance; and though the manners and general turn of the composition were altered so as to suit modern times, the author remained fettered by many peculiarities derived from the original style of romantic fiction. These may be chiefly traced in the conduct of the narrative, and the tone of sentiment attributed to the fictitious personages. On the first point, although

> The talisman and magic wand were broke,
> Knights, dwarfs, and genii vanish'd into smoke,

still the reader expected to peruse a course of adventures of a nature more interesting and extraordinary than those which occur in his own life, or that of his next-door neighbours. The hero no longer defeated armies by his single sword, clove giants to the chine, or gained kingdoms. But he was expected to go through perils by sea and land, to be steeped in poverty, to be tried by temptation, to be exposed to the alternate vicissitudes of adversity and prosperity, and his life was a troubled scene of suffering and achievement. Few novelists, indeed, adventured to deny to the hero his final hour of tranquillity and happiness, though it was the prevailing fashion never to relieve him out of his last and most dreadful distress until

the finishing chapters of his history; so that although his prosperity
in the record of his life was short, we were bound to believe it was
long and uninterrupted when the author had done with him. The
heroine was usually condemned to equal hardships and hazards.
She was regularly exposed to being forcibly carried off like a Sabine
virgin by some frantic admirer. And even if she escaped the terrors
of masked ruffians, an insidious ravisher, a cloak wrapped forcibly
around her head, and a coach with the blinds up driving she could
not conjecture whither, she had still her share of wandering, of
poverty, of obloquy, of seclusion, and of imprisonment, and was
frequently extended upon a bed of sickness, and reduced to her
last shilling before the author condescended to shield her from
persecution. In all these dread contingencies the mind of the reader
was expected to sympathize, since by incidents so much beyond
the bounds of his ordinary experience, his wonder and interest ought
at once to be excited. But gradually he became familiar with the
land of fiction, the adventures of which he assimilated not with
those of real life, but with each other. Let the distress of the hero
or heroine be ever so great, the reader reposed an imperturable confidence in the talents of the author, who, as he had plunged them
into distress, would in his own good time, and when things, as Tony
Lumkin says, were in a concatenation accordingly, bring his
favourites out of all their troubles. Mr. Crabbe has expressed his
own and our feelings excellently on this subject.

> For should we grant these beauties all endure
> Severest pangs, they've still the speediest cure;
> Before one charm be wither'd from the face,
> Except the bloom which shall again have place,
> In wedlock ends each wish, in triumph all disgrace.
> And life to come, we fairly may suppose,
> One light bright contrast to these wild dark woes.

In short, the author of novels was, in former times, expected to
tread pretty much in the limits between the concentric circles of
probability and possibility: and as he was not permitted to transgress
the latter, his narrative, to make amends, almost always went
beyond the bounds of the former. Now, although it may be urged
that the vicissitudes of human life have occasionally led an individual

through as many scenes of singular fortune as are represented in the most extravagant of these fictions, still the causes and personages acting on these changes have varied with the progress of the adventurer's fortune, and do not present that combined plot, (the object of every skilful novelist,) in which all the more interesting individuals of the dramatis personae have their appropriate share in the action and in bringing about the catastrophe. Here, even more than in its various and violent changes of fortune, rests the improbability of the novel. The life of man rolls forth like a stream from the fountain, or it spreads out into tranquillity like a placid or stagnant lake. In the latter case, the individual grows old among the characters with whom he was born, and is contemporary,—shares precisely the sort of weal and woe to which his birth destined him,—moves in the same circle,—and, allowing for the change of seasons, is influenced by, and influences the same class of persons by which he was originally surrounded. The man of mark and of adventure, on the contrary, resembles, in the course of his life, the river whose mid-current and discharge into the ocean are widely removed from each other, as well as from the rocks and wild flowers which its fountains first reflected; violent changes of time, of place, and of circumstances, hurry him forward from one scene to another, and his adventures will usually be found only connected with each other because they have happened to the same individual. Such a history resembles an ingenious, fictitious narrative, exactly in the degree in which an old dramatic chronicle of the life and death of some distinguished character, where all the various agents appear and disappear as in the page of history, approaches a regular drama, in which every person introduced plays an appropriate part, and every point of the action tends to one common catastrophe.

We return to the second broad line of distinction between the novel, as formerly composed, and real life,—the difference, namely, of the sentiments. The novelist professed to give an imitation of nature, but it was, as the French say, *la belle nature*. Human beings, indeed, were presented, but in the most sentimental mood, and with minds purified by a sensibility which often verged on extravagance. In the serious class of novels, the hero was usually

A knight of love, who never broke a vow.

And although, in those of a more humorous cast, he was permitted a license, borrowed either from real life or from the libertinism of the drama, still a distinction was demanded even from Peregrine Pickle, or Tom Jones; and the hero, in every folly of which he might be guilty, was studiously vindicated from the charge of infidelity of the heart. The heroine was, of course, still more immaculate; and to have conferred her affections upon any other than the lover to whom the reader had destined her from their first meeting, would have been a crime against sentiment which no author, of moderate prudence, would have hazarded, under the old *régime*.

Here, therefore, we have two essential and important circumstances, in which the earlier novels differed from those now in fashion, and were more nearly assimilated to the old romances. And there can be no doubt that, by the studied involution and extrication of the story, by the combination of incidents new, striking and wonderful beyond the course of ordinary life, the former authors opened that obvious and strong sense of interest which arises from curiosity; as by the pure, elevated, and romantic cast of the sentiment, they conciliated those better propensities of our nature which loves [*sic*] to contemplate the picture of virtue, even when confessedly unable to imitate its excellences.

But strong and powerful as these sources of emotion and interest may be, they are, like all others, capable of being exhausted by habit. The imitators who rushed in crowds upon each path in which the great masters of the art had successively led the way, produced upon the public mind the usual effect of satiety. The first writer of a new class is, as it were, placed on a pinnacle of excellence, to which, at the earliest glance of a surprized admirer, his ascent seems little less than miraculous. Time and imitation speedily diminish the wonder, and each successive attempt establishes a kind of progressive scale of ascent between the lately deified author, and the reader, who had deemed his excellence inaccessible. The stupidity, the mediocrity, the merit of his imitators, are alike fatal to the first inventor, by shewing how possible it is to exaggerate his faults and to come within a certain point of his beauties.

Materials also (and the man of genius as well as his wretched imitator must work with the same) become stale and familiar. Social life, in our civilized days, affords few instances capable of being painted in the strong dark colours which excite surprize and horror; and robbers, smugglers, bailiffs, caverns, dungeons, and mad-houses, have been all introduced until they ceased to interest. And thus in the novel, as in every style of composition which appeals to the public taste, the more rich and easily worked mines being exhausted, the adventurous author must, if he is desirous of success, have recourse to those which were disdained by his predecessors as unproductive, or avoided as only capable of being turned to profit by great skill and labour.

Accordingly a style of novel has arisen, within the last fifteen or twenty years, differing from the former in the points upon which the interest hinges; neither alarming our credulity nor amusing our imagination by wild variety of incident, or by those pictures of romantic affection and sensibility, which were formerly as certain attributes of fictitious characters as they are of rare occurrence among those who actually live and die. The substitute for these excitements, which had lost much of their poignancy by the repeated and injudicious use of them, was the art of copying from nature as she really exists in the common walks of life, and presenting to the reader, instead of the spendid scenes of an imaginary world, a correct and striking representation of that which is daily taking place around him.

In adventuring upon this task, the author makes obvious sacrifices, and encounters peculiar difficulty. He who paints from *le beau idéal*, if his scenes and sentiments are striking and interesting, is in a great measure exempted from the difficult task of reconciling them with the ordinary probabilities of life: but he who paints a scene of common occurrence, places his composition within that extensive range of criticism which general experience offers to every reader. The resemblance of a statue of Hercules we must take on the artist's judgment; but every one can criticize that which is presented as the portrait of a friend, or neighbour. Something more than a mere sign-post likeness is also demanded. The portrait must have spirit and character, as well as resemblance; and being deprived of all that, according to Bayes, goes 'to elevate and surprise,' it must make amends by displaying depth of knowledge and dexterity of execution. We, therefore, bestow no mean compliment upon the author of Emma, when we say that, keeping close to common incidents, and to such characters as occupy the ordinary walks of life, she has produced sketches of such spirit and originality, that we never miss the excitation which depends upon a narrative of uncommon events, arising from the consideration of minds, manners, and sentiments, greatly above our own. In this class she stands almost alone; for the scenes of Miss Edgeworth are laid in higher life, varied by more romantic incident, and by her remarkable power of embodying and illustrating national character. But the author of Emma confines herself chiefly to the middling classes of society; her most distinguished characters do not rise greatly above well-bred country gentlemen and ladies; and those which are sketched with most originality and precision, belong to a class rather below that standard. The narrative of all her novels is composed of such common occurrences as may have fallen under the observation of most folks; and her dramatis personæ conduct themselves upon the motives and principles which the readers may recognize as ruling their own and that of most of their acquaintances. The kind of moral, also, which these novels inculcate, applies equally to the paths of common life, as will best appear from a short notice of the author's former works, with a more full abstract of that which we at present have under consideration.

[Scott then summarizes the plots of *Sense and Sensibility, Pride and Prejudice,* and *Emma.*]

. . . Such is the simple plan of a story [*Emma*] which we peruse with pleasure, if not with deep interest, and which perhaps we might more willingly resume than one of those narratives where the attention is strongly riveted, during the first perusal, by the powerful excitement of curiosity.

The author's knowledge of the world, and the peculiar tact with which she presents characters that the reader cannot fail to recognize, reminds us something of the merits of the Flemish school of painting. The subjects are not often elegant, and certainly never grand; but they are finished up to nature, and with a precision which delights the reader. This is a merit which it is very difficult to illustrate by extracts, because it pervades the whole work, and is not to be comprehended from a single passage.

[Scott then quotes a long passage beginning "While they were thus comfortably occupied . . . " and ending " . . . and Jane Fairfax, though no great favorite with her in general, she was at that moment very happy to assist in praising" from Chapter Twelve of *Emma*.]

Perhaps the reader may collect from the preceding specimen both the merits and faults of the author. The former consists much in the force of a narrative conducted with much neatness and point, and a quiet yet comic dialogue, in which the characters of the speakers evolve themselves with dramatic effect. The faults, on the contrary, arise from the minute detail which the author's plan comprehends. Characters of folly or simplicity, such as those of old Woodhouse and Miss Bates, are ridiculous when first presented, but if too often brought forward or too long dwelt upon, thire prosing is apt to become as tiresome in fiction as in real society. Upon the whole, the turn of this author's novels bears the same relation to that of the sentimental and romantic cast, that cornfields and cottages and meadows bear to the highly adorned grounds of a show mansion, or the rugged sublimities of a mountain landscape. It is neither so captivating as the one, nor so grand as the other, but it affords to those who frequent it a pleasure nearly allied with the experience of their own social habits; and what is of some importance, the youthful wanderer may return from his promenade to the ordinary business of life, without any chance of having his head turned by the recollection of the scene through which he has been wandering.

One word, however, we must say in behalf of that once powerful divinity, Cupid, king of gods and men, who in these times of revolution, has been assailed, even in his own kingdom of romance, by the authors who were formerly his devoted priests. We are quite aware that there are few instances of first attachment being brought to a happy conclusion, and that it seldom can be so in a state of society so highly advanced as to render early marriages among the better class, acts, generally speaking, of imprudence. But the youth of this realm need not at present be taught the doctrine of selfishness. It is by no means their error to give the world or the good things of the world all for love; and before the authors of moral fiction couple Cupid indivisibly with calculating prudence, we would have them reflect, that they may sometimes

lend their aid to substitute more mean, more sordid, and more
selfish motives of conduct, for the romantic feelings which their
predecessors perhaps fanned into too powerful a flame. Who is it, that
in his youth has felt a virtuous attachment, however romantic or
however unfortunate, but can trace back to its influence much that
his character may possess of what is honourable, dignified, and
disinterested? If he recollects hours wasted in unavailing hope, or
saddened by doubt and disappointment; he may also dwell on
many which have been snatched from folly or libertinism, and
dedicated to studies which might render him worthy of the object
of his affection, or pave the way perhaps to that distinction necessary to raise him to an equality with her. Even the habitual indulgence of feelings totally unconnected with ourself and our own
immediate interest, softens, graces, and amends the human mind;
and after the pain of disappointment is past, those who survive (and
by good fortune those are the greater number) are neither less
wise nor less worthy members of society for having felt, for a time,
the influence of a passion which has been well qualified as the
'tenderest, noblest and best.'

3 Jane Austen

FROM A Letter to John Murray[1]

I return you the 'Quarterly Review' with many thanks. The Authoress of 'Emma' has no reason, I think, to complain of her
treatment in it, except in the total omission of 'Mansfield Park.'
I cannot but be sorry that so clever a man as the Reviewer of
'Emma' should consider it as unworthy of being noticed. You will
be pleased to hear that I have received the Prince's thanks for the
handsome copy I sent him of 'Emma.' Whatever he may think of
my share of the work, yours seems to have been quite right.

1. R. W. Chapman, ed., *Jane Austen's Letters,* by permission of the Clarendon
Press, Oxford, 1932, vol. II, p. 453.

FROM A Correspondence with James Stanier Clarke[1]

(November 15, 1815)

Sir:

I must take the liberty of asking you a question.—Among the many flattering attentions which I rec^d from you at Carlton House on Monday last, was the Information of my being at liberty to dedicate any future work to HRH. [His Royal Highness] the P. R. [Prince Regent] without the necessity of any solicitation on my part. Such at least, I believed to be your word; but as I am very anxious to be quite certain of what was intended, I intreat you to have the goodness to inform me how such a Permission is to be understood, & whether it is incumbent on me to shew my sense of the Honour, by inscribing the Work now in the Press, to H.R.H.—I sh^d be equally concerned to appear either Presumptuous or Ungrateful.—

* * *

(November 16, 1815)

Dear Madam:

It is certainly not *incumbent* on you to dedicate your work now in the Press to His Royal Highness: but if you wish to do the Regent that honour either now or at any future period, I am happy to send you that permission which need not require any more trouble or solicitation on your Part.

Your late Works, Madam, and in particular Mansfield Park reflect the highest honour on your Genius & your Principles; in every new work your mind seems to increase its energy and powers of discrimination. The Regent has read & admired all your publications.

Accept my sincere thanks for the pleasure your Volumes have given me: in the perusal of them I felt a great inclination to write & say so. And I also dear Madam wished to be allowed to ask you, to delineate in some future Work the Habits of Life and Character

1. Reprinted from R. W. Chapman, ed., *Jane Austen's Letters*, by permission of the Clarendon Press, Oxford, 1932, vol. II, pp. 429–430, 442–443, 452–453.

and enthusiasm of a Clergyman—who should pass his time between the metropolis & the Country—who should be something like Beatties Minstrel

> Silent when glad, affectionate tho' shy
> And now his look was most demurely sad
> & now he laughd aloud yet none knew why—

Neither Goldsmith—nor La Fontaine in his Tableau de Famille— have in my mind quite delineated an English Clergyman, at least of the present day—Fond of, & entirely engaged in Literature—no man's Enemy but his own. Pray dear Madam think of these things.

> Believe me at all times
> With sincerity & respect
> Your faithful & obliged Servant
> J. S. Clarke
> Librarian.

* * *

(December 11, 1815)

Dear Sir:

My 'Emma' is now so near publication that I feel it right to assure you of my not having forgotten your kind recommendation of an early copy for Carlton House, and that I have Mr. Murray's promise of its being sent to His Royal Highness, under cover to you, three days previous to the work being really out. I must make use of this opportunity to thank you, dear Sir, for the very high praise you bestow on my other novels. I am too vain to wish to convince you that you have praised them beyond their merits. My greatest anxiety at present is that this fourth work should not disgrace what was good in the others. But on this point I will do myself the justice to declare that, whatever may be my wishes for its success, I am strongly haunted with the idea that to those readers who have preferred 'Pride and Prejudice' it will appear inferior in wit, and to those who have preferred 'Mansfield Park' inferior in good sense. Such as it is, however, I hope you will do me the favour of accepting a copy. Mr. Murray will have directions for sending one. I am quite honoured by your thinking me capable of drawing such a clergyman as you gave the sketch of in your note of Nov. 16th. But I assure you I am *not*. The comic part of the character I might be equal to, but not the good, the enthusiastic, the literary. Such a man's conversation must at times be on subjects of science and philosophy, of which I know nothing; or at least be occasionally abundant in quotations and allusions which a woman who, like me, knows only her own mother tongue, and has read little in that, would be totally without the power of giving. A classical education, or at any rate a very extensive acquaintance with English literature, ancient and modern, appears to me quite indispensable for the person who would do any justice to your clergyman; and I think I may boast myself to be, with all possible vanity, the most unlearned and uninformed female who ever dared to be an authoress.

Believe me, dear Sir,
Your obliged and faithful hum^{bl} Ser^t.

Jane Austen

* * *

(April 1, 1816)

You are very kind in your hints as to the sort of composition which might recommend me at present, and I am fully sensible that an historical romance, founded on the House of Saxe Cobourg, might be much more to the purpose of profit or popularity than such pictures of domestic life in country villages as I deal in. But I could no more write a romance than an epic poem. I could not sit seriously down to write a serious romance under any other motive than to save my life; and if it were indispensable for me to keep it up and never relax into laughing at myself or at other people, I am sure I should be hung before I had finished the first chapter. No, I must keep to my own style and go on in my own way; and though I may never succeed again in that, I am convinced that I should totally fail in any other.

I remain, my dear Sir,
Your very much obliged, and sincere friend,

J. Austen

4 [*Archbishop Richard Whately*]

FROM *Quarterly Review,*
January, 1821[1]

The times seem to be past when an apology was requisite from
reviewers for condescending to notice a novel; when they felt
themselves bound in dignity to deprecate the suspicion of paying
much regard to such trifles, and pleaded the necessity of occasionally
stooping to humour the taste of their fair readers. The delights of
fiction, if not more keenly or more generally relished, are at least
more readily acknowledged by men of sense and taste; and we have
lived to hear the merits of the best of this class of writings earnestly
discussed by some of the ablest scholars and soundest reasoners of
the present day.

We are inclined to attribute this change, not so much to an
alteration in the public taste, as in the character of the productions
in question. Novels may not, perhaps, display more genius now than
formerly, but they contain more solid sense; they may not afford
higher gratification, but it is of a nature which men are less
disposed to be ashamed of avowing. We remarked, in a former
Number, in reviewing a work of the author now before us, that 'a
new style of novel has arisen, within the last fifteen or twenty years,
differing from the former in the points upon which the interest
hinges; neither alarming our credulity nor amusing our imagination
by wild variety of incident, or by those pictures of romantic affection
and sensibility, which were formerly as certain attributes of fictitious
characters as they are of rare occurrence among those who actually
live and die. The substitute for these excitements, which had lost
much of their poignancy by the repeated and injudicious use of
them, was the art of copying from nature as she really exists in the
common walks of life, and presenting to the reader, instead of the
splendid scenes of an imaginary world, a correct and striking representation of that which is daily taking place around him.'

Now, though the origin of this new school of fiction may probably
be traced, as we there suggested, to the exhaustion of the mines

1. Vol. XXIV, pp. 352–376.

from which materials for entertainment had been hitherto extracted, and the necessity of gratifying the natural craving of the reader for variety, by striking into an untrodden path; the consequences resulting from this change have been far greater than the mere supply of this demand. When this Flemish painting, as it were, is introduced—this accurate and unexaggerated delineation of events and characters—it necessarily follows, that a novel, which makes good its pretensions of giving a perfectly correct picture of common life, becomes a far more *instructive* work than one of equal or superior merit of the other class; it guides the judgment, and supplies a kind of artificial experience. It is a remark of the great father of criticism, that poetry (i.e. narrative, and dramatic poetry) is of a more philosophical character than history; inasmuch as the latter details what has actually happened, of which many parts may chance to be exceptions to the general rules of probability, and consequently illustrate no general principles; whereas the former shews us what must naturally, or would probably, happen under given circumstances; and thus displays to us a comprehensive view of human nature, and furnishes general rules of practical wisdom. It is evident, that this will apply only to such fictions as are quite *perfect* in respect of the probability of their story; and that he, therefore, who resorts to the fabulist rather than the historian, for instruction in human character and conduct, must throw himself entirely on the judgment and skill of his teacher, and give him credit for talents much more rare than the accuracy and veracity which are the chief requisites in history. We fear, therefore, that the exultation which we can conceive some of our gentle readers to feel, at having Aristotle's warrant for (what probably they had never dreamed of) the *philosophical character* of their studies, must, in practice, be somewhat qualified, by those sundry little violations of probability which are to be met with in most novels; and which so far lower their value, as models of real life, that a person who had no other preparation for the world than is afforded by them, would form, probably, a less accurate idea of things as they are, than he would of a lion from studying merely the representations on China tea-pots.

Accordingly, a heavy complaint has long lain against works of fiction, as giving a false picture of what they profess to imitate, and disqualifying their readers for the ordinary scenes and every-day duties of life. And this charge applies, we apprehend, to the generality of what are strictly called novels, with even more justice than to romances. When all the characters and events are very far removed from what we see around us,—when, perhaps, even supernatural agents are introduced, the reader may indulge, indeed, in occasional day-dreams, but will be so little reminded of what he has been reading, by any thing that occurs in actual life, that though he may perhaps feel some disrelish for the tameness of the scene before him, compared with the fairy-land he has been visiting, yet at least his judgment will not be depraved, nor his expectations misled; he will not apprehend a meeting with Algerine banditti on English shores, nor regard the old woman who shews him about an antique country seat, as either an enchantress or the keeper of an imprisoned damsel. But it is otherwise with those fictions which differ from common life in little or nothing but the improbability of the occurrences: the reader is insensibly led to calculate upon some of those lucky incidents and opportune coincidences of which he has been so much accustomed to read, and which, it is undeniable, *may* take place in real life; and to feel a sort of confidence, that however romantic his conduct may be, and in whatever difficulties it may involve him, all will be sure to come right at last, as is invariably the case with the hero of a novel.

On the other hand, so far as these pernicious effects fail to be produced, so far does the example lose its influence, and the exercise of poetical justice is rendered vain. The reward of virtuous conduct being brought about by fortunate accidents, he who abstains (taught, perhaps, by bitter disappointments) from reckoning on such accidents, wants that encouragement to virtue, which alone has been held out to him. 'If I were *a man in a novel,*' we remember to have heard an ingenious friend observe, 'I should certainly act so and so, because I should be sure of being no loser by the most heroic self-devotion, and of ultimately succeeding in the most daring enterprises.'

It may be said, in answer, that these objections apply only to the *unskilful novelist,* who, from ignorance of the world, gives an unnatural representation of what he professes to delineate. This is partly true, and partly not; for there is a distinction to be made between the *unnatural* and the merely *improbable:* a fiction is unnatural when there is some assignable reason against the events taking place as described,—when men are represented as acting contrary to the character assigned them, or to human nature in general; as when a young lady of seventeen, brought up in ease, luxury and retirement, with no companions but the narrow-minded and illiterate, displays (as a heroine usually does) under the most trying circumstances, such wisdom, fortitude, and knowledge of the world, as the best instructors and the best examples can rarely produce without the aid of more mature age and longer experience.— On the other hand, a fiction is still *improbable*, though *not unnatural*, when there is no reason to be assigned why things should not take place as represented, except that the *overbalance of chances is* against it . . .

Now, though an author who understands human nature is not likely to introduce into his fictions any thing that is unnatural, he will often have much that is improbable: he may place his personages, by the intervention of accident, in striking situations, and lead them through a course of extraordinary adventures; and yet, in the midst of all this, he will keep up the most perfect consistency of character, and make them act as it would be natural for men to act in such situations and circumstances. Fielding's novels are a good illustration of this: they display great knowledge of mankind; the characters are well preserved; the persons introduced all act as one would naturally expect they should, in the circumstances in which they are placed; but these circumstances are such as it is incalculably improbable should ever exist: several of the events, taken singly, are much against the chances of probability; but the combination of the whole in a connected series, is next to impossible. Even the romances which admit a mixture of supernatural agency, are not more unfit to prepare men for real life, than such novels as these; since one might just as reasonably calculate on the intervention of a fairy, as on the train of lucky chances which combine first to involve Tom Jones in his difficulties, and afterwards to extricate him. Perhaps, indeed, the supernatural fable is of the two not only (as we before remarked) the less mischievous in its moral effects, but also the more correct kind of composition in point of taste: the author lays down a kind of hypothesis of the existence of ghosts, witches, or fairies, and professes to describe what would take place under that hypothesis; the novelist, on the contrary, makes no demand of extraordinary machinery, but professes to describe what may actually take place, according to the existing laws of human affairs: if he therefore present us with a series of events quite unlike any which ever do take place, we have reason to complain that he has not made good his professions.

When, therefore, the generality, even of the most approved novels, were of this character, (to say nothing of the heavier charges brought, of inflaming the passions of young persons by warm descriptions, weakening their abhorrence of profligacy by exhibiting it in combination with the most engaging qualities, and presenting vice in all its allurements, while setting forth the triumphs of 'virtue rewarded') it is not to be wondered that the grave guardians of youth should have generally stigmatized the whole class, as 'serving only to fill young people's heads with romantic love-stories, and rendering them unfit to mind any thing else.' That this censure and caution should in many instances be indiscriminate, can surprize no one, who recollects how rare a quality discrimination is; and how much better it suits indolence, as well as ignorance, to lay down a rule, than to ascertain the exceptions to it: we are acquainted with a careful mother whose daughters, while they never in their lives read a *novel* of any kind, are permitted to peruse, without reserve, any *plays* that happen to fall in their way; and with another, from whom no lessons, however excellent, of wisdom and piety, contained in a *prose-fiction*, can obtain quarter; but who, on the other hand, is no less indiscriminately indulgent to her children in the article of tales in *verse*, of whatever character.

The change, however, which we have already noticed, as having taken place in the character of several modern novels, has operated in a considerable degree to do away this prejudice; and has elevated this species of composition, in some respects at least, into a much higher class. For most of that instruction which used to be presented to the world in the shape of formal dissertations, or shorter and more desultory moral essays, such as those of the Spectator and Rambler, we may now resort to the pages of the acute and judicious, but not less amusing, novelists who have lately appeared. If their views of men and manners are no less just than those of the essayists who preceded them, are they to be rated lower because they present to us these views, not in the language of general description, but in the form of well-constructed fictitious narrative? If the practical lessons they inculcate are no less sound and useful, it is surely no diminution of their merit that they are conveyed by example instead of precept: nor, if their remarks are neither less wise nor less important, are they the less valuable for being represented as thrown out in the course of conversations suggested by the circumstances of the speakers, and perfectly in character. The praise and blame of the moralist are surely not the less effectual for being bestowed, not in general declamation, on classes of men, but on individuals representing those classes, who are so clearly delineated and brought into action before us, that we seem to be acquainted with them, and feel an interest in their fate.

Biography is allowed, on all hands, to be one of the most attractive and profitable kinds of reading: now such novels as we have been speaking of, being a kind of fictitious biography, bear the same relation to the real, that epic and tragic poetry, according to Aristotle, bear to history: they present us (supposing, of course, each perfect in its kind) with the general, instead of the particular,—the probable, instead of the true; and, by leaving out those accidental irregularities, and exceptions to general rules, which constitute the many improbabilities of real narrative, present us with a clear and *abstracted* view of the general rules themselves; and thus concentrate, as it were, into a small compass, the net result of wide experience.

Among the authors of this school there is no one superior, if equal, to the lady whose last production is now before us, and whom we have much regret in finally taking leave of: her death (in the prime of life, considered as a writer) being announced in this the first publication to which her name is prefixed. We regret the failure not only of a source of innocent amusement, but also of that supply of practical good sense and instructive example, which she would probably have continued to furnish better than any of her contemporaries. . .

Miss Austin [sic] has the merit (in our judgment most essential) of being evidently a Christian writer: a merit which is much enhanced, both on the score of good taste, and of practical utility, by her religion being not at all obtrusive. She might defy the most

fastidious critic to call any of her novels, (as Cœlebs was desig-
nated, we will not say altogether without reason,) a 'dramatic
sermon.' The subject is rather alluded to, and that incidentally, than
studiously brought forward and dwelt upon. In fact she is more
sparing of it than would be thought desirable by some persons; perhaps even by herself, had she consulted merely her own sentiments;
but she probably introduced it as far as she thought would be generally acceptable and profitable: for when the purpose of inculcating
a religious principle is made too palpably prominent, many readers,
if they do not throw aside the book with disgust, are apt to fortify
themselves with that respectful kind of apathy with which they
undergo a regular sermon, and prepare themselves as they do to
swallow a dose of medicine, endeavouring to *get it down* in large
gulps, without tasting it more than is necessary.

The moral lessons also of this lady's novels, though clearly and
impressively conveyed, are not offensively put forward, but spring
incidentally from the circumstances of the story; they are not forced
upon the reader, but he is left to collect them (though without any
difficulty) for himself: hers is that unpretending kind of instruction which is furnished by real life; and certainly no author has ever
conformed more closely to real life, as well in the incidents, as in the
characters and descriptions. Her fables appear to us to be, in their
own way, nearly faultless; they do not consist (like those of some
of the writers who have attempted this kind of common-life novel
writing) of a string of unconnected events which have little or no
bearing on one main plot, and are introduced evidently for the sole
purpose of bringing in characters and conversations; but have all
that compactness of plan and unity of action which is generally produced by a sacrifice of probability: yet they have little or nothing
that is not probable; the story proceeds without the aid of extraordinary accidents; the events which take place are the necessary
or natural consequences of what has preceded; and yet (which is a
very rare merit indeed) the final catastrophe is scarcely ever
clearly foreseen from the beginning, and very often comes, upon
the generality of readers at least, quite unexpected. We know not
whether Miss Austin ever had access to the precepts of Aristotle;
but there are few, if any, writers of fiction who have illustrated
them more successfully.

The vivid distinctness of description, the minute fidelity of detail, and air of unstudied ease in the scenes represented, which are no less necessary than probability of incident, to carry the reader's imagination along with the story, and give fiction the perfect appearance of reality, she possesses in a high degree; and the object is accomplished without resorting to those deviations from the ordinary plan of narrative in the third person, which have been patronized by some eminent masters. We allude to the two other methods of conducting a fictitious story, viz. either by narrative in the first person, when the hero is made to tell his own tale, or by a series of letters; both of which we conceive have been adopted with a view of heightening the resemblance of the fiction to reality. At first sight, indeed, there might appear no reason why a story told in the first person should have more the air of a real history than in the third; especially as the majority of real histories actually are in the third person; nevertheless, experience seems to show that such is the case: provided there be no want of skill in the writer, the resemblance to real life, of a fiction thus conducted, will approach much the nearest (other points being equal) to a deception, and the interest felt in it, to that which we feel in real transactions. We need only instance Defoe's Novels, which, in spite of much improbability, we believe have been oftener mistaken for true narratives, than any fictions that ever were composed. Colonel Newport is well known to have been cited as an historical authority; and we have ourselves found great difficulty in convincing many of our friends that Defoe was not himself the citizen, who relates the plague of London. The reason probably is, that in the ordinary form of narrative, the writer is not content to exhibit, like a real historian, a bare detail of such circumstances as might actually have come under his knowledge; but presents us with a description of what is passing in the minds of the parties, and gives an account of their feelings and motives, as well as their most private conversations in various places at once. All this is very amusing, but perfectly unnatural: the merest simpleton could hardly mistake a fiction of *this* kind for a true history, unless he believed the writer to be endued with omniscience and omnipresence, or to be aided by familiar spirits, doing the office of Homer's Muses, whom he invokes to tell him all that could not otherwise be known.

. . . Let the events, therefore, which are detailed, and the characters described, be ever so natural, the way in which they are presented to us is of a kind of supernatural cast, perfectly unlike any real history that ever was or can be written, and thus requiring a greater stretch of imagination in the reader. On the other hand, the supposed narrator of his own history never pretends to dive into the thoughts and feelings of the other parties; he merely describes his own, and gives his conjectures as to those of the rest, just as a real autobiographer might do; and thus an author is enabled to assimilate his fiction to reality, without withholding that delineation of the inward workings of the human heart, which is so much coveted. Nevertheless novels in the first person have not succeeded so well as to make that mode of writing become very general. It is objected to them, not without reason, that they want a *hero*: the person intended to occupy that post being the narrator himself, who of course cannot so describe his own conduct and character as to make the reader thoroughly acquainted with him; though the attempt frequently produces an offensive appearance of egotism.

The plan of a fictitious correspondence seems calculated in some measure to combine the advantages of the other two; since by allowing each personage to be the speaker in turn, the feelings of each may be described by himself, and his character and conduct by another. But these novels are apt to become excessively tedious; since, to give the letters the appearance of reality, (without which the main object proposed would be defeated,) they must contain a very large proportion of matter which has no bearing at all upon the story. There is also generally a sort of awkward disjointed appearance in a novel which proceeds entirely in letters, and holds together, as it were, by continual splicing.

Miss Austin, though she has in a few places introduced letters with great effect, has on the whole conducted her novels on the ordinary plan, describing, without scruple, private conversations and uncommunicated feelings: but she has not been forgetful of the important maxim, so long ago illustrated by Homer, and afterwards enforced by Aristotle, of saying as little as possible in her own person, and giving a dramatic air to the narrative, by introducing frequent conversations; which she conducts with a regard to character hardly exceeded even by Shakspeare himself. Like him, she shows as admirable a discrimination in the characters of fools as of people of sense; a merit which is far from common. To invent, indeed, a conversation full of wisdom or of wit, requires that the writer should himself possess ability; but the converse does not hold good: it is no fool that can describe fools well; and many who have succeeded pretty well in painting superior characters, have failed in giving individuality to those weaker ones, which it is necessary to introduce in order to give a faithful representation of real life: they exhibit to us mere folly in the abstract, forgetting that to the eye of a skilful naturalist the insects on a leaf present as wide differences as exist between the elephant and the lion. Slender, and Shallow, and Aguecheek, as Shakspeare has painted them, though equally fools, resemble one another no more than Richard, and Macbeth, and Julius Cæsar; and Miss Austin's Mrs. Bennet, Mr. Rushworth, and Miss Bates, are no more alike than her Darcy, Knightley, and Edmund Bertram. Some have complained, indeed, of finding her fools too much like nature, and consequently tiresome; there is no disputing about tastes; all we can say is, that such critics must (whatever deference they may outwardly pay to received opinions) find the Merry Wives of Windsor and Twelfth Night very tiresome; and that those who look with pleasure at Wilkie's pictures, or those of the Dutch school, must admit that excellence of imitation may confer attraction on that which would be insipid or disagreeable in the reality.

Her minuteness of detail has also been found fault with; but even where it produces, at the time, a degree of tediousness, we know not whether that can justly be reckoned a blemish, which is absolutely essential to a very high excellence. Now, it is absolutely impossible, without this, to produce that thorough acquaintance with the characters, which is necessary to make the reader heartily interested in them. . . .

We ventured, in a former article, to remonstrate against the dethronement of the once powerful God of Love, in his own most especial domain, the novel; and to suggest that, in shunning the ordinary fault of recommending by examples a romantic and uncalculating extravagance of passion, Miss Austin had rather fallen into the opposite extreme of exclusively patronizing what are called prudent matches, and too much disparaging sentimental enthusiasm. We urged, that, mischievous as is the extreme on this side, it is not the one into which the young folks of the present day are the most likely to run: the prevailing fault is not now, whatever it may have been, to sacrifice all for love:

'Venit enim magnum donandi parca juventus,
Nec tantum Veneris quantum studiosa culinæ.'

On the whole, Miss Austin's works may safely be recommended, not only as among the most unexceptionable of their class, but as combining, in an eminent degree, instruction with amusement, though without the direct effort at the former, of which we have complained, as sometimes defeating its object. For those who cannot, or will not, *learn* any thing from productions of this kind, she has provided entertainment which entitles her to thanks; for mere innocent amusement is in itself a good, when it interferes with no greater; especially as it may occupy the place of some other that may *not* be innocent. The Eastern monarch who proclaimed a reward to him who should discover a new pleasure, would have deserved well of mankind had he stipulated that it should be blameless. Those, again, who delight in the study of human nature, may improve in the knowledge of it, and in the profitable application of that knowledge, by the perusal of such fictions as those before us.

5 [*George Henry Lewes*]

FROM "The Novels of Jane Austen," *Blackwood's,*
July, 1859[1]

For nearly half a century England has possessed an artist of the highest rank, whose works have been extensively circulated, whose merits have been keenly relished, and whose name is still unfamiliar in men's mouths. One would suppose that great excellence and real

1. Vol. LXXXVI, pp. 99–109, 112–113.

success would inevitably produce a loud reputation. Yet in this particular case such a supposition would be singularly mistaken. So far from the name of Miss Austen being constantly cited among the glories of our literature, there are many well-informed persons who will be surprised to hear it mentioned among the best writers. If we look at Hazlitt's account of the English novelists, in his *Lectures on the Comic Writers,* we find Mrs Radcliff, Mrs Inchbald, Mrs Opie, Miss Burney, and Miss Edgeworth receiving due honour, and more than is due; but no hint that Miss Austen has written a line. If we cast a glance over the list of English authors republished by Baudry, Galignani, and Tauchnitz, we find there writers of the very smallest pretensions, but not the author of *Emma,* and *Mansfield Park.* Mention the name of Miss Austen to a cultivated reader, and it is probable that the sparkle in his eye will at once flash forth sympathetic admiration, and he will perhaps relate how Scott, Whately, and Macaulay prize this gifted woman, and how the English public has bought her works; but beyond the literary circle we find the name almost entirely unknown; and not simply unknown in the sense of having no acknowledged place among the remarkable writers, but unremembered even in connection with the very works which are themselves remembered. We have met with many persons who remembered to have read *Pride and Prejudice,* or *Mansfield Park,* but who had altogether forgotten by whom they were written. "Miss Austen? Oh, yes; she translates from the German, doesn't she?" is a not uncommon question—a vague familiarity with the name of Mrs. Austin being uppermost. From time to time also the tiresome twaddle of lady novelists is praised by certain critics, as exhibiting the "quiet truthfulness of Miss Austen."

That Miss Austen is an artist of high rank, in the most rigorous sense of the word, is an opinion which in the present article we shall endeavour to substantiate. That her novels are very extensively read, is not an opinion, but a demonstrated fact; and with this fact we couple the paradoxical fact, of a fine artist, whose works are widely known and enjoyed, being all but unknown to the English public, and quite unknown abroad. The causes which have kept her name in comparative obscurity all the time that her works have been extensively read, and her reputation every year has been settling itself more firmly in the minds of the better critics, may well be worth an inquiry. It is intelligible how the blaze of Scott should have thrown her into the shade, at first: beside his frescoes her works are but miniatures; exquisite as miniatures, yet incapable of ever filling that space in the public eye which was filled by his massive and masterly pictures. But although it is intelligible why Scott should have eclipsed her, it is not at first so easy to understand why Miss Edgeworth should have done so. Miss Austen, indeed, has taken her revenge with posterity. She will doubtless be read as long as English novels find readers; whereas Miss Edgeworth is already little more than a name, and only finds a public for her children's books. But contemporaries, for the most part, judged otherwise; and in consequence Miss Edgeworth's name has become familiar all over the three kingdoms. Scott, indeed, and Archbishop Whately, at once perceived the superiority of Miss Austen to her more fortunate rival;* but the *Quarterly* tells us that "her fame has grown fastest since she died: there was no *éclat* about her first appearance: the public took time to make up its mind; and she, not having staked her hopes of happiness on success or failure, was content to wait for the decision of her claims. Those claims have been long established beyond a question; but the merit of *first* recognising them belongs less to reviewers than to general readers." There is comfort in this for authors who see the applause of reviewers lavished on works of garish effect. Nothing that is really good can fail, at last, in securing its audience; and it is evident that Miss Austen's works must possess elements of indestructible excellence, since, although never "popular," she survives writers who were very popular; and forty years after her death, gains more recognition than she gained when alive. Those who, like ourselves, have read and re-read her works several times, can understand this duration, and this increase of her fame. But the fact that her name is not even now a household word proves that her excellence must be of an unobtrusive kind, shunning the glare of popularity, not appealing to temporary tastes and vulgar sympathies, but demanding culture in its admirers. Johnson wittily says of somebody, "Sir, he managed to make himself public without making himself known." Miss Austen has made herself known without making herself public. There is no portrait of her in

---

* See the notices in LOCKHART'S *Life of Scott;* and the reviews in the *Quarterly*, No. 27, by SCOTT, and No. 48, by Dr. WHATELY. (Lewes' note.)

the shop windows; indeed, no portrait of her at all. But she is cherished in the memories of those whose memory is fame. . . .

One might gather from her works that she was personally attractive, and we are told in the memoir that this was the case. "Her stature rather exceeded the middle height; her carriage and deportment were quiet but graceful; her features were separately good; their assemblage produced an unrivalled expression of that cheerfulness, sensibility, and benevolence which were her real characteristics; her complexion was of the finest texture—it might with truth be said that her eloquent blood spoke through her modest cheek; her voice was sweet; she delivered herself with fluency and precision; indeed, she was formed for elegant and rational society, excelling in conversation as much as in composition." We may picture her as something like her own sprightly, natural, but by no means perfect Elizabeth Bennett, in *Pride and Prejudice,* one of the few heroines one would seriously like to marry.

We have no means of ascertaining how many copies of these exquisite pictures of English life have been circulated, but we know that the number is very large. Twice or thrice have the railway editions been out of print; and Mr Bentley's edition is stereotyped. This success implies a hold on the Public, all the more certainly because the popularity is "not loud but deep." We have re-read them all four times; or rather, to speak more accurately, they have been read aloud to us, one after the other; and when it is considered what a severe test that is, how the reading aloud permits no skipping, no evasion of weariness, but brings both merits and defects into stronger relief by forcing the mind to dwell on them, there is surely something significant of genuine excellence when both reader and listener finish their fourth reading with increase of admiration. The test of reading aloud applied to *Jane Eyre,* which had only been read once before, very considerably modified our opinion of that remarkable work; and, to confess the truth, modified it so far that we feel as if we should never open the book again. The same test applied to such an old favourite as *Tom Jones,* was also much more damaging than we should have anticipated—bringing the defects and shortcomings of that much overrated work into very distinct prominence, and lessening our pleasure in its effective, but, on the whole, coarse painting. Fielding has greater vigour of mind, greater experience, greater attainments, and a more effective *mise en scène*, than Miss Austen; but he is not only immeasurably inferior to her in the highest department of art—the representation of character—he is also inferior to her, we think, in real humour; and in spite of his "construction," of which the critics justly speak in praise, he is inferior to her in the construction and conduct of his story, being more commonplace and less artistic. He has more invention of situation and more vigour, but less truth and subtlety. This is at any rate our individual judgment, which the reader is at liberty to modify as he pleases. In the course of the fifteen years which have elapsed since we first read *Emma*, and *Mansfield Park*, we have outlived many admirations, but have only learned to admire Miss Austen more; and as we are perfectly aware of *why* we so much admire her, we may endeavour to communicate these reasons to the reader.

If, as probably few will dispute, the art of the novelist be the representation of human life by means of a story; and if the *truest* representation, effected by the *least expenditure* of means, constitutes the highest claim of art, then we say that Miss Austen has carried the art to a point of excellence surpassing that reached by any of her rivals. Observe we say "the art;" we do not say that she equals many of them in the *interest* excited by the art; that is a separate question. It is probable, nay certain, that the interest excited by the *Antigone* is very inferior to that excited by *Black-eyed Susan*. It is probable that *Uncle Tom* and *Dred* surpassed in interest the *Antiquary* or *Ivanhoe*. It is probable that *Jane Eyre* produced a far greater excitement than the *Vicar of Wakefield*. But the critic justly disregards these fervid elements of immediate success, and fixes his attention mainly on the art which is of eternal substance. Miss Austen has nothing fervid in her works. She is not capable of producing a profound agitation in the mind. In many respects this is a limitation of her powers, a deduction from her claims. But while other writers have had more power over the emotions, more vivid imaginations, deeper sensibilities, deeper insight, and more of what is properly called invention, no novelist has approached her in what we may style the "economy of art," by which is meant the easy adaptation of means to ends, with no aid from extraneous or superfluous elements. Indeed, paradoxical as the juxtaposition of the names may perhaps appear to those who have not reflected much on this subject, we venture to say that the only names we can place above Miss Austen, in respect of this economy of art, are Sophocles and Molière (in *Le Misanthrope*). And if any one will examine the terms of the definition, he will perceive that almost all defects in works of art arise from neglect of this economy. When the *end* is the representation of human nature in its familiar aspects, moving amid every-day scenes, the *means* must likewise be furnished from every-day life: romance and improbabilities must be banished as rigorously as the grotesque exaggeration of peculiar characteristics, or the representation of abstract types. It is easy for the artist to choose a subject from every-day life, but it is *not* easy for him so to represent the characters and their actions that they shall be at once lifelike and interesting; accordingly, whenever ordinary people are introduced, they are either made to speak a language never spoken out of books, and to pursue conduct never observed in life; or else they are intolerably wearisome. But Miss Austen is like Shakespeare: she makes her very noodles inexhaustibly amusing, yet accurately real. We never tire of her characters. They become equal to actual experiences. They live with us, and form perpetual topics of comment. We have so personal a dislike to Mrs Elton and Mrs Norris, that it would gratify our savage feeling to hear of some calamity befalling them. We think of Mr Collins and John Thorpe with such a mixture of ludicrous enjoyment and angry contempt, that we alternately long and dread to make their personal acquaintance. The heroines—at least Elizabeth, Emma, and Catherine Morland—are truly *lovable,* flesh-and-blood young women; and the good people are all really good, without being goody. Her reverend critic in the *Quarterly* truly says, "She herself compares her productions to a little bit of ivory, two inches wide, worked upon with a brush so fine that little effect is produced with much labour. It is so: her portraits are perfect likenesses, admirably finished, many of them gems; but it is all miniature-painting; and having satisfied herself with being inimitable in one line, she never essayed canvass and oils; never tried her hand at a majestic daub." This is very true: it at once defines her position and lowers her claims. When we said that in the highest department of the novelist's art—namely, the truthful representation of character—Miss Austen was without a superior, we ought to have added that in this department she did

not choose the highest range; the truth and felicity of her delineation
are exquisite, but the characters delineated are not of a high rank.
She belongs to the great dramatists; but her dramas are of homely
common quality. It is obvious that the nature of the thing represented will determine degrees in art. Raphael will always rank
higher than Teniers; Sophocles and Shakespeare will never be low-
ered to the rank of Lope de Vega and Scribe. It is a greater effort
of genius to produce a fine epic than a fine pastoral; a great
drama, than a perfect lyric. There is far greater strain on the intellectual effort to create a Brutus or an Othello, than to create a
Vicar of Wakefield or a Squire Western. The higher the aims, the
greater is the strain, and the nobler is success. . . .

To return to Miss Austen: her delineation is unsurpassed, but the
characters delineated are never of a lofty or impassioned order, and
therefore make no demand on the highest faculties of the intellect.
Such genius as hers is excessively rare; but it is not the highest kind
of genius. . . . Miss Austen's two-inch bit of ivory is worth a gallery
of canvass by eminent R.A.'s, but it is only a bit of ivory after all.
"Her two inches of ivory," continues the critic recently quoted, "just
describes her preparations for a tale in three volumes. A village—
two families connected together—three or four interlopers, out of
whom are to spring a little *tracasserie;* and by means of village or
country-town visiting and gossiping, a real plot shall thicken, and
its 'rear of darkness' never be scattered till six pages off *finis.*

. . . The work is all done by half-a-dozen people; no person, scene,
or sentence is ever introduced needless to the matter in hand: no
catastrophes, or discoveries, or surprises of a grand nature are allowed—neither children nor fortunes are found or lost by accident—
the mind is never taken off the level surface of life—the reader
breakfasts, dines, walks, and gossips with the various worthies, till a
process of transmutation takes place in him, and he absolutely
fancies himself one of the company. . . . The secret is, Miss Austen
was a thorough mistress in the knowledge of human character; how
it is acted upon by education and circumstance, and how, when
once formed, it shows itself through every hour of every day, and
in every speech of every person. Her conversations would be tiresome
but for this; and her personages, the fellows to whom may be met
in the streets, or drank tea with at half an hour's notice, would

excite no interest; but in Miss Austen's hands we see into their hearts and hopes, their motives, their struggles within themselves; and a sympathy is induced which, if extended to daily life and the world at large, would make the reader a more amiable person; and we must think it that reader's own fault who does not close her pages with more charity in his heart towards unpretending, if prosing worth; with a higher estimation of simple kindness and sincere good-will; with a quickened sense of the duty of bearing and forbearing in domestic intercourse, and of the pleasure of adding to the little comforts even of persons who are neither wits nor beauties." It is worth remembering that this is the deliberate judgment of the present Archbishop of Dublin, and not a careless verdict dropping from the pen of a facile reviewer. There are two points in it to which especial attention may be given: *first,* The indication of Miss Austen's power of representing life; and, *secondly,* The indication of the effect which her sympathy with ordinary life produces. . . .

But the real secret of Miss Austen's success lies in her having the exquisite and rare gift of dramatic creation of character. Scott says of her, "She had a talent for describing the involvements, and feelings, and characters of ordinary life, which is to me the most wonderful I ever met with. The big bow-wow strain I can do myself like any now going; but the exquisite touch, which renders ordinary commonplace things and characters interesting, from the truth of the description and the sentiment, is denied me. What a pity such a gifted creature died so early!" Generously said; but high as the praise is, it is as much below the real excellence of Miss Austen, as the "big bow-wow strain" is below the incomparable power of the Waverley Novels. Scott felt, but did not define, the excellence of Miss Austen. The very word "describing" is altogether misplaced and misleading. She seldom describes anything, and is not felicitous when she attempts it. But instead of *description,* the common and easy resource of novelists, she has the rare and difficult art of *dramatic presentation:* instead of telling us what her characters are, and what they feel, she presents the people, and they reveal themselves. In this she has never perhaps been surpassed, not even by Shakespeare himself. If ever living beings can be said to have moved across the page of fiction, as they lived, speaking as they spoke, and feeling as they felt, they do so in *Pride and Prejudice, Emma,* and *Mansfield Park*. What incomparable noodles she exhibits for our astonishment and laughter! What silly, good-natured women! What softly-selfish men! What lively, amiable, honest men and women, whom one would rejoice to have known!

But all her power is dramatic power; she loses her hold on us directly she ceases to speak through the *personæ;* she is then like a great actor *off* the stage. When she is making men and women her mouthpieces, she is exquisitely and inexhaustibly humorous; but when she speaks in her own person, she is apt to be commonplace, and even prosing. Her dramatic ventriloquism is such that, amid our tears of laughter and sympathetic exasperation at folly, we feel it almost impossible that she did not hear those very people utter those very words. In many cases this was doubtless the fact. The best invention does not consist in finding *new* language for characters, but in finding the *true* language for them. It is easy to invent a language never spoken by any one out of books; but it is so far from easy to invent—that is, to find out—the language which certain characters would speak and did speak, that in all the thousands of volumes written since Richardson and Fielding, every difficulty is more frequently overcome than *that*. If the reader fails to perceive the extraordinary merit of Miss Austen's representation of character, let him try himself to paint a portrait which shall be at once many-sided and interesting, without employing any but the commonest colours, without calling in the aid of eccentricity, exaggeration, or literary "effects;" or let him carefully compare the writings of Miss Austen with those of any other novelist, from Fielding to Thackeray.

It is probably this same dramatic instinct which makes the construction of her stories so admirable. And by construction, we mean the art which, selecting what is useful and rejecting what is superfluous, renders our interest unflagging, because one chapter evolves the next, one character is necessary to the elucidation of another. In what is commonly called "plot" she does not excel. Her invention is wholly in character and motive, not in situation. Her materials are of the commonest every-day occurrence. Neither the emotions of tragedy, nor the exaggerations of farce, seem to have the slightest attraction for her. The reader's pulse never throbs, his curiosity is never intense; but his interest never wanes for a moment. The action begins; the people speak, feel, and act; everything that is said, felt, or done tends towards the entanglement or disentanglement of the plot; and we are almost made actors as well as spectators of the little drama. One of the most difficult things in dramatic writing is so to construct the story that every scene shall advance the denouement by easy evolution, yet at the same time give scope to the full exhibition of the characters. In dramas, as in novels, we almost always see that the action stands still while the characters are being exhibited, and the characters are in abeyance while the action is being unfolded. For perfect specimens of this higher construction demanded by art, we would refer to the jealousy-scenes of *Othello*, and the great scene between Célimène and Arsinoé in *Le Misanthrope;* there is not in these two marvels of art a verse which does not exhibit some *nuance* of character, and thereby, at the same time, tends towards the full development of the action.

So entirely dramatic, and so little descriptive, is the genius of Miss Austen, that she seems to rely upon what her people say and do for the whole effect they are to produce on our imaginations. She no more thinks of describing the physical appearance of her people than the dramatist does who knows that his persons are to be represented by living actors. This is a defect and a mistake in art: a defect, because, although every reader must necessarily conjure up to himself a vivid image of people whose characters are so vividly presented; yet each reader has to do this for himself without aid from the author, thereby missing many of the subtle connections between physical and mental organisation. It is not enough to be told that a young gentleman had a fine countenance and an air of fashion; or that a young gentlewoman was handsome and elegant. As far as any direct information can be derived from the authoress, we might imagine that this was a purblind world, wherein nobody ever saw anybody, except in a dim vagueness which obscured all peculiarities. It is impossible that Mr Collins should not have been endowed by nature with an appearance in some way heralding the delicious folly of the inward man. Yet *all* we hear of this fatuous curate is, that "he was a tall heavy-looking young man of five-and-twenty. His air was grave and stately, and his manners were very formal." Balzac or Dickens would not have been content without making the reader *see* this Mr Collins. Miss Austen is content to make us *know* him, even to the very intricacies of his inward man. It is not stated whether she was shortsighted, but the absence of all sense of the outward world—either scenery or personal appearance—is more remarkable in her than in any writer we remember.

We are touching here on one of her defects which help to an explanation of her limited popularity, especially when coupled with her deficiencies in poetry and passion. She has little or no sympathy with what is picturesque and passionate. This prevents her from painting what the popular eye can see, and the popular heart can feel. The struggles, the ambitions, the errors, and the sins of energetic life are left untouched by her; and these form the subjects most stirring to the general sympathy. Other writers have wanted this element of popularity, but they have compensated for it by a keen sympathy with, and power of representing, the adventurous, the romantic, and the picturesque. Passion and adventure are the sources of certain success with the mass of mankind. The passion may be coarsely felt, the romance may be ridiculous, but there will always be found a large majority whose sympathies will be awakened by even the coarsest daubs. Emotion is in its nature sympathetic and uncritical: a spark will ignite it. Types of villany never seen or heard of out of books, or off the stage, types of heroism and virtue not less hyperbolical, are eagerly welcomed and *believed* in by a public which would pass over without notice the subtlest creations of genius, and which would even *resent* the more truthful painting as disturbing its emotional enjoyment of hating the bad, and loving the good. The nicer art which mingles goodness with villany, and weakness with virtue, as in life they are always mingled, causes positive distress to young and uncultivated minds. The mass of men never ask whether a character is true, or the events probable; it is enough for them that they are moved; and to move them strongly, black must be very black, and white without a shade. Hence it is that caricature and exaggeration of all kinds—inflated diction and daubing delineation—are, and always will be, popular: a certain breadth and massiveness of effect being necessary to produce a strong impression on all but a refined audience. In the works of the highest genius we sometimes find a breadth and massiveness of effect which make even these works popular, although the qualities most highly prized by the cultivated reader are little appreciated by the public. The *Iliad*, Shakespeare and Molière, *Don Quixote* and *Faust,* affect the mass powerfully;

but how many admirers of Homer would prefer the *naïveté* of the original to the epigrammatic splendour of Pope?

The novelist who has no power of broad and massive effect can never expect to be successful with the great public. He may gain the suffrages of the highest minds, and in course of time become a classic; but we all know what the *popularity* of a classic means. Miss Austen is such a novelist. Her subjects have little intrinsic interest; it is only in their treatment that they become attractive; but treatment and art are not likely to captivate any except critical and refined tastes. Every reader will be amused by her pictures, because their very truth carries them home to ordinary experience and sympathy; but this amusement is of a tepid nature, and the effect is quickly forgotten. Partridge expressed the general sentiment of the public when he spoke slightingly of Garrick's "Hamlet," because Garrick did just what he, Partridge, would have done in presence of a ghost; whereas the actor who performed the king powerfully impressed him by sonorous elocution and emphatic gesticulation: *that* was acting, and required art; the other was natural, and not worth alluding to.

The absence of breadth, picturesqueness, and passion, will also limit the appreciating audience of Miss Austen to the small circle of cultivated minds; and even these minds are not always capable of greatly relishing her works. We have known very remarkable people who cared little for her pictures of every-day life; and indeed it may be anticipated that those who have little sense of humour, or whose passionate and insurgent activities demand in art a reflection of their own emotions and struggles, will find little pleasure in such homely comedies. Currer Bell[1] may be taken as a type of these. She was utterly without a sense of humour, and was by nature fervid and impetuous. In a letter published in her memoirs she writes,—"Why do you like Miss Austen so very much? I am puzzled on that point. . . . I had not read *Pride and Prejudice* till I read that sentence of yours, and then I got the book. And what did I find? An accurate daguerreotyped portrait of a commonplace face; a carefully-fenced, highly-cultivated garden, with neat borders and delicate flowers; but no glance of a bright, vivid physiognomy, no open country, no fresh air, no blue hill, no bonny beck. I should

1. Pseudonym for Charlotte Bronte.

hardly like to live with her elegant ladies and gentlemen, in their elegant but confined houses." The critical reader will not fail to remark the almost contemptuous indifference to the art of truthful portrait-painting which this passage indicates; and he will understand, perhaps, how the writer of such a passage was herself incapable of drawing more than characteristics, even in her most successful efforts. Jane Eyre, Rochester, and Paul Emmanuel, are very vigorous sketches, but the reader observes them from the *outside,* he does not penetrate their souls, he does not know them. What is said respecting the want of open country, blue hill, and bonny beck, is perfectly true; but the same point has been more felicitously touched by Scott, in his review of *Emma:* "Upon the whole," he says, "the turn of this author's novels bears the same relation to that of the sentimental and romantic cast, that cornfields and cottages and meadows bear to the highly-adorned grounds of a show mansion, or the rugged sublimities of a mountain landscape. It is neither so captivating as the one, nor so grand as the other; but it affords those who frequent it a pleasure nearly allied with the experience of their own social habits." Scott would also have loudly repudiated the notion of Miss Austen's characters being "mere daguerreotypes." Having himself drawn both ideal and real characters, he knew the difficulties of both; and he well says, "He who paints from *le beau idéal,* if his scenes and sentiments are striking and interesting, is in a great measure exempted from the difficult task of reconciling them with the ordinary probabilities of life; but he who paints a scene of common occurrence, places his composition within that extensive range of criticism which general experience offers to every reader. . . Something more than a mere sign-post likeness is also demanded. The portrait must have spirit and character as well as resemblance; and being deprived of all that, according to Bayes, goes to 'elevate and surprise,' it must make amends by displaying depth of knowledge and dexterity of execution. . . ."

Miss Austen has generally but an indifferent story to tell, but her art of telling it is incomparable. Her characters, never ideal, are not of an eminently attractive order; but her dramatic ventriloquism and power of presentation is little less than marvellous. Macaulay declares his opinion that in this respect she is second only to Shakespeare. "Among the writers," he says, "who, in the point we have noticed, have approached nearest the manner of the great master, we have no hesitation in placing Jane Austen, a woman of whom England is justly proud. She has given us a multitude of characters, all, in a certain sense, commonplace—all such as we meet every day. Yet they are all as perfectly discriminated from each other as if they were the most eccentric of human beings. . . . . And all this is done by touches so delicate that they elude analysis, that they defy powers of description, and that we only know them to exist by the general effect to which they have contributed.[1]

The art of the novelist consists in telling the story and representing the characters; but besides these, there are other powerful though extraneous sources of attraction often possessed by novels, which are due to the literary talent and culture of the writer. There is, for example, the power of description, both of scenery and of character. Many novels depend almost entirely on this for their effect. It is a lower kind of power, and consequently much more frequent than what we have styled the *art* of the novelist; yet it may be very puissant in the hands of a fine writer, gifted with a real sense of the picturesque. Being very easy, it has of late become the resource of weak writers; and the prominent position it has usurped has tended in two ways to produce weariness—first, by encouraging incompetent writers to do what is easily done; and, secondly, by seducing writers from the higher and better method of dramatic exposition.

Another source of attraction is the general vigour of mind exhibited by the author, in his comments on the incidents and characters of his story: these comments, when proceeding from a fine insight or a large experience, give additional charm to the story, and make the delightful novel a delightful book. It is almost superfluous to add, that this also has its obverse: the comments too often painfully exhibit a general weakness of mind. Dr Johnson refused to take tea with some one because, as he said, "Sir, there is no vigour in his talk." This is the complaint which must be urged against the majority of novelists: they put too much water in their ink. And even when the talk is good, we must remember that it is, after all, only one of the side-dishes of the feast. All the literary and philo-

1. "Madame D' Arblay," *Edinburgh Review*, LXXVII, (January, 1843), pp. 561–562.

sophic culture which an author can bring to bear upon his work will *tend* to give that work a higher value, but it will not really make it a better novel. To suppose that culture can replace invention, or literature do instead of character, is as erroneous as to suppose that archæological learning and scenical splendour can raise poor acting to the level of fine acting. Yet this is the common mistake of literary men. They are apt to believe that mere writing will weigh in the scale against artistic presentation; that comment will do duty for dramatic revelation; that analysing motives with philosophic skill will answer all the purpose of creation. But whoever looks closely into this matter will see that literature—that is, the writing of thinking and accomplished men—is excessively cheap, compared with the smallest amount of invention or creation; and it is cheap because more easy of production, and less potent in effect. This is apparently by no means the opinion of some recent critics, who evidently consider their own *writing* of more merit than *humour* and *invention,* and who are annoyed at the notion of "mere serialists," without "solid acquirements," being regarded all over Europe as our most distinguished authors. Yet it may be suggested that writing such as that of the critics in question can be purchased in abundance, whereas humour and invention are among the rarest of products. If it is a painful reflection that genius should be esteemed more highly than solid acquirements, it should be remembered that learning is only the diffused form of what was *once* invention. "Solid acquirement" is the genius of wits, which has become the wisdom of reviewers.

Be this as it may, we acknowledge the great attractions which a novel may receive from the general vigour and culture of the author; and acknowledge that such attractions form but a very small element in Miss Austen's success. Her pages have no sudden illuminations. There are neither epigrams nor aphorisms, neither subtle analyses nor eloquent descriptions. She is without grace or felicity of expression; she has neither fervid nor philosophic comment. Her charm lies solely in the art of representing life and character, and that is exquisite. . . .

The reader who has yet to make acquaintance with these novels, is advised to begin with *Pride and Prejudice* or *Mansfield Park;* and if these do not captivate him, he may fairly leave the others unread. In *Pride and Prejudice* there is the best story, and the greatest variety of character: the whole Bennet family is inimitable: Mr Bennet, caustic, quietly, indolently selfish, but honourable, and in some respects amiable; his wife, the perfect type of a gossiping, weak-headed, fussy mother; Jane a sweet creature; Elizabeth a sprightly and fascinating flesh-and-blood heroine; Lydia a pretty, but vain and giddy girl; and Mary, plain and pedantic, studying "thorough bass and human nature." Then there is Mr Collins, and Sir William Lucas, and the proud foolish old lady Catherine de Bough, and Darcy, Bingley, and Wickham, all admirable. From the first chapter to the last there is a succession of scenes of high comedy, and the interest is unflagging. *Mansfield Park* is also singularly fascinating, though the heroine is less of a favourite with us than Miss Austen's heroines usually are; but aunt Norris and Lady Bertram are perfect; and the scenes at Portsmouth, when Fanny Price visits her home after some years' residence at the Park, are wonderfully truthful and vivid. The private theatricals, too, are very amusing; and the day spent at the Rushworths' is a masterpiece of art. If the reader has really tasted the flavour of these works, he will need no other recommendation to read and re-read the others. Even *Persuasion,* which we cannot help regarding as the weakest, contains exquisite touches, and some characters no one else could have surpassed.

We have endeavoured to express the delight which Miss Austen's works have always given us, and to explain the sources of her success by indicating the qualities which make her a model worthy of the study of all who desire to understand the art of the novelist. But we have also indicated what seem to be the limitations of her genius, and to explain why it is that this genius, moving only amid the quiet scenes of every-day life, with no power over the more stormy and energetic activities which find vent even in every-day life, can never give her a high rank among great artists. Her place is among great artists, but it is not high among them. She sits in the House of Peers, but it is as a simple Baron. The delight derived from her pictures arises from our sympathy with ordinary characters, our relish of humour, and our intellectual pleasure in art for art's sake. But when it is admitted that she never stirs the deeper emotions, that she never fills the soul with a noble aspiration, or brightens it with a fine idea, but, at the utmost, only teaches us charity for the ordinary failings of ordinary people, and sympathy with their goodness, we have admitted an objection which lowers her claims to rank among the great benefactors of the race; and this sufficiently explains why, with all her excellence, her name has not become a household word. Her fame, we think, must endure. Such art as hers can never grow old, never be superseded. But, after all, miniatures are not frescoes, and her works are miniatures. Her place is among the Immortals; but the pedestal is erected in a quiet niche of the great temple.

6 [George Henry Lewes]

FROM "The Lady Novelists," *Westminster Review,* July, 1862[1]

Having said thus much on the general subject of female novel writing, let us glance rapidly, and without pretence of exhaustive criticism, at some of the novelists; doing in careless prose what Leigh Hunt has done in genial verse in his "Blue Stocking Revels." We have been great readers and great admirers of female novels; and although it is difficult to give authors a *satisfactory* reason for not including their names among the most celebrated, we beg our fair novelists to put the most generous construction upon all our "omissions," and to believe that when we are ungallant and omissive, there is "a design under it" as profound as that under Swift's dulness. To include *all* would obviously be impossible in these limits; and we shall purposely exclude some names of undoubted worth and renown, in order not even to seem invidious.

First and foremost let Jane Austen be named, the greatest artist that has ever written, using the term to signify the most perfect mastery over the means to her end. There are heights and depths in human nature Miss Austen has never scaled nor fathomed, there are

1. Vol. LVIII, pp. 73–74.

worlds of passionate existence into which she has never set foot; but although this is obvious to every reader, it is equally obvious that she has risked no failures by attempting to delineate that which she had not seen. Her circle may be restricted, but it is complete. Her world is a perfect orb, and vital. Life, as it presents itself to an English gentlewoman peacefully yet actively engaged in her quiet village, is mirrored in her works with a purity and fidelity that must endow them with interest for all time. To read one of her books is like an actual experience of life; you know the people as if you had lived with them, and you feel something of personal affection towards them. The marvellous reality and subtle distinctive traits noticeable in her portraits has led Macaulay to call her a prose Shakspeare. If the whole force of the distinction which lies in that epithet *prose* be fairly appreciated, no one, we think, will dispute the compliment; for out of Shakspeare it would be difficult to find characters so typical yet so nicely demarcated within the limits of their kind. We do not find such profound psychological insight as may be found in George Sand (not to mention male writers), but taking the type to which the characters belong, we see the most intimate and accurate knowledge in all Miss Austen's creations.

Only cultivated minds fairly appreciate the exquisite art of Miss Austen. Those who demand the stimulus of "effects;" those who can only see by strong lights and shadows, will find her tame and uninteresting. We may illustrate this by one detail. Lucy Steele's bad English, so delicately and truthfully indicated, would in the hands of another have been more obvious, more "effective" in its exaggeration, but the loss of this comic effect is more than replaced to the cultivated reader by his relish of the nice discrimination visible in its truthfulness. And so of the rest. *Strong* lights are unnecessary, *true* lights being at command. The incidents, the characters, the dialogue —all are of every day life, and so truthfully presented, that to appreciate the art we must try to imitate it, or carefully compare it with that of others.

We are but echoing an universal note of praise in speaking thus highly of her works, and it is from no desire of simply swelling that chorus of praise that we name her here, but to call attention to the peculiar excellence at once womanly and literary which has earned this reputation. Of all imaginative writers she is the most *real*. Never does she transcend her own actual experience, never does her pen trace a line that does not touch the experience of others. Herein we recognise the first quality of literature. We recognise the second and more special quality of womanliness in the tone and point of view; they are novels written by a woman, an Englishwoman, a gentle-woman; no signature could disguise that fact; and because she has so faithfully (although unconsciously) kept to her own womanly point of view, her works are durable. There is nothing of the *doctrinaire* in Jane Austen; not a trace of woman's "mission;" but as the most truthful, charming, humorous, pure-minded, quick-witted, and unexaggerated of writers, female literature has reason to be proud of her.

Sir Walter Scott
The Heart of Midlothian
1818

1

FROM "Proceedings in the Trial of William Maclauchlane," March, 1737[1]

William Maclauchlane, late servant of the Countess of Wemyss, prisoner in the castle of Edinburgh, pannel. INDICTED and ACCUSED at the instance of Duncan Forbes of Culloden, Esquire, his Majesty's Advocate for his Highness's interest, for the crimes of murder and fire raising, and others, as is more fully mentioned in the indictment raised against him thereanent. Making mention, THAT WHEREAS, by the law of God, the common law, the municipal laws and practice of this kingdom, and the laws of all other well-governed realms, privy conspiracies to raise, procure, and move, and the raising, pro-

1. Reprinted from *Criminal Trials Illustrative of the Tale Entitled "The Heart of Mid-Lothian," Published from the Original Record*, Edinburgh: Archibald Constable, 1818, pp. 205–211, 290–291, 295–297, 303–305, 314–316, 318–321.

curing, or moving seditious commotions of the people, mobs or tumults, in violation of the laws, repose, and tranquillity of the kingdom, or any part thereof; the convocating the lieges by beat of drum; and their assembling themselves riotously and tumultuously together, armed with guns, Lochaber-axes, or other warlike weapons whatsoever, within burgh, without the special license of the Sovereign, or the Magistrates of the same; the surprising, invading, or seizing of the guard room of any burgh or city, by force or violence, disarming and driving out the soldiers placed there, for the preservation of the public peace, and the taking away their arms; the violent and masterful seizing and securing the gates of any city or burgh, by numbers of dissolute and disorderly persons, riotously assembled, whereby the lives and property of the inhabitants were put under the power, and exposed to the rage and caprice of the giddy and profligate part of the people; the insulting, stoning, and resisting Magistrates in the due execution of their offices; the raising wilful fire, and forcibly breaking open the doors of public prisons, and by force, threats, or terrors, extorting the keys from the lawful keepers, and setting at large prisoners lawfully confined for capital or other heinous crimes; and the committing wilful and deliberate murder, under cloud of night, in derision of public justice, in open defiance and contempt of his Majesty's laws and authority; and attended with circumstances of brutal cruelty, were most enormous and detestable; crimes destructive of the public peace; dangerous to the lives, liberties, and property of the subject; subversive of all laws, government, and society; odious and abominable in the sight of God and man, and most severely punishable: NEVERTHELESS, it was of verity, That the said William Maclauchlane had presumed to commit, and was guilty of all or one or other of the foresaid abominable crimes, aggravated as aforesaid: IN SO FAR AS, upon the 7th day of September 1736, or one or other of the days of the said month, certain seditious and blood-thirsty persons, shaking off all fear of God, regard and reverence to his Majesty's laws and authority, guided by disloyal and diabolical principles, or instigated by dangerous and desperate incendiaries, having feloniously conspired unlawfully to raise, move, and procure mobs and tumults, insult the laws and public authority, and in an outrageous manner to break and disturb the public peace in the city of Edinburgh; to do murder, and commit the other black and odious crimes after mentioned: Did assemble themselves together, within the said city and county of Edinburgh, about the hour of nine, or some other hour that night; and being armed with clubs and other offensive weapons, seized a drum, in the possession of the drummer of Portsburgh, part of the suburbs of Edinburgh, and by beating the same within the said burgh, convocated and brought together great numbers of dissolute, profligate, and disorderly persons, who, proceeding to the Netherbow Port of the said city, by force and violence seized upon the keeper and keys thereof, shut and locked the gate, and marching to the guard room, where the city guard, constituted by act of Parliament, was in use to be kept, by force and violence seized the sentinel standing at the door, entered the same, and disarmed and drove out the soldiers placed there by the authority of the Magistrates, for the preservation of the public peace, and arming themselves with the guns, halberts, Lochaber-axes, and other weapons kept in the said room, for the defence of the city; sent parties to the several ports, and took possession of the same, shutting the gates, nailing, or rolling stones to secure the said gates: And having thus made themselves masters of the city, to the great fear, terror, and trouble, of his Majesty's lieges, to the imminent danger of shedding much blood, pillaging, plundering, and burning the houses of the inhabitants; they advanced towards the public prison of the said city, and planted some of their accomplices, armed as a guard, from the north side of the said prison, commonly called Purses, across the High Street, to stop all who did not unlawfully associate themselves with them, from passing to the prison gate; and with fore-hammers beat on the door of the said prison, in order to break it open; and among the rioters so planted as a guard, and at the prison door, and in divers other places during the said tumult and sedition, he, the said William Maclauchlane, armed with a Lochaber-axe, or other offensive weapon, was unlawfully and riotously assembled with them. And when the Magistrates of the city, as in duty bound, went in a body toward the said prison, to disperse this riotous and unlawful assembly, showers of large stones were by him, the said William Laclauchlane, or his accomplices, poured upon them, whereby some of them were bruised, and all of them under great terror, were obliged to fly and save themselves from the fury of an armed mob: AND FURTHER, he, the said William Maclauchlane, or his accomplices, by burning torches, links, whins, or other combustible matter, wilfully and maliciously set fire to the said prison door, to the great danger of the adjacent wooden houses, and other houses and shops; and having burnt and beat the same open, seized the keeper, and, by force and fear, extorted the keys of the rooms of the said prison from him, and dismissed William Grinsell, imprisoned there for murder; James Ratcliff, imprisoned for theft, robbery, and housebreaking; and divers other persons there, also committed by lawful warrants: And he, the said William Maclauchlane, having conceived a deadly hatred and malice against John Porteous, commonly called Captain Porteous, there also confined under sentence of death, the execution whereof, by the amiable power and prerogative of the Crown to shew mercy to subjects condemned, had been respited by her sacred Majesty the Queen, then guardian of the kingdom, he, the said William Maclauchlane, or his said accomplices, laid violent hands upon him, with intent to murder and bereave him of his life; and having dragged him by the heels down the said tolbooth stair, crying for mercy for Christ's sake, lengthening out their cruelty towards him, alternately led, dragged, and carried him, fainting and falling on the street, to the Grassmarket, within the said city of Edinburgh, the place of common execution, in derision of public justice, and making a stand at the gallows-stone, where the gibbet was usually placed, they consulted together in what manner to put him to death; and about the hour of eleven, or some other hour that night, having hurried him to a dyster's tree near the said place, while, in the most moving manner, he was supplicating for a little time to recollect himself, a dying man, and to beg mercy from God, he, the said William Maclauchlane, or his wicked accomplices, renouncing all Christian compassion, and even human nature, fixing a rope about his neck, instantly drew him up upon the said tree; and when he endeavoured to save himself, by catching hold of the rope with his hands, he, the said William Maclauchlane, or one or other of his vile associates, barbarously beat them down with a padle, or other instrument, and brutally struck him upon the face with a Lochaber-axe, or other weapon; and wantoning in their wickedness, making loose the rope that was fixed about the said dyer's tree, he, the said William Maclauchlane, or some of his accomplices, let him down to the ground, and pulled him up again, where he hung by the neck till he was dead: All which detestable facts and crimes were impudently, wickedly, and maliciously done and committed by the said dissolute and disorderly persons, riotously and tumultuously assembled in manner above described; and the said John Porteous was cruelly murdered at the time and place aforesaid, in a daring and outrageous manner, to the dishonour of God, the contempt of his Majesty's laws and authority, and to the lasting infamy of the barbarous and bloody actors; and he, the said William Maclauchlane, was art and part of all, or one or other of the foresaid crimes, aggravated as aforesaid; which facts, or part thereof, or his being art and part in all or any of the foresaid crimes, being found proven by the verdict of an assize, before the Lords Justice General, Justice Clerk, and Commissioners of Justiciary, he, the said William Maclauchlane, ought to be most examplary punished with the pains of law, to the terror of others to commit the like in time coming.

. . . .

. . . The pursuer, for proving the libel, adduced the witnesses after deponing, viz.

PATRICK WEIR, shoemaker and drummer in Portsburgh, part of the suburbs of Edinburgh, aged forty-six years or thereby, married, solemnly sworn, purged of malice, partial counsel, examined and interrogate, deponed, That the time libelled, and about half an hour after nine o'clock at night, a number of persons came riotously and beat open the deponent's door, and called Bougar, give us out the drums; and the deponent having asked them, What they were to do with the drums? they said they were going to sacrifice Captain Porteous; and thereafter, having seized one of the drums, they put it by force about the deponent's son's neck, and forced him to beat the alarm, and dragged him along with them within the port of the Grassmarket, which some time thereafter they shut, commonly called the Westport; which port being thereafter opened about twelve o'clock at night the deponent came in and saw the deceased Captain Porteous hanging upon a dyster's tree, near the place of common execution, and then he was dead. *Causa scientiae patet.* And this was truth, as he should answer to God. And declared he could not write. (Signed)   ANDW. FLETCHER.

JOHN LEARMOND, keeper of the Netherbow Port of Edinburgh, aged seventy years or thereby, married, solemnly sworn, purged of malice, partial counsel, examined and interrogated, deponed, That the time libelled, the mob that that night was riotously assembled, a part of them came to the Netherbow Port about the hour of ten; and the deponent having the custody of the keys of the Netherbow Port, they came to his house, and forced from him the keys, and therewith did lock fast the said port, and carry the keys away with them. At this time the deponent had the occasion only of seeing a few of them, no more than what filled the stair up to the deponent's house, whom he observed only to be armed with clubs and staves. After their removal from the said port, he did not observe that they had placed any guard or sentinels there; but thereafter did observe every now and then some of the said mob come down and visit the said port. *Causa scientiæ patet.* And this was the truth, as he should answer to God.

(Signed)   JOHN LEARMOND.
DA. ERSKINE.

DOUGALL CAMPBELL, soldier in the city-guard of Edinburgh, aged forty-four years or thereby, married, solemnly sworn, purged of malice, partial counsel, examined and interrogated, deponed, That at the time libelled, a little before ten at night, the deponent was standing sentinel at the guard-door with a Lochaber-axe in his hand: That there was at that time a great crowd of people going up and down the street, some of them with staves in their hands: That one of them seized the deponent's Lochaber-axe, and desired him to part with it; which the deponent being unwilling to do, they struggled about it, but some other of the mob having joined the man who first seized it, they took it from him by force; whereupon the deponent going into the guard-room, a great number of the mob rushed in and seized the soldiers' arms, and turned them out of the guard. *Causa scientiæ patet.* And this was the truth, as he should answer to God. And declared he could not write.

(Signed)   JA. MACKENZIE.

GEORGE WILSON, indweller and workman in Edinburgh, aged thirty-one years or thereby, married, solemnly sworn, purged of malice, partial counsel, examined and interrogated, deponed, That time and place libelled, the deponent came about eleven o'clock at night to the Tolbooth-door, where he saw two faggots of broom brought by some of the mob, and with which two faggots, fire was set to the said door until it was burnt, and there the deponent waited till he saw Captain Porteous brought down by the mob, and after that the mob carried him up the Lawnmarket, until they came to Stewart's sign-post, near the Bowhead, over which some of the mob proposed to hang Captain Porteous, but others were against it. After this, the said Captain Porteous was carried up until he came to the Weigh-house, where some of the mob proposed to hang him over the Weigh-house stair, but this proposal was also rejected; and by this time the deponent happened to get pretty near to Captain Porteous; and as the mob was carrying the said Captain Porteous down the Bow, one of the mob, in a woman's dress, knocked the deponent down; and that as they were going alongst before this, the deponent interceded with the mob to give Captain Porteous some time to pray. The answer made by the mob was, that the said Captain Porteous never prayed for himself, and did not give them time to pray that he had killed, and that he should be damned before he got time to pray. Deponed, That after this, the deponent was run over by a good many of the mob, and that after he had recovered himself, he went down to the Grassmarket, following the said mob; and there he saw a man set up a halbert upon the stone, the common place of execution; and the person who did so was not the pannel; and that the person who did so had a hat upon his head, and a dark coloured coat, and taller than the pannel: That at the above place where the halbert was fixed, there was a good many in arms about Captain Porteous, and which arms the mob kept always until they came to that place, and there they threw them down: That the deponent heard some of the mob cry, Let us carry him hence, for we have a rope for him in another place. Accordingly he was carried to the dyer's tree, where he was hanged; but before hie execution, the deponent again interceded to give him some time to pray, he having by this time got again pretty near him, Captain Porteous; but the mob cried out much to the same purpose, as is above mentioned. Deponed, That he saw Captain Porteous deliver to John Carmichael a purse, which he desired him to deliver to his brother, and that he saw the rope put about Captain Porteous's neck, and afterwards drawn up; but he was not drawn up until they heard that the military were coming from the Canongate, in by the hospital, at the foot of Leith wynd; and that Captain Porteous was three times hung up, and twice let down again. The first time it happened that the rope was not right about his neck, whereupon he was let down, and afterwards hung up, and then let down a second time, upon the mob's observing that he had not something upon his face; then his shirt was hung over his face, and then he was drawn up, upon hearing of the above rumour, and hung there till he was dead. Deponed, That the first time Captain Porteous was hung up, he heard some of the mob make a proposal of cutting his ears out, and others proposed to geld him; and at the last time he was hung up, he saw some of the mob strike him upon the face with a Lochaber-axe; and that during the whole period, from the time the fire was first set to the Tolbooth-door, till the time that Captain Porteous was hung up upon the dyer's tree, the deponent did not remember to have seen William Maclauchlane, pannel. *Causa scientiæ patet.* And this was truth, as he should answer to God.

(Signed) George Wilson.
Alex. Fraser.

Robert Mackinlay, indweller in Edinburgh, and son to the deceased David Mackinlay, waterman there, aged twenty-one years or thereby, unmarried, solemnly sworn, purged of malice, partial counsel, examined and interrogate, deponed, That the time libelled, the deponent saw a great crowd of people on the north side of the Tolbooth, near the Purses, and that there was severals of them armed with guns, Lochaber-axes, and halberts: That they stood across the street from the Tolbooth to the other side of the street, and that they stopped people who were going along: That some of the mob forced the deponent to put a drum about his neck and beat it: That amongst the men who were so armed, as aforesaid, he saw the pannel with a halbert in his hand, but saw him do nothing: That he appeared to be drunk and staggering, and not stand still in one place. Deponed, That he saw Captain Porteous, after he was brought out of prison by the mob, near the head of Libberton Wynd: That he saw the pannel, William Maclauchlane, before them in the Lawnmarket, with a halbert in his hand, and a great mob being betwixt the said Maclauchlane and Captain Porteous: That when the mob carried Captain Porteous to the Cornmarket they made a stand there, and that he saw the pannel there with a hatchet; and being asked how near Captain Porteous was then to the pannel? deponed, There would have been six people between them: And being interrogated, Where he, the deponent, was when Captain Porteous was at the gallow's stone, as aforesaid? deponed, That he, the deponent, was a little above the well at the foot of the Bow. *Causa scientiae patet*. And this was the truth, as he should answer to God. And declared he could not write.

(Signed) JA. MACKENZIE.

Thereafter, the pannel adduced the witnesses, after deponing, for proving his exculpation, *viz.*

JOHN SAMUELL, change-keeper near the Parliament Close, Edinburgh, aged thirty-eight years or thereby, married, solemnly sworn, purged of malice, partial counsel, examined and interrogate, deponed, That at the time libelled, and about a quarter after nine o'clock at night, the pannel came into the deponent's cellar, near the Cross, where he staid about a quarter of an hour, called for a bottle of ale and drank a part of it, and then leaned his head to the wall; he appeared to the deponent to be very drunk, for when he went up the stair going to the street again, he stumbled and fell forward. *Causa scientiae patet*. And this was the truth, as he should answer to God.

(Signed) JOHN SAMUELL.
GILB. ELLIOT.

JEAN MITCHELL, spouse to William Maclellan, servant to Thomas Marshall, vintner in Edinburgh, aged twenty-six years or thereby, married, solemnly sworn, purged of malice, partial counsel, examined and interrogated, deponed, That the time libelled, about eleven o'clock at night, the deponent saw William Maclauchlane, the pannel, at the head of Dunbar's Close, and there coming a great rush and noise from the Tolbooth, the deponent and some others ran down the said close, and the pannel followed them down the said close for refuge, where he fell twice, and after the noise was gone, William Maclauchlane, the pannel, went up the said close, having a halbert the whole time in his hand, and the deponent went up also; and when she came to the head of the close, she saw a woman take the halbert out of the pannel's hand and run away with it; and that the pannel was so mortally drunk that he could not stand alone, and that having once fallen she and some others lifted him up. *Causa scientiae patet.* And this was the truth, as she should answer to God.

(Signed) J. M.

ALEX. FRASER.

The said Lords ordained the assize instantly to inclose in this place, and return their verdict the morrow at twelve o'clock forenoon, and the haill fifteen to be then present, each person under the pain of law, and the pannel to be carried to the place from whence he came.

. . . .

. . . The persons who passed upon the assize of the said William Maclauchlane, returned their verdict in presence of the said Lords, whereof the tenor follows:

The above assize having inclosed, and chosen Mr Charles Hope Weir of Craigiehall to be their Chancellor, and William Hamilton, brewer in Edinburgh, to be their clerk, and having considered the indictment at the instance of Duncan Forbes of Culloden, Esq. His Majesty's Advocate for his Highness' interest, against William Maclauchlane, pannel, with the Lord Justice-Clerk and Lords Commissioners of Justiciary, their interlocutor thereupon, and the depositions of the witnesses adduced for proving thereof, and the depositions of the witnesses adduced for proving the pannel's behaviour; they, all in one voice, did find the said William Maclauchlane, pannel, *Not Guilty.* In witness whereof, their said Chancellor and Clerk have subscribed these presents in their names, at Edinburgh, the twenty-first day of March seventeen hundred and thirty-seven years.

CH. HOPE WEIR, *Chancellor.*
WM. HAMILTON *Clerk.*

The Lord Justice-Clerk and Lords Commissioners of Justiciary having considered the foregoing verdict of assize, they, in respect thereof, assoilzied the said William Maclauchlane *simpliciter,* and dismissed him from the bar.

(Signed)   AND. FLETCHER, *I. P. D.*

2 *Lady Louisa Stuart*

FROM A Letter to Sir Walter Scott,
August 11, 1818[1]

Now for it, dear Mr. Scott. I can speak to the purpose, as I have not only read it myself, but am in a house where everybody is tearing it out of each other's hands, and talking of nothing else. So much for its success,—the more flattering because it overcomes a prejudice. People were beginning to say the author would wear himself out; it was going on too long in the same key, and no striking notes could possibly be produced. On the contrary, I think the interest is stronger here than in any of the former ones (always excepting my first love *Waverley*), and one may congratulate you upon having effected what many have tried to do and nobody yet succeeded in,—making the perfectly good character the most interesting. Of late days especially, since it has been the fashion to write

1. Reprinted from *Familiar Letters of Sir Walter Scott,* Boston: Houghton, Mifflin, 1894, vol. II, pp. 18–22.

moral and even religious novels, one might almost say of some of
the wise good heroines what a lively girl once did to me of her
well-meaning aunt, "Upon my word, she is enough to make anybody wicked." And, though beauty and talents are heaped on the
right side, the writer in spite of himself is sure to put agreeableness
on the wrong; the person from whose errors he means you should
take warning runs away with your secret partiality in the meantime.

Had this very story been conducted by a common hand, Effie
would have attracted all our concern and sympathy, Jeanie only cold
approbation. Whereas Jeanie, without youth, beauty, genius, warm
passions, or any other novel perfection, is here our object from beginning to end. This is "inlisting the affections in the cause of virtue" ten times more than ever Richardson did, for whose male and
female pedants, all-excelling as they are, I never could care half so
much as I found myself inclined to do for Jeanie before I finished
the first volume. Is it possible that you had at all in your eye what
my wishes pointed to, when I wrote to you last winter? If not, you
will think the question strange; yet with all the differences of situation, improvement, refinement, etc., nay, with all the power to charm
and dazzle, there was a strong likeness of character: the same steady
attachment to rectitude, the same simplicity and singleness of heart,
the same inward humility, the same forgetfulness of self, the same
strong, plain, straightforward understanding always hitting exactly
right. Superficial observers took for granted this last could not be
where there was so much wit and taste, but thus it was notwithstanding. Let me dream that you designed this resemblance, whether
you did or not; I would rather be indulged in the thought than set
right, and I should like it the better for being so veiled by circumstances that the rest of the world would pass it without observation.

You know I tell you my opinion just as I should do to a third
person, and I trust the freedom is not unwelcome. I was a little tired
of your Edinburgh lawyers in the introduction; mere English people
will be more so, as well as impatient of the passages alluding to
Scotch law throughout. Mr. Saddletree will not entertain them. The
latter part of fourth volume unavoidably flags to a certain degree;
after Jeanie is happily settled at Roseneath we have no more to
wish for. But the chief fault I have to find relates to the reappear-
ance and shocking fate of the boy. I hear on all sides, "Oh, I do

not like that." I cannot say what I would have had instead, but that I do not like either; it is a lame, huddled conclusion. I know you so well in it, by the bye! You grow tired yourself, want to get rid of the story, and hardly care how. Sir George Staunton finishes his career very fitly; he ought not to die in his bed, and for Jeanie's sake one would not have him hanged. It is unnatural, though, that he should ever have gone within twenty miles of the Tolbooth, or shown his face in the streets of Edinburgh, or dined at a public meeting, if the Lord Commissioner had been his brother. Here ends my *per contra* account. The opposite page would make my letter too long if I entered equally into particulars. Carlisle and Corby castles in *Waverley* did not affect me more deeply than the prison and trial scenes. The end of poor Madge Wildfire is also most pathetic; the meeting at Muschat's Cairn most tremendous. Dumbiedikes and Rory Bean are delightful; and I shall own that my old family prejudices were secretly gratified by the light in which you place Uncle John of Argyle, whom Mr. Coxe so ran down to please Lord Orford. You have drawn him to the very life. I heard so much of him in my youth, so many anecdotes, so often—"as the Duke of Argyle used to say"—that I really believe I am almost as good a judge as if I had seen and lived with him. My grandfather, dying very young, left his sons to the guardianship of their mother's brothers, who placed my father at Eton School when he was seven years old, and took him themselves in his holidays, while their sister lived in Bute with her daughters. John, having a wife and family and country-seats in England, my father was of course mostly under his roof, and had the feelings of a son rather than a nephew towards him. My grandmother Wortley too, as you may see by her letters, particularly admired him; and my beloved mother has told me that when she married (in 1737, the very time) he was still remarkably handsome, with manners more graceful and engaging than she ever saw in any one else, the most agreeable person in conversation, the best teller of a story. When fifty-seven thus captivates eighteen, the natural powers of pleasing must be extraordinary. You have likewise colored Queen Caroline exactly right, but I was bred up in another creed about Lady Suffolk, of whom, as a very old deaf woman, I have some faint recollection. My mother knew her intimately, and never would allow she had been the King's mistress, though she owned it was currently believed. She said he had just enough liking for her to make the Queen very civil to her, and very jealous and spiteful; the rest remained always uncertain, at most,—like a similar scandal in our days, where I, for one, imagine love of seeming influence on one side, and love of lounging, of an easy house, and a good dinner on the other, to be all the criminal passions concerned. However, I confess my mother had that in herself which made her not ready to think the worst of her fellow-women.

Did you ever hear the history of John, Duke of Argyle's marriage, and constant attachment before and after to a woman not handsomer or much more elegant than Jeanie Deans, though very unlike her in understanding? I can give it you, if you wish it, for it is at my fingers' ends. I was so much the youngest of a numerous family that I had no playfellow, and for that reason listened with all my ears to the grown people's conversation, most especially when my mother and the friends of her youth got upon old stories; nor did I lose my taste for them when I grew old enough to converse with her on equal terms, and enquire into particulars. Now I am an ancient tabby myself, I should be a great treasure of anecdote to anybody who had the same humor, but I meet with few who have. They read vulgar tales in books, Wraxall and so forth, what the footmen and maids only gave credit to at the moment, but they desire no farther information. I dare swear many of your readers never heard of the Duke of Argyle before. "Pray who was Sir Robert Walpole?" they ask me, "and when did he live?"—or perhaps, "Was not the great Lord Chatham in Queen Anne's days?"

Amongst the persons most pleased here is Lady Charlotte Lindsay. She has the true North humor and love of humor, and she does enjoy it heartily. They have, to help them, an exemplification on two legs in their country apothecary, whom you have painted over and over without the honor of knowing him: an old, dry, arguing, prosing, obstinate Scotchman, very shrewd, rather sarcastic, a sturdy whig and presbyterian, *tirant un peu sur le démocrat*. Your books are bird-lime to him, however; he hovers about the house to obtain a volume when others have done with it. I long to ask him whether douce Davie was anyway sib to him. He acknowledges he would not now go to Muschat's Cairn at night for any money, he had such a horror of it sixty years ago when a laddie.

3

FROM "Tales of My Landlord, Second Series,"
The Monthly Review, December, 1818[1]

The productions of this author have rendered society better
acquainted with him in his literary than in his personal capacity;
and, as the present volumes comprise no more than a single tale,
they form the longest work which he has yet offered to our notice.
This increase in the *length,* however, is so far from being attended
by a proportional augmentation in the *merit* of his story, that we
cannot attribute the absence of interest, with which we crawl on to
its conclusion, to any other cause than the prolixity of the narrative
itself; and which, in the last two of these volumes, becomes so
tedious as to detract much not only from the sympathy that we
ought to feel, but also from the probability and *vrai-semblance*
which ought to exist, in the circumstances that are detailed. The
same censure applies in a trifling degree to the two commencing volumes: but *there* it is more than compensated by the admirable connection of the incidents, the natural delineation of the characters,
and the deep yet simple pathos of the narrative. We should be glad
to add that the two latter volumes were rescued from condemnation
by the possession of similar merits, but this unfortunately we cannot
say; for on the contrary we regard them as unworthy of the high
reputation which their author has acquired, and destitute of any virtue that is necessary to ensure admiration and success. Though they
sometimes discover a glimpse of that vigorous genius and fervid
imagination which have elsewhere afforded such genuine satisfaction,
it appears like a ray of light in the midst of darkness; it no sooner
glances across the horizon than it is lost in its obscurity, and only
renders the surrounding gloom more distinct and visible. Melancholy
as this statement is, we must, nevertheless, observe that the commencement of the 'Heart of Mid-Lothian' (for such is the name of
the tale) is almost as excellent as its conclusion is "lame and impotent;" and we do not think that this story could be better typified

1. Vol. LXXXVII, pp. 356–364, 366–367.

than by comparing it to one of those "monstrous and prodigious things," which Horace has described as decked with all the attributes of feminine proportion above, but as ending below in an obscene and disgusting fish. . . .

Before we enter into a farther examination of this work, we shall take the opportunity of making a few remarks on the literary merits of its author; and, in order to exhibit them in clear and striking colours, we shall investigate those peculiarities of *subject, style,* and *character,* by which he is exalted so far above the range of ordinary novelists. These latter writers, with a few honourable exceptions, devote themselves to the representation of a passion, which from its frequent recurrence is more easily developed, and from its universal nature is more generally attractive, than any other to which man is liable,—we mean the passion of love; from it they make the whole of their incidents to proceed, and on it the whole interest of their narratives to depend; and they depict every personage, who is a stranger to its influence, as equally a stranger to the action and business of their story, and a reluctant accessary to its final development. The present author has obtained his reputation by applying the exuberance of his genius to very different objects: on first entering the literary arena, he found all the ordinary subjects of fiction either monopolized or exhausted: but, instead of suffering the powers of his mind to be depressed to despondency by the difficulties which thus seemed to oppose his progress, he considered them as incentives to greater exertions, determined to persevere in seeking for fresh materials, and was successful in his search. He dug down into the mine of human nature, and discovered in it a new and inexhaustible vein of instruction and amusement; he traced the passions to their fountain-head; and then, instead of continuing to confine them in one channel, he demolished the dams which stopped their current, and employed the various streams, into which it immediately branched, to enrich and fertilize the course of his own narrations. Love, which his predecessors deemed the only subject worthy of their consideration, and which was almost beginning to lose the power to please from the want of grandeur and novelty in its portraits, was not indeed entirely banished from his productions: but it was so far removed for the introduction of stronger and nobler emotions, as to form nothing more than an episode to divert the attention, or an interlude to relax the mind, after it had been strung up to the highest pitch of intensity by witnessing the effects of the more grave and agitating feelings. In no instance has he rendered his incidents subservient to its development, though in several he has rendered its development subservient to his incidents.

. . . In the present work, the anxiety and solicitude, which we feel for the fate of its principal characters, originate in sources very different from any of those which we have hitherto noticed. We see even from the first moment how all the love-story will conclude; and, as our interest dies at the same instant that our uncertainty ceases, we never care a straw about it. The entertainment, which these volumes afford, is derived from the strong emotions of pity and terror, with which we follow the recital of the Porteous-riots, and the misfortunes and trial of the fair Euphemia, or Effie. With that recital, our pleasure ceases; and it ceases only because the author chuses to play with the spindle of Omphale after he has been wielding the club of Hercules, and to wind a tedious journey round the foot of the mountain when he should have exerted his strength to carry his reader by a short passage over all its clefts, precipices, and acclivities.

The peculiarity, which we have just been pointing out, is one of those striking features that distinguish this author, as we said before, from the common mass of the writers of fiction; and from this peculiarity in the subject to which he directs his own and our attention, one of his principal excellences in our opinion is derived. While he carefully guards himself against touching, except incidentally, on the passion of love, and the refined sensibilities which are so intimately connected with it, he places himself under the necessity of recurring to those fierce and grand and terrible emotions of the soul, which he alone can depict as ably as he can ably controul and govern them.

Another peculiarity also appears in his manner of treating his subject, which is worthy of our observation. The remark, which Madame de Stael makes on epic poetry, that there is something in it too certain and something too unexpected, *(quelque chose d'inattendu,)* is equally just when applied to the generality of modern novels. The *too great certainty* occurs when the reader sees not only the "cork-jacket which is to carry the hero safe over all the billows of affliction," but also the occasions and the manner of its being used to ensure his preservation; and this entirely destroys all the pleasure, which would otherwise proceed from our fears regarding the destiny of its wearer. The something *too unexpected* is when, by an effect diametrically opposite to the too great certainty of the future, we are deprived of the pleasure of foreseeing the course of events at all; and it occurs whenever witchcraft and demonology are employed to unravel the mysteries and obviate the difficulties of romance. Under such circumstances, nothing takes place according to the ordinary transaction of human affairs, but all depends on supernatural agency; which can as easily render abortive all the measures of skill and the precautions of prudence, as it can give victory and fame to those plans which, according to all moderate calculation, could experience only defeat and ignominy from their inherent absurdity. Of both these faults, the unknown writer now before us has steered wonderfully clear. We are not admitted to view the *denouement* of his stories immediately on commencing them, nor to discern the manner in which every difficulty is to be overcome at the same time that we first observe its appearance, but are carried on to the conclusion through a series of adventures and a chain of incidents, which rise so naturally out of each other that we have no wish to look beyond that which is immediately before us; and which are so well rivetted together, that our attention never flags and our curiosity is never wearied during the perusal of them. We attribute this excellence generally to all his novels, without deeming it necessary to enter into any minute or particular proofs of it; and at the same time we remark that he never either creates mystery for mere mystery's sake, or involves his heroes in any difficulties from which he cannot extricate them by human skill and human exertions. Thus, while he avoids the *too great certainty* by the admirable arrangement of his story, he also escapes the other fault of excessive *unexpectedness* by the just conception of what is suitable to his characters; and the union of these two qualifications, which, even separately, are sufficient to prevent any writer from transgressing the probabilities that ought always to exist in fictitious adventures, not only preserves inviolate the magic influence on which their illusion depends, but increases it to an extraordinary extent.

This is high encomium, because the excellence which elicits it is rare: yet it yields in dignity to another topic of praise, to which we shall immediately challenge attention.—It is without doubt an arduous task to give a correct delineation of men and manners, as they *now* exist: but it is much more arduous to draw a true portrait of society as it was, and as it has just ceased to be,—to arrest the shades of habits, prejudices, and opinions, which are fast evanescing from public view,—and to give substance and solidity to that which is in itself so volatile, as almost to defy the grasp of thought. The difficulty in the former case is diminished by the author having the object, of which he is to form a copy, perpetually before his eye on all occasions, and by having to write on subjects which have an interest of their own, independent of any that is created by skill or management; while, in the latter case, the difficulty is increased, because the whole of the interest is to be generated by himself, and because he is writing on customs and subjects which have ceased to be entertaining. Besides, should he in any instance doubt the correctness of his resemblance, he cannot trust to experience, but must reason from analogy: he cannot refer to the great living book of human nature, but must have recourse to books of ethics, or books of history; he can only judge of what no longer exists by the most delusive of all tests, that which exists at the present moment. We have not heard of any author who has been so successful in this Herculean labour, as the writer whose merits we are now discussing. He convinces us by the representation of scenes and characters which have long been withdrawn from the gaze of the world, that he is not less acquainted with the passions and prejudices of mankind as they now subsist, than he is with them as they subsisted a century ago. He exhibits himself as the intimate acquaintance at one and the same time of the dead and the living; and the characters, whom he calls from the grave to figure in his pages, start forth into new life, perfect in all the mien, form, and lineaments of human beings, and warm with all the blood and freshness of animated existence. He thus stamps the impress of originality and of genius on his productions, and raises himself from the general mass of novelists to sit on the same bench with the annalists of his country.

In this enumeration of his merits, we cannot forget the strong nationality of all his publications, which forms the distinguishing feature of his style and characters. All his novels are Scotch, even

to the back-bone; and the vices and virtues of his countrymen are
coloured in them with such warmth of feeling and such glow of
imagination, as could arise only from an entire conviction of their
existence, acquired by a long abode in their habitations and by a
frequent and varied intercourse with every class of society among
them. His portrait of the higher orders is the production of a master's hand, and displays a very correct resemblance of their general
customs, habits, and opinions; yet it is inferior to the picture which
he has sketched of the honest and humble and industrious peasantry
of his native land: a picture which, though invariably favourable
to their moral and civil excellence, bears about it no marks of exaggeration, and evinces no blindness to their faults and imperfections.
It is to this charm of nationality, and to the more than dramatic
representations of the thoughts, words, manners, and actions of his
countrymen, which always attend his exemplification of it, that
the success which his narratives have obtained is principally owing;
though we must allow that another cause of it is also to be found
in his exquisite and appropriate adaptation of the Scotish language
to the personages and purposes of his numerous fictions. We have
heard that this insertion of the dialogues of Scotchmen in their own
peculiar dialect has been made an engine of attack against him, as if
it were improper (as Theocritus has observed) for the natives of
Doris to speak Doric; and the introduction of it into the various
tales of this writer has been said to subtract materially from the delight which every English reader experiences in perusing them. How
it may be with the supporters of this charge, we do not know: but
for ourselves, as we do not find the Scotch so stiff as to require
much trouble in deciphering, and can perceive all its variations and
inflections in the original construction of the English language, we
must say that we relish these works much more highly than we
otherwise should do, on account of the Scotish phraseology with
which they abound. It gives us a more full and complete idea of
rustic simplicity and honesty, than any which we could possibly
acquire by reading the same sentiments expressed in the most refined and polished English: it detaches us from the localities of
present associations; and it enhances the feelings with which we
peruse it, by transporting us to other regions, where we are mere
sojourners, and in which we find every thing attractive because it is
new and strange to our perception. We are even inclined to go

farther, and to assert that the Doricism of the language inspires an English bosom with an intensity of sympathy, interest, and curiosity, which no North-Briton himself can ever attain; because the illusion, which we have before stated the dialect to create in our minds, is destroyed in his by the frequency with which he hears it repeated. The sounds, to which we attach ideas of purity and rural virtue, in spite of all the contrary suggestions of reason, will convey to him no other ideas than those which they are intended to communicate; and the representations, which to us seem so inimitable, of the modes and habits of our Caledonian rustics, lose a great part of their effect on him, if incorrect in any of the slightest particular. He is enabled by daily experience and observation to detect the delusions which the author has thrown around his subject: whereas we are induced, as much by our own ignorance of any thing to the contrary, as by the great powers of the writer and the extraordinary skill which he displays in the use of them, to believe circumstances to be as he has pourtrayed them; and are inclined, by the general consistency of his narratives, by his faithful and accurate representation of all that has fallen beneath our own notice, and by the ingenious manner in which he has blended fiction with reality and reality with fiction, to accept his delineations as correct, without examining too closely into the grounds on which they may be founded. . . .

All this is told[1] in a very striking and affecting manner; and, if it were not most strangely connected with the Porteous-riots, (at Edinburgh, 1736) which, though described in a very vivid style, have little to do with the main business of the story, its effect would be still more electric than it is at present. That effect, however, receives farther diminution from the prolix detail by which it is succeeded: we are not now alluding to the long and tedious recital of the Rev. Mr. and Mrs. Butler's wedded happiness, so much as to the "moonlight flitting" which the pardoned culprit makes from her father's house, even before she has poured out her soul in gratitude to the excellent being who had delivered her from a premature and disgraceful death. We maintain that this step shews not merely a want of natural affection in Effie Deans, which we have no reason for expecting, but also a most pointed inconsistency of

1. In the original review, the paragraph preceding this one is a summary of the story of Effie up to the point where she is pardoned.

character, of which the author in the haste in which he has concocted a part of these volumes may probably not have been aware. If Effie could before her trial muster virtuous resolution sufficient to remain in a prison, whence she could have effected her escape, when she knew that nothing less than death awaited her by remaining in it,—and if she could defend her resolution on the principle that life, deprived of honour, was not worth preserving,—on what motive can she be supposed to have acted in voluntarily flying with Robertson from a comfortable home, within three days of the time at which she was so unexpectedly restored to it? We see none; and therefore, independently of the breach of morality of which some readers have accused the author in allowing this procedure, we must beg leave to denounce it as inconsistent with the whole tenor of the previous narrative. The guilt, which Effie had to incur in eloping with her seducer, was the same in both cases; while the inducement to take such a measure was so strong in one instance that it would have almost excused it, and in the other was so much weakened that it scarcely formed any temptation.

Other remarks on this novel must naturally press on the consideration of every person who reads it; such as the impropriety of transforming Effie Deans into Lady Staunton, and delineating her as a favourite with the Duke of Argyle, to whose intercession she had been indebted for life; and also the extraordinary conclusion to which it is brought by the murder of George Robertson, (who has undergone a curious metamorphosis into a Sir George Staunton) by the offspring of his own criminal intrigue with Effie.

4 William Hazlitt

"The Waverley Notes," The Atlas, June 7, 1829[1]

The London Magazine, speaking of Sir Walter Scott's notes on the Waverley novels, observes:

1. Reprinted, by permission of the publisher, from P. P. Howe, ed., *The Complete Works of William Hazlitt,* London and Toronto: J. M. Dent, 1930–1934, vol. XX, pp. 231–233.

'We think Sir Walter has been unwise in letting us see the machinery of his scenery—which from the front had so beautiful an effect—and showing us some of the reality of characters which, as he had put them on the scene, were so admirable in their several natures. Why would not he leave—not well, but admirably—alone? Why show us the warp and woof of that tapestry which, in its unbetrayed state, was so perfect? In *Waverley,* this is less disadvantage than it will be anon. Oh! how we dread his giving us the *pleadings* in the *Heart of Mid-Lothian.*'

This is addressed to the imagination only, not to the judgment. The charms of a work professing to copy nature cannot be destroyed by the evidence that proves it to be founded upon truth; and, least of all, the Waverley novels. In showing us the reality of his characters, Sir Walter will not alter their nature; he will rather confirm it. Fiction is not necessarily the mere production of fancy, although much fancy is to be found in works of fiction; nor is it essential that fiction should be untrue, for the materials of our best fictions are principally drawn from fact. It is not a stage illusion, nor a magic lanthern, presenting shadows and spectacles that either burlesque or flatter humanity; but a transcript from nature, in which the truth is preserved not *literally,* but *poetically.* And this is the difference between the notes and the text. The notes are the literal facts, the text the poetical transcript, in which the original is elaborated into a more continuous and imaginative series of impressions, and written out into more passionate and vivid language. Our enjoyment is not to be spoiled by a new means of estimating the author's skill; by that which will enable us to compare the finished statue with the clay from which it was formed. The plain fact will not constitute a novel; there must be the creative spirit to work up all its parts into an embellished picture, and superadd such matters as, although not actually true, are deducible from that which is, and are relatively consistent; and in proportion to the amount of truth will be the effect and value of the performance. The question then is, how far our pleasure will be interrupted by the assurance that certain portions are real, and how far our confidence in the rest will be thereby shaken. To know that Effie Deans lived and was accused, is not likely to produce a disbelief in the remaining parts of her story, which if not literally true might have been so, and seem as if they could not be dispensed with without violating the congruity of the whole. Her history is not the less touching because historical evidence does not attest it scene by scene; while its appeal to our feelings is enhanced by our knowledge that the main incident did happen, from which all the other details and circumstances appear to spring naturally. The disclosure of the sources of pleasure cannot philosophically be argued as a diminution of enjoyment. There is no person who believes the puppets of the Petit Lazary to be men and women, yet the fact that they are made of wood and paint increases our wonder and delight. Could we see the machinery by which they are worked—which overstretches the analogy—we would wonder still more how so much effect could be so simply produced. To be vexed at the shock our first enthusiasm might receive would be weakness or vanity; we should have known that there was a secret process going forward; if we did not know it, it is our vanity that is hurt at the exposure. Such vexation, however, would resemble the resentment of those who were deceived by the Shakespeare forgeries—they were annoyed that their want of penetration should be detected, and never forgave Ireland. But not even their indignation at the impious cheat upon the bard, could obtain them credit for possessing a sense of poetry. A true relish for nature can neither be deceived by a bad fiction, nor dissipated by the most prosaic illustrations.

Emily Brontë
Wuthering Heights
1847

𝕭 *1*

FROM "The Bridegroom of Barna," *Blackwood's Edinburgh Magazine,* November, 1840[1]

IV.

. . . From an early age we have seen that Lawlor was left his own master. Endued with feelings of high susceptibility and strong passions, he unfortunately lacked a guide to restrain them when they could alone be taught control. Then came his inauspicious attachment to Ellen Nugent. The long, and bitter, and hopeless opposition that attachment had to undergo, no doubt gave his spirit an inflexibility and sullenness that gradually hardened a heart not naturally

1. Vol. XLVIII, pp. 697–700, 702–704. Leicester Bradner has shown that the story from which these extracts are taken is probably one of the sources of *Wuthering Heights* ("The Growth of *Wuthering Heights*," *Publications of the Modern Language Association of America,* vol. XLVIII, March, 1933, pp. 139–141, 143–145).

ill-disposed, and imparted to it a selfishness by which it was finally corrupted. To his lonely and affectionate spirit, Ellen was all the world—the only living thing that he felt necessary to his existence; and, as he grew to manhood, the potency of this master-passion affected more or less all his social proceedings, until the possession of his mistress became with him almost as much an object by which his skill in baffling his foes (for so he deemed all who did not favour his suit) was to be estimated, as one that was to confirm the happiness of his life. By degrees the impediments to that happiness gave way. The wounded brother of his beloved recovered to fall by the slower but surer hand of disease. The irritated mother, too, resigned her enmity and her breath together. But then came White Will, with his impressive purse and his long train of persecutions; and if ever a crime, by its dreadful originality, indicated the revenge of a master-spirit, it was that by which Lawlor, so fatally for himself, resolved to cross his enemy. The deed was done. By the death of Byrne, Redmond was reduced to comparative poverty, and with his wealth subsided his pretensions to claim Ellen Nugent as the bride of his son; and the desperate but devoted lover at once effected the humiliation of his enemy, and secured the hand of his long-worshipped mistress.

V.

Months passed away, and Lawlor still continued to elude the officers of justice—but this was all that could be ascertained of his fate; and Time, that veers alike through the most buoyant hours of bliss and the profoundest nights of affliction, saw his hapless bride revive to a state of languid health and mournful resignation. She again attempted to resume the little daily round of domestic duties, and to whisper peace to her infirm father, when she knew there was no peace in the sinking heart that prompted her. From the fatal evening of her nuptials, she never pronounced the name of her husband, nor was it ever breathed in her hearing. She had loved him with a love surpassing that of women. She had for his sake long encountered the stern anger of her brother—the loss of her father's confidence—the reproachful upbraidings of her mother, whose dying injunction, sealed with a solemn curse, that she should not wed with Lawlor, she had disregarded. The more loud the whispers of calumny spread, that his life was irregular—that his pursuits were unlawful—the more perseveringly she fought in his cause, with all that generous devotion and fidelity that none but her glorious sex can feel or practise. "Were Hugh here," she would scornfully say to his detractors, "you dared not insinuate in his presence the stories with which you are so ready to wound the feelings of his only defender. Pronounce them to his face, and I will judge by your boldness whether they are deserving of belief." And now—that idolized one, no longer her lover, but her husband, was, like the first murderer, a fugitive upon the earth, with a curse as deep as Cain's pursuing his footsteps; and she—but no—she had no more to hear of him in blame or obloquy; for, coarse as the people were by whom she was surrounded, their hearts too deeply sympathized in her early sorrows not to respect the eternal silence that sealed her lips. Of one thing only, connected with Lawlor's fate, it was thought she could not be ignorant—that her abode was watched by the emissaries of justice, from a supposition that she was so passionately beloved by the criminal, that he would at some period attempt to visit her: but on this subject too, it is needless to say, she never ventured a remark; perhaps she felt the current of her existence drying away too surely, to care further about any event by which it might be momentarily ruffled or illumined.

It was far in summer. At the close of a sweet evening in July, Ellen sat alone in the window of her chamber that opened upon the deep soft grass and refreshing umbrage of the orchard by which the greater part of the mansion was overshadowed. The air was sweet with the fragrance of lime-trees, and slumberous with the lulling hum of the bees that clustered in the branches. The melancholy girl had thrown the window entirely open, and sat reclined, with her head thrown back, resting in a reverie against the wainscot, scarce conscious of the departing sunset, whose lingering tints, as they fell upon her wan, fair forehead, and the long locks of paly gold that descended to her shoulders, invested her whole aspect with that mournful and spiritual beauty that subdues us in the immortal pencillings of Guido. To a careless eye she would have seemed intently listening to the mellow song of the blackbird, that gushed at intervals upon her ear; but the sweetest sounds of earth had no longer charms for Ellen. Her spirit was far away, in petitions to Him who had chosen, for His own wise purposes, to break so bruised a reed as her pining and tortured heart. The warm tint of evening faded from her face, and the twilight night of summer came down amid the green recesses of the orchard, and still she sat motionless, drinking the holy peace of the scene. All at once she was roused by a shadow encroaching on the faint light admitted through the window; and, starting up, she saw the tall figure of a woman standing close to it. It was Nanse, the fortune-teller, who curtsied low when she saw that she was perceived, but preserved that respectful silence by which, with innate good sense or taste, the Irish peasantry evince the sense of the sorrows of their superiors, when they feel that they are beyond human consolation. . . .

"Mother of Him whom you watched upon the cross through the long and killing night!" murmured the distracted girl, when again alone, "look down upon me with pity; you, whose sinless soul was wrung with more than mortal agony, teach a helpless and erring creature to struggle with the lot that is wearing her to the grave!" and she raised her eyes to the brightening stars. When she dropped them again, Lawlor was standing close to her; his very breath almost mingling with the rich shadows of her hair. One frantic shriek, as she sprang with an electric shiver from the spot, gushed to her lips; but, with an instinctive sense of the result, she stifled it ere it passed them, and with a groan sank upon her knees before the window, her hands in vain motioning the intruder to depart.

"Ellen," he murmured, "Ellen, hear me!"

She made no reply, but remained bent in an attitude of supplication and dismay, until she perceived him attempting to enter the apartment; with a stifled sob she rushed forward and essayed to close the window against him.

"Very well," he said, "it is a matter of indifference to me; for you and for your love I have become what I am—I have lost them both, and life is intolerable; here, then, I remain until I am observed and given up to justice."

"No, no!" she almost shrieked, "do not drive me to distraction— wretched, sinful, outcast man, what have I done to deserve this trial?"

"Ellen, my life, my bride, hear me!—the world and all its prizes— pleasure, wealth, fair fame, are to me henceforward what they are to the dead. I had long ceased to value them; one thing alone, your affection, bound me to earth; that, that is, gone too, this terrible hour convinces me. What, then, have I to dread?—No; here I remain—let me die at least within the air you breathe."

"Madman! will you kill me?—Every path about the house is beset by armed men thirsting for your blood."

"I know it, Ellen, yet I have ventured, and dared them all. Oh, darling! what have I not dared, in this world and the next, to be for ever within sight of the beauty from which I am debarred for ever? Yet one hour with you, only *one hour*, Ellen, if it were but once in the long dreary year, and I could bear to live."

"May God assist me!" cried the frenzied girl.—Oh, Hugh! live —live to repent what has come between us, and left us blackened, and withered wretches upon God's fair world."

"Give me one sign, one proof then, Ellen," said the impassioned criminal, "that you still have not lost all the fond love you so often vowed me; let me clasp you once more to this breaking heart, and, degraded and branded as I am, I will be more boundlessly happy than thrones could make me out of your sight. Say that you disclaim me, that I am not your husband, wedded in the sight of that church you reverence so deeply; shut me out from your presence, all of heaven I have long dared to hope for, and give me up to a shameful death; or afford me one hour's shelter in peace and rapture by your side—May I enter?"

There was no reply—he sprang through the window and extended his arms—shuddering, she recoiled from him, but only for an instant —with one broken gasp she darted forward and fell senseless on his bosom. . . .

VII.

The delicate constitution of Ellen Nugent never recovered the repeated shocks of that trying and terrible night. On awaking from the long swoon into which she had not fallen until the loud knocking of the police for admission assured her of the escape of Lawlor, she was seized with fever and delirium, which threatened for several days a fatal termination. During this time she raved incessantly about her unhappy husband, whom she seemed to see constantly by her side, and to whose imaginary entreaties, that she would fly with him to some foreign land, she answered with expressions of the most impassioned devotion. Sometimes she fancied she beheld him in the hands of justice, and prayed and supplicated to be allowed to watch his fate and share his grave. Her disorder, however, yielded to the skill of the physicians—reason again assumed its control—and she once more became rigidly silent respecting the name and the affection for which her heart was breaking. As the lovely autumnal season of her native island set in with unusual mildness, it was hoped that with care her health would be re-established; but when winter came, symptoms of consumption—a disease that had already been fatal to more than one of her family—appeared, and it was evident that her days were numbered. The sweet patient herself was the first to feel the conviction; and the smile of satisfied resignation and thankfulness with which she received its confirmation from the lips of the physician, showed that Hope—that last seed to wither in the hearts of the young and gentle—had long perished in hers. "What have I to do with earth and earthly things?" she said, "my poor old father will not long stay after me, when he misses his spoiled Ellen from his lonely hearth—and then we will sleep together in the same quiet grave, and I shall know what it is to be at peace at last." Winter passed away—the faint perfumes of the early flowers of spring arose from the neglected garden; and ere they had disappeared, one more frail and fair than they was gathered to the dust. Her grave lies in the old churchyard of Abbeymahon; its soft turf is ever bright and green, though the rude letters on the stone by her gentle head are fast becoming illegible:—

"PRAY FOR THE SOUL OF
ELLEN ——,
ONLY DAUGHTER OF DAVID NUGENT
OF BARNA,
WHO DEPARTED THIS LIFE
THE 2D DAY OF APRIL 1821,
AGED NINETEEN YEARS."

... Early in the evening, the men comprising the little force stationed at Capparue, headed by their officer, and under the guidance of Bush, set out upon the excursion. By their starting so early, it was evident their destination was a distant one. They were reinforced, as they proceeded, by the men at two stations in advance on their route. As night darkened, the party no longer confined themselves to the main roads of the country, but struck forward on those which led to the mountains by the least circuitous routes. This, however, rendered their journey tedious and fatiguing, and would have made it, without the escort of a guide, an impracticable one, from the nature of the country to be traversed. The paths, for the most part, lay through swampy moorland, and not unfrequently across vast tracts of bog, where all traces of a footway disappeared; and where, without the aid of one thoroughly acquainted with the way, a single step to the right or left would have buried the whole party in the deep watery slough that spread far and wide around. It had rained heavily on the preceding day, which served still the more to impede their exertions, and a sharp spring frost, which was setting in, made the slowness of their progress doubly irksome. At length they crossed the chain of wild hills that divides the county of Tipperary, on the south, from that of Cork; but, despite of all their efforts, the moon had long risen above the stupendous range of the Galty mountains—through which their road now wound—before they came in sight of the spot which their officer at length informed them was to be the termination of their march—the churchyard of Abbeymahon. They could see it plainly at a considerable distance—the ruined tower of the Abbey, and the grey walls by which it was surrounded, crowning the summit of a lonely hill directly before them, and glancing white in the broadening moon.

On approaching the place they halted; and Bush, motioning them to preserve unbroken silence, crept stealthily up the ancient road that led, by a winding and steep ascent, to the burial-ground. After a short absence he reappeared, and beckoned to the party to follow. Imitating the stealthy pace of their conductor, and pressing silently forward without waking a single echo by their tread, they reached the wall of the grave-yard, outside of which the officer disposed his men so as to form an unbroken line of sentinels around the enclosure.

Advancing to a rude stile that led into the cemetery, the spy directed the officer's attention to a scene within it, which, when fully comprehended by the spectator's astonished gaze, made the blood run tingling and freezing through his veins.

By the side of Ellen Nugent's new-made grave sat the murderer Lawlor, enclosing in his arms the form that had once comprised all earth's love and beauty for him, and which, like a miser, with mild and maniac affection, he had unburied once more to clasp and contemplate. The shroud had fallen from the upper part of the body, upon which decay had as yet made slight impression. The delicate head lay reclined upon that shoulder which had been its home so often, and over which now streamed the long bright hair like a flood of loosened gold, the wan face turned up to his as if it still could thrill to the mad kisses in which he steeped it, while he had twined one of the white arms frantically about his neck.

"Ellen!" he said, "Ellen, speak to your murderer! speak to him who now for the first time holds you to his heart without one answering throb—without one word from those lips that never allowed me to kiss them, and kept that cheek so white, before. Darling! remember the hour in the happy summer-house when you first pledged your faith to mine, with my lips on those eyelids that all the warmth of my heart will never waken into life again. Remember this, and say upon this grave, that you forgive the wretch who killed you because he could not live without your love!"

"Now's your time, captain," whispered Bush, "this is the second night of his comin' an' takin' her up—give the word an' we're on him."

"Advance, men!" said the chief constable, and sprang into the enclosure.

Lawlor was on his feet in an instant—his frenzied eyes glaring with the fierceness of a roused tiger—grasping a carbine, which until then had lain unperceived with the mattock and other implements he had used in opening the grave. The moment he rose he saw Bush advancing with the officer—he levelled and fired—and fell himself, at the same instant, dead by the side of his unburied bride. One of the men, alarmed at the danger to which his officer was exposed, had discharged his musket at him from behind, but not before Bush, the informer, had fallen beneath the unerring aim of the foe he had betrayed.

The remains of Ellen Nugent were recommitted to the earth. An inquest was held on the spot upon the body of her husband, and a report thereof transmitted to Government. Hugh Lawlor was the last of his family, and his corpse was unclaimed by friend or relative;

but the strangers who dug his grave did not venture to separate in death the hapless pair who in life could never be united.

 2

FROM A Review, *Britannia* [1848][1]

There are scenes of savage wildness in nature which, though they inspire no pleasurable sensations, we are yet well satisfied to have seen. In the dark green of overhanging vegetation, the dank, moist underground and tangled net work of weeds and bushes, even the harsh cry of solitary birds, the cries of wild animals, and the startling motion of the snake as it springs away scared by the intruder's foot—there is an image of primeval rudeness which has much to fascinate, though nothing to charm the mind. The elements of beauty are round us in the midst of gloom and danger, and some forms are the more picturesque from their distorted growth amid so many obstacles. A tree clinging to the side of a precipice may more attract the eye than the pride of a plantation.

The principle may, to some extent, be applied to life. The uncultured freedom of native character presents more rugged aspects than we meet with in educated society. Its manners are not only more rough, but its passions are more violent. It knows nothing of those breakwaters to the fury of tempest which civilized training establishes to subdue the harsher workings of the soul. Its wrath is unsustained by reflection; the lips curse and the hand strikes with the first impulse to anger. It is more subject to brutal instinct than to divine reason.

It is humanity in this wild state that the author of "Wuthering Heights" essays to depict. His work is strangely original. It bears a resemblance to some of those irregular German tales in which the writers, giving the reins to their fancy, represent personages as swayed

1. Reprinted, by permission of the publisher, from Edith M. Weir, "Contemporary Reviews of the First Brontë Novels," *Brontë Society Publications, Transactions,* vol. XI, part LVII, 1947, pp. 93–94. This article states (p. 90) that "it can be inferred" that the review "appeared early in 1848."

and impelled to evil by supernatural influences. But they gave spiritual identity to evil impulses, while Mr. Bell[1] more naturally shows them as the natural offspring of the unregulated heart. He displays considerable power in his creations. They have all the angularity of mis-shapen growth, and form in this respect a striking contrast to those regular forms we are accustomed to meet with in English fiction. They exhibit nothing of the composite character. There is in them no trace of ideal models. They are so new, so grotesque, so entirely without art, that they strike us as proceeding from a mind of limited experience but of original energy and of a singular and distinctive cast.

In saying this we indicate both the merits and faults of the tale. It is in parts very unskilfully constructed; many passages in it display neither the grace of art nor the truth of nature, but only the vigour of one positive idea—that of passionate ferocity. It blazes forth in the most unsuitable circumstances and from persons the least likely to be animated by it. The author is a Salvator Rosa with his pen. He delineates forms of savage grandeur when he wishes to represent sylvan beauty. His Griseldas are furies and his swains Polyphemi. For this reason his narrative leaves an unpleasant effect on the mind. There are no green spots in it on which the mind can linger with satisfaction. The story rushes onwards with impetuous force, but it is the force of a dark and sullent torrent, flowing between high and rugged rocks. . . .

We must suppose that the characters are drawn from the very lowest of life; that they are the inhabitants of an isolated and un-civilized district, or that they are of some demoniac influence. It is difficult to pronounce any decisive judgment on a work in which there is so much rude ability displayed yet in which there is so much matter for blame. The scenes of brutality are unnecessarily long and unnecessarily frequent; and as an imaginative writer the author has to learn the first principles of his art. But there is singular power in his portraiture of strong passion. He exhibits it as convulsing the whole frame of nature, distracting the intellect to madness, and snapping the heartstrings. The anguish of Heathcliff on the death of Catherine approaches to sublimity. . . .

We do not know whether the author writes with any purpose; but we can speak of one effect of his production. The story shows the

1. The Brontë sisters adopted the pseudonym "Bell."

brutalizing influence of unchecked passion. His characters are a commentary on the truth that there is no tyranny in the world like that which thoughts of evil exercise in the daring and reckless breast.

 3

FROM "Novels of the Season," *The North American Review*, October, 1848[1]

Acton,[2] when left altogether to his own imaginations, seems to take a morose satisfaction in developing a full and complete science of human brutality. In Wuthering Heights he has succeeded in reaching the summit of this laudable ambition. He appears to think that spiritual wickedness is a combination of animal ferocities, and has accordingly made a compendium of the most striking qualities of tiger, wolf, cur, and wild-cat, in the hope of framing out of such elements a suitable brute-demon to serve as the hero of his novel. Compared with Heathcote [*sic*], Squeers is considerate and Quilp humane. He is a deformed monster, whom the Mephistopheles of Goethe would have nothing to say to, whom the Satan of Milton would consider as an object of simple disgust, and to whom Dante would hesitate in awarding the honor of a place among those whom he has consigned to the burning pitch. This epitome of brutality, disavowed by man and devil, Mr. Acton Bell attempts in two whole volumes to delineate, and certainly he is to be congratulated on his success. As he is a man of uncommon talents, it is needless to say that it is to his subject and his dogged manner of handling it that we are to refer the burst of dislike with which the novel was received. His mode of delineating a bad character is to narrate every offensive act and repeat every vile expression which are characteristic. Hence, in Wuthering Heights, he details all the ingenuities of animal malignity, and exhausts the whole rhetoric of stupid blasphemy, in order that there may be no mistake as

1. Vol. LXVII, pp. 358–359.
2. "Acton Bell" was Anne Brontë's pseudonym. The reviewer believes "Acton" to be the author of *Wuthering Heights*.

to the kind of person he intends to hold up to the popular gaze. Like all spendthrifts of malice and profanity, however, he overdoes the business. Though he scatters oaths as plentifully as sentimental writers do interjections, the comparative parsimony of the great novelists in this respect is productive of infinitely more effect. It must be confessed that this coarseness, though the prominent, is not the only characteristic of the writer. His attempt at originality does not stop with the conception of Heathcote, but he aims further to exhibit the action of the sentiment of love on the nature of the being whom his morbid imagination has created. This is by far the ablest and most subtle portion of his labors, and indicates that strong hold upon the elements of character, and that decision of touch in the delineation of the most evanescent qualities of emotion, which distinguish the mind of the whole family.[1] For all practical purposes, however, the power evinced in Wuthering Heights is power thrown away. Nightmares and dreams, through which devils dance and wolves howl, make bad novels.

4 Sidney Dobell

FROM "Currer Bell," *The Palladium,*
September, 1850[2]

Laying aside 'Wildfell Hall,' we open 'Wuthering Heights,' as at once the earlier in date and ruder in execution. We look upon it as the flight of an impatient fancy fluttering in the very exultation of young wings; sometimes beating against its solitary bars, but turning, rather to exhaust, in a circumscribed space, the energy and agility which it may not yet spend in the heavens—a youthful story, written for oneself in solitude, and thrown aside till other successes recall the eyes to

1. The "Bells," that is, the Brontës.
2. Reprinted from E[mily] J[olly], ed., *The Life and Letters of Sidney Dobell,* London: Smith, Elder, 1878, pp. 169–172, 174–176. "Currer Bell" is Charlotte Brontë's pseudonym. Despite her disclaimer in the preface to the third edition of *Jane Eyre,* Dobell is convinced that *Wuthering Heights* is one of "Currer Bell's" early works.

it in hope. In this thought let the critic take up the book; lay it down in what thought he will, there are some things in it he can lay down no more.

That Catherine Earnshaw—at once so wonderfully fresh, so fearfully natural—new, 'as if brought from other spheres,' and familiar as the recollection of some woeful experience—what can surpass the strange compatibility of her simultaneous loves; the involuntary art with which her two natures are so made to co-exist, that in the very arms of her lover we dare not doubt her purity; the inevitable belief with which we watch the oscillations of the old and new elements in her mind, and the exquisite truth of the last victory of nature over education, when the past returns to her as a flood, sweeping every modern landmark from within her, and the soul of the child, expanding, fills the woman?

Found at last, by her husband, insensible on the breast of her lover, and dying of the agony of their parting, one looks back upon her, like that husband, without one thought of accusation or absolution; her memory is chaste as the loyalty of love, pure as the air of the Heights on which she dwelt.

Heathcliff *might* have been as unique a creation. The conception in his case was as wonderfully strong and original, but he is spoilt in detail. The authoress has too often disgusted, where she should have terrified, and has allowed us a familiarity with her fiend which had ended in unequivocal contempt. If 'Wuthering Heights' had been written as lately as 'Jane Eyre,' the figure of Heathcliff, symmetrised and elevated, might have been one of the most natural and most striking portraits in the gallery of fiction.

Not a subordinate place or person in this novel but bears more or less the stamp of high genius. Ellen Dean is the ideal of the peasant playmate and servant of 'the family.' The substratum in which her mind moves is finely preserved. Joseph, as a specimen of the sixty years' servitor of 'the house,' is worthy a museum case. We feel that if Catherine Earnshaw bore her husband a child, it must be that Cathy Linton, and no other. The very Jane Eyre, of quiet satire, peeps out in such a paragraph as this:—'He told me to put on my cloak, and run to Gimmerton for the doctor and the parson. I went through wind and rain, and brought one, the doctor, back with me: the other said, *he would come in the morning*.' What terrible truth, what nicety of touch, what 'uncanny' capacity for mental aberration in the first symptoms of Catherine's delirium. 'I'm not wandering; you're mistaken, or else I should believe you really *were* that withered hag, and I should think I *was* under Penistone Crags: and I'm conscious it's night, and there are two candles on the table making the black press shine like jet.' What an unobtrusive, unexpected sense of *keeping* in the hanging of Isabella's dog.

The book abounds in such things. But one looks back at the whole story as to a world of brilliant figures in an atmosphere of mist; shapes that come out upon the eye, and burn their colours into the brain, and depart into the enveloping fog. It is the unformed writing of a giant's hand: the 'large utterance' of a baby god. In the sprawling of the infant Hercules, however, there must have been attitudes from which the statuary might model. In the early efforts of unusual genius, there are not seldom unconscious felicities which maturer years may look back upon with envy. The child's hand wanders over the strings. It cannot combine them in the chords and melodies of manhood; but its separate notes are perfect in themselves, and perhaps sound all the sweeter for the Æolian discords from which they come.

We repeat, that there are passages in this book of 'Wuthering Heights' of which any novelist, past or present, might be proud. Open the first volume at the fourteenth page, and read to the sixty-first. There are few things in modern prose to surpass these pages for native power. We cannot praise too warmly the brave simplicity, the unaffected air of intense belief, the admirable combination of extreme likelihood with the rarest originality, the nice provision of the possible even in the highest effects of the supernatural, the easy strength and instinct of keeping with which the accessory circumstances are grouped, the exquisite but unconscious art with which the chiaro-scuro of the whole is managed, and the ungenial frigidity of place, time, weather, and persons, is made to heighten the unspeakable pathos of one ungovernable outburst.

The *thinking out* of some of the pages . . . is the masterpiece of a poet, rather than the hybrid creation of the novelist. The mass of readers will probably yawn over the whole; but, in the memory of those whose remembrance makes *fame,* the images in these pages will live—when every word that conveyed them is forgotten—as a recollection of *things heard and seen.* This is the highest triumph of description; and perhaps every creation of the fancy is more or less faulty, so long as, in a mind fitted to reproduce them, the images co-exist only with the words that called them up. The spiritual structure is not complete till the scaffolding can be safely struck away.

... When Currer Bell writes her next novel, let her remember, as far as possible, the frame of mind in which she sat down to her first. She cannot now commit the faults of that early effort; it will be well for her if she be still capable of the virtues. She will never sin so much against consistent keeping as to draw another Heathcliff; she is too much *au fait* of her profession to make again those sacrifices to machinery which deprive her early picture of any claim to be ranked as a work of art. Happy she, if her next book demonstrate the unimpaired possession of those powers of insight, that instinctive obedience to the nature within her, and those occurrences of infallible inspiration which astound the critic in the young author of 'Wuthering Heights.' She will not let her next dark-haired hero babble away the respect of her reader and the awe of his antecedents; nor will she find another housekeeper who remembers two volumes *literatim*. Let her rejoice if she can again give us such an elaboration of a rare and fearful form of mental disease—so terribly strong, so exquisitely subtle—with such nicety in its transitions, such intimate symptomatic truth in its details, as to be at once a psychological and medical study. It has been said of Shakespeare, that he drew cases which the physician might study; Currer Bell has done no less. She will not, again, employ her wonderful pencil on a picture so destitute of moral beauty and human worth. Let her exult, if she can still invest such a picture with such interest. We stand painfully before her portraits; but our eyes are drawn towards them by the irresistible ties of blood relationship. Let her exult, if she can still make us weep with the simple pathos of that fading face, which looked from the golden crocuses on her pillow to the hills which concealed the old home and the churchyard of Gimmerton. . . .

Let Currer Bell prize the young intuition of character which dictated Cathy's speech to Ellen . . . There is a deep, unconscious philosophy in it. There are minds whose crimes and sorrows are not so much the result of intrinsic evil as of a false position in the scheme of things, which clashes their energies with the arrangements of surrounding life. It is difficult to cure such a soul from *within*. The point of view, not the eye or the landscape, is in fault. Move *that,* and as at the changing of a stop, the mental machine assumes its proper relative place, and the powers of discord become, in the same measure, the instruments of harmony. It was a fine instinct which saw this. Let Currer Bell be passing glad if it is as vigorous now as then; and let her thank God if she can now draw the apparition of the 'Wanderer of the Moor.'

5 E[lizabeth] C[leghorn] Gaskell

FROM *The Life of Charlotte Brontë,* 1858[1]

FOR a right understanding of the life of my dear friend, Charlotte Brontë, it appears to me more necessary in her case than in most others, that the reader should be made acquainted with the peculiar forms of population and society amidst which her earliest years were passed, and from which both her own and her sisters' first impressions of human life must have been received. I shall endeavour, therefore, before proceeding further with my work, to present some idea of the character of the people of Haworth, and the surrounding districts.

Even an inhabitant of the neighbouring county of Lancaster is struck by the peculiar force of character which the Yorkshiremen display. This makes them interesting as a race; while, at the same time, as individuals, the remarkable degree of self-sufficiency they possess gives them an air of independence rather apt to repel a stranger. I use this expression, "self-sufficiency" in the largest sense. Conscious of the strong sagacity and the dogged power of will which seem almost the birthright of the natives of the West Riding, each man relies upon himself, and seeks no help at the hands of his neighbour. From rarely requiring the assistance of others, he comes to doubt the power of bestowing it; from the general success of his efforts, he grows to depend upon them, and to over-esteem his own energy and power. He belongs to that keen, yet short-sighted class, who consider suspicion of all whose honesty is not proved as a sign of wisdom. The practical qualities of a man are held in great respect; but the want of faith in

1. New York: Appleton, pp. 9–11, 13–19. The date of the first English edition is 1857.

strangers and untried modes of action, extends itself even to the manner in which the virtues are regarded; and if they produce no immediate and tangible result, they are rather put aside as unfit for this busy, striving world; especially if they are more of a passive than an active character. The affections are strong, and their foundations lie deep: but they are not—such affections seldom are—wide-spreading; nor do they show themselves on the surface. Indeed, there is little display of any of the amenities of life among this wild, rough population. Their accost is curt; their accent and tone of speech blunt and harsh. Something of this may, probably, be attributed to the freedom of mountain air and of isolated hill-side life; something be derived from their rough Norse ancestry. They have a quick perception of character, and a keen sense of humour; the dwellers among them must be prepared for certain uncomplimentary, though most likely true, observations, pithily expressed. Their feelings are not easily roused, but their duration is lasting. Hence there is much close friendship and faithful service; and for a correct exemplification of the form in which the latter frequently appears, I need only refer the reader of "Wuthering Heights" to the character of "Joseph."

From the same cause come also enduring grudges, in some cases amounting to hatred, which occasionally has been bequeathed from generation to generation. I remember Miss Brontë once telling me that it was a saying round about Haworth, "Keep a stone in thy pocket seven year; turn it, and keep it seven year longer, that it may be ever ready to thine hand when thine enemy draws near."

The West Riding men are sleuth-hounds in pursuit of money. Miss Brontë related to my husband a curious instance illustrative of this eager desire for riches. A man that she knew, who was a small manufacturer, had engaged in many local speculations, which had always turned out well, and thereby rendered him a person of some wealth. He was rather past middle age, when he bethought him of insuring his life; and he had only just taken out his policy, when he fell ill of an acute disease which was certain to end fatally in a very few days. The doctor, half-hesitatingly, revealed to him his hopeless state. "By jingo!" cried he, rousing up at once into the old energy, "I shall *do* the insurance company! I always was a lucky fellow!"

These men are keen and shrewd; faithful and persevering in following out a good purpose, fell in tracking an evil one. They are not emotional; they are not easily made into either friends or enemies; but once lovers or haters, it is difficult to change their feeling. They are a powerful race both in mind and body, both for good and for evil. . . .

The parish of Halifax touches that of Bradford, in which the chapelry of Haworth is included; and the nature of the ground in the two parishes is much of the same wild and hilly description. The abundance of coal, and the number of mountain streams in the district, make it highly favourable to manufactures; and accordingly, as I stated, the inhabitants have for centuries been engaged in making cloth, as well as in agricultural pursuits. But the intercourse of trade failed, for a long time, to bring amenity and civilization into these outlying hamlets, or widely scattered dwellings. Mr. Hunter, in his "Life of Oliver Heywood," quotes a sentence out of a memorial of one James Rither, living in the reign of Elizabeth, which is partially true to this day—

"They have no superior to court, no civilities to practise: a sour and sturdy humour is the consequence, so that a stranger is shocked by a tone of defiance in every voice, and an air of fierceness in every countenance."

Even now, a stranger can hardly ask a question without receiving some crusty reply, if indeed, he receive any at all. Sometimes the sour rudeness amounts to positive insult. Yet, if the "foreigner" takes all this churlishness good-humouredly, or as a matter of course, and makes good any claim upon their latent kindliness and hospitality, they are faithful and generous, and thoroughly to be relied upon. As a slight illustration of the roughness that pervades all classes in these out-of-the-way villages, I may relate a little adventure which happened to my husband and myself, three years ago, at Addingham . . . a village not many miles from Haworth.

We were driving along the street, when one of those ne'er-do-well lads who seem to have a kind of magnetic power for misfortunes, having jumped into the stream that runs through the place, just where all the broken glass and bottles are thrown, staggered naked and nearly covered with blood into a cottage before us. Besides receiving another bad cut in the arm, he had completely laid open the artery, and was in a fair way of bleeding to death—which, one of his relations comforted him by saying, would be likely to "save a deal o' trouble."

When my husband had checked the effusion of blood with a strap that one of the bystanders unbuckled from his leg, he asked if a surgeon had been sent for.

"Yoi," was the answer; "but we dunna think he'll come."

"Why not?"

"He's owd, yo seen, and asthmatic, and it's up-hill."

My husband, taking a boy for his guide, drove as fast as he could to the surgeon's house, which was about three-quarters of a mile off, and met the aunt of the wounded lad leaving it.

"Is he coming?" inquired my husband.

"Well, he didna' say he wouldna' come."

"But tell him the lad may bleed to death."

"I did."

"And what did he say?"

"Why, only, 'D——n him; what do I care.' "

It ended, however, in his sending one of his sons, who, though not brought up to "the surgering trade," was able to do what was necessary in the way of bandages and plaisters. The excuse made for the surgeon was, that "he was near eighty, and getting a bit doited, and had had a matter o' twenty childer."

Among the most unmoved of the lookers-on was the brother of the boy so badly hurt; and while he was lying in a pool of blood on the flag floor, and crying out how much his arm was "warching," his stoical relation stood coolly smoking his bit of black pipe, and uttered not a single word of either sympathy or sorrow.

Forest customs, existing in the fringes of dark wood, which clothed the declivity of the hills on either side, tended to brutalize the population until the middle of the seventeenth century. Execution by beheading was performed in a summary way upon either men or women who were guilty of but very slight crimes; and a dogged, yet in some cases fine, indifference to human life was thus generated. The roads were so notoriously bad, even up to the last thirty years, that there was little communication between one village and another; if the produce of industry could be conveyed at stated times to the cloth market of the district, it was all that could be done; and, in lonely houses on the distant hill-side, or by the small magnates of secluded hamlets, crimes might be committed almost unknown, certainly without any great uprising of popular indignation calculated to bring down the strong arm of the law. It must be remembered that in those days there was no rural constabulary; and the few magistrates left to themselves, and generally related to one another, were most of them inclined to tolerate eccentricity, and to wink at faults too much like their own.

Men hardly past middle life talk of the days of their youth, spent in this part of the country, when, during the winter months, they rode up to the saddle-girths in mud; when absolute business was the only reason for stirring beyond the precincts of home; and when that business was conducted under a pressure of difficulties which they themselves, borne along to Bradford market in a swift first-class carriage, can hardly believe to have been possible. For instance, one woollen manufacturer says that, not five-and-twenty years ago, he had to rise betimes to set off on a winter's morning in order to be at Bradford with the great waggon-load of goods manufactured by his father: this load was packed over-night, but in the morning there was great gathering around it, and flashing of lanterns, and examination of horses' feet, before the ponderous waggon got under weigh; and then some one had to go grouping here and there, on hands and knees, and always sounding with a staff down the long, steep, slippery brow, to find where the horses might tread safely, until they reached the comparative easy going of the deep rutted main road. People went on horseback over the upland moors, following the tracks of the packhorses that carried the parcels, baggage, or goods from one town to another, between which there did not happen to be a highway.

But in the winter, all such communication was impossible, by reason of the snow which lay long and late on the bleak high ground. I have known people who, travelling by the mail-coach over Blackstone Edge, had been snowed up for a week or ten days at the little inn near the summit, and obliged to spend both Christmas and New Year's Day there, till the store of provisions laid in for the use of the landlord and his family falling short before the inroads of the unexpected visitors, they had recourse to the turkeys, geese, and Yorkshire pies with which the coach was laden; and even these were beginning to fail, when a fortunate thaw released them from their prison.

Isolated as the hill villages may be, they are in the world, compared with the loneliness of the grey ancestral houses to be seen here and there in the dense hollows of the moors. These dwellings are not large, yet they are solid and roomy enough for the accommodation of those who live in them and to whom the surrounding estates belong. The land has often been held by one family since the days of the Tudors; the owners are, in fact, the remains of the old yeomanry—small squires, who are rapidly becoming extinct as a class, from one of two causes. Either the possessor falls into idle, drinking habits, and so is obliged eventually to sell his property: or he finds, if more shrewd and adventurous, that the "beck" running down the mountain side, or the minerals beneath his feet, can be turned into a new source of wealth: and leaving the old plodding life of a landowner with small capital, he turns manufacturer, or digs for coal, or quarries for stone.

Still there are those remaining of this class—dwellers in the lonely houses far away in the upland districts—even at the present day, who sufficiently indicate what strange eccentricity—what wild strength of will—nay, even what unnatural power of crime was fostered by a mode of living in which a man seldom met his fellows, and where public opinion was only a distant and inarticulate echo of some clearer voice sounding behind the sweeping horizon.

A solitary life cherishes mere fancies until they become manias. And the powerful Yorkshire character which was scarcely tamed into subjection by all the contact it met with in "busy town or crowded mart," has before now broken out into strange wilfulness in the remoter districts. A singular account was recently given me of a landowner (living it is true, on the Lancashire side of the hills, but of the same blood and nature as the dwellers on the other) who was supposed to be in the receipt of seven or eight hundred a year, and whose house bore marks of handsome antiquity, as if his forefathers had been for a long time people of consideration. My informant was struck with the appearance of the place, and proposed to the countryman who was accompanying him, to go up to it and take a nearer inspection. The reply was, "Yo'd better not; he'd threap yo down th' loan. He's let fly at some folks' legs, and let shot lodge in 'em afore now, for going too near to his house." And finding, on closer inquiry, that such was really the inhospitable custom of this moorland squire, the gentleman gave up his purpose. I believe that the savage yeoman is still living.

Another squire, of more distinguished family and larger property—one is thence led to imagine of better education, but that does not always follow—died at his house, not many miles from Haworth, only a few years ago. His great amusement and occupation had been cockfighting. When he was confined to his chamber with what he knew would be his last illness, he had his cocks brought up there, and watched the bloody battle from his bed. As his mortal disease increased, and it became impossible for him to turn so as to follow the combat, he had looking-glasses arranged in such a manner around and above him, as he lay, that he could still see the cocks fighting. And in this manner he died.

These are merely instances of eccentricity compared to the tales of positive violence and crime that have occurred in these isolated dwellings, which still linger in the memories of the old people of the district, and some of which were doubtless familiar to the authors of "Wuthering Heights" and "The Tenant of Wildfell Hall.'

6 Algernon Charles Swinburne

FROM "Emily Brontë," *The Athenaeum,* June 16, 1883[1]

To the England of our own time, it has often enough been remarked, the novel is what the drama was to the England of Shakespeare's. The same general interest produces the same incessant demand for the same inexhaustible supply of imaginative produce, in a shape more suited to the genius of a later day and the conditions of a changed society. Assuming this simple explanation to be sufficient for the obvious fact that in the modern world of English letters the novel is everywhere and the drama is nowhere, we may remark one radical point of difference between the taste of playgoers in the age of Shakespeare and the taste of novel-readers in our own. Tragedy was then at least as popular as either romantic or realistic comedy; whereas nothing would seem to be more unpopular with the run of modern readers than the threatening shadow of tragedy projected across the whole length of a story, inevitable and unmistakable from the lurid harshness of its dawn to the fiery softness of its sunset. The objection to a novel in which the tragic element has

1. Pp. 762–73.

an air of incongruity and caprice—in which a tragic surprise is, as it were, sprung upon the reader, with a jarring shock such as might be given by the actual news of some unforeseen and grievous accident—this objection seems to me thoroughly reasonable, grounded on a true critical sense of fitness and unfitness; but the distaste for high and pure tragedy, where the close is in perfect and simple harmony with the opening, seems not less thoroughly pitiable and irrational.

A recent work of singular and admirable power, in which the freshness of humour is as real and vital as the fervour of passion, was at once on its appearance compared with Emily Brontë's now famous story. And certainly not without good cause; for in point of local colour 'Mehalah' is, as far as I know, the one other book which can bear and may challenge the comparison. Its pages, for one thing, reflect the sterile glitter and desolate fascination of the salt marshes, their minute splendours and barren beauties and multitudinous monotony of measureless expanse, with the same instinctive and unlaborious accuracy which brings all the moorland before us in a breath when we open any chapter of 'Wuthering Heights.' And the humour is even better; and the passion is not less genuine. But the accumulated horrors of the close, however possible in fact, are wanting in the one quality which justifies and ennobles all admissible horror in fiction: they hardly seem inevitable; they lack the impression of logical and moral certitude. All the realism in the world will not suffice to convey this impression; and a work of art which wants it wants the one final and irreplaceable requisite of inner harmony. Now in 'Wuthering Heights' this one thing needful is as perfectly and triumphantly attained as in 'King Lear' or 'The Duchess of Malfi,' in 'The Bride of Lammermoor' or 'Notre-Dame de Paris.' From the first we breathe the fresh dark air of tragic passion and presage; and to the last the changing wind and flying sunlight are in keeping with the stormy promise of the dawn. There is no monotony, there is no repetition, but there is no discord. This is the first and last necessity, the foundation of all labour and the crown of all success, for a poem worthy of the name; and this it is that distinguishes the hand of Emily from the hand of Charlotte Brontë. All the works of the elder sister are rich in poetic spirit, poetic feeling, and poetic detail; but the younger sister's work is essentially and definitely a poem in the fullest and most positive sense of the term. . . .

It is a fine and accurate instinct that has inevitably led Miss Robinson[1] to cite in chosen illustration of the book's quality at its highest those two incomparable pictures of dreamland and delirium which no poet that ever lived has ever surpassed or equalled for passionate and lifelike beauty of imaginative truth. But it is even somewhat less than exact to say that the latter scene "is given with a masterly pathos that Webster need not have made more strong, nor Fletcher more lovely and appealing." Fletcher could not have made it as lovely and appealing as it is; he would have made it exquisitely pretty and effectively theatrical; but the depth, the force, the sincerity, recalling here so vividly, the "several forms of distraction" through which Webster's Cornelia passes after the murder of her son by his brother, excel everything else of the kind in imaginative art; not excepting, if truth may be spoken on such a subject, the madness of Ophelia or even of Madge Wildfire.

. . . As a woman we never knew her so well as now that we have to welcome this worthy record of her life, with deeper thanks and warmer congratulations to the writer than can often be due even to the best of biographers and critics. As an author she has not perhaps even yet received her full due or taken her final place. Again and again has the same obvious objection been taken to that awkwardness of construction or presentation which no reader of 'Wuthering Heights' can undertake to deny. But, to judge by the vigour with which this objection is urged, it might be supposed that the rules of narrative observed by all great novelists were of an almost legal or logical strictness and exactitude with regard to probability of detail. Now most assuredly the indirect method of relation through which the story of Heathcliff is conveyed, however unlikely or clumsy it may seem from the realistic point of view, does not make this narrative more liable to the charge of actual impossibility than others of the kind. Defoe still remains the one writer of narrative in the first person who has always kept the stringent law of possibilities before the eye of his invention. Even the admirable ingenuity and the singular painstaking which distinguish the method of Mr. Wilkie

1. Agnes M. F. Robinson, whose biography of Emily Brontë, published in 1883, was the occasion for this essay.

Collins can only give external and transient plausibility to the record of long conversations overheard or shared in by the narrator only a few hours before the supposed date of the report drawn up from memory. The very greatest masters in their kind, Walter Scott and Charles Dickens, are of all narrators the most superbly regardless of this objection. From 'Rob Roy' and 'Redgauntlet,' from 'David Copperfield' and 'Bleak House,' we might select at almost any stage of the autobiographic record some instance of detail in which the violation of plausibility, probability, or even possibility, is at least as daring and as glaring as any to be found in the narrative of Nelly Dean. Even when that narrative is removed, so to speak, yet one degree further back—even when we are supposed to be reading a minute detail of incident and dialogue transcribed by the hand of the lay figure Mr. Lockwood from Nelly Dean's report of the account conveyed to her years ago by Heathcliff's fugitive wife or gadding servant, each invested for the nonce with the peculiar force and distinctive style of the author—even then we are not asked to put such an overwhelming strain on our faculty of imaginative belief as is exacted by the great writer who invites us to accept the report drawn up by Mr. Pendennis of everything that takes place—down even to the minutest points of dialogue, accent, and gesture—in the household of the Newcomes or the Firmins during the absence no less than in the presence of their friend the reporter. Yet all this we gladly and gratefully admit, without demur or cavil, to be thoroughly authentic and credible, because the whole matter of the report, however we get at it, is found when we do get at it to be vivid and lifelike as an actual experience of living fact. Here, if ever anywhere, the attainment of the end justifies the employment of the means. If we are to enjoy imaginative work at all, we must "assume the virtue" of imagination, even if we have it not; we must, as children say, "pretend" or make believe a little as a very condition of the game.

A graver and perhaps a somewhat more plausible charge is brought against the author of 'Wuthering Heights' by those who find here and there in her book the savage note or the sickly symptom of a morbid ferocity. Twice or thrice especially the details of deliberate or passionate brutality in Heathcliff's treatment of his victims make the reader feel for a moment as though he were reading a police report or even a novel by some French "naturalist" of the latest and brutallest order. But the pervading atmosphere of the book is so high and healthy that the effect even of those "vivid and fearful scenes" which impaired the rest of Charlotte Brontë is almost at once neutralized—we may hardly say softened, but sweetened, dispersed, and transfigured—by the general impression of noble purity and passionate straightforwardness, which removes it at once and for ever from any such ugly possibility of association or comparison. The whole work is not more incomparable in the effect of its atmosphere or landscape than in the peculiar note of its wild and bitter pathos; but most of all is it unique in the special and distinctive character of its passion. The love which devours life itself, which devastates the present and desolates the future with unquenchable and raging fire, has nothing less pure in it than flame or sunlight. And this passionate and ardent chastity is utterly and unmistakably spontaneous and unconscious. Not till the story is ended, not till the effect of it has been thoroughly absorbed and digested, does the reader even perceive the simple and natural absence of any grosser element, any hint or suggestion of a baser alloy in the ingredients of its human emotion than in the splendour of lightning or the roll of a gathered wave. Then, as on issuing sometimes from the tumult of charging waters, he finds with something of wonder how absolutely pure and sweet was the element of living storm with which his own nature has been for a while made one; not a grain in it of soiling sand, not a waif of clogging weed. As was the author's life, so is her book in all things: troubled and taintless, with little of rest in it, and nothing of reproach. It may be true that not many will ever take it to their hearts; it is certain that those who do like it will like nothing very much better in the whole world of poetry or prose.

William Makepeace Thackeray
Vanity Fair
1848

1 *William Makepeace Thackeray*

FROM *The Book of Snobs,* 1848[1]

CHAPTER VI

ON SOME RESPECTABLE SNOBS

Having received a great deal of obloquy for dragging monarchs, princes, and the respected nobility into the Snob category, I trust to please everybody in the present chapter, by stating my firm opinion that it is among the *respectable* classes of this vast and happy empire that the greatest profusion of Snobs is to be found. I pace down my beloved Baker Street (I am engaged on a life of Baker,

1. Reprinted from *The Works of William Makepeace Thackeray,* The Biographical Edition, New York and London: Harper, 1898–99, vol. II, pp. 323–325, 330–333. The original version of *The Book of Snobs,* entitled *The Snobs of England,* appeared serially in *Punch* in 1846–47.

founder of this celebrated street), I walk in Harley Street (where every other house has a hatchment), Wimpole Street, that is as cheerful as the Catacombs—a dingy Mausoleum of the genteel:—I rove round Regent's Park, where the plaster is patching off the house walls; where Methodist preachers are holding forth to three little children in the green enclosures, and puffy valetudinarians are cantering in the solitary mud:—I thread the doubtful zigzags of Mayfair, where Mrs. Kitty Lorimer's brougham may be seen drawn up next door to old Lady Lollipop's belozenged family coach;—I roam through Belgravia, that pale and polite district, where all the inhabitants look prim and correct, and the mansions are painted a faint whity-brown; I lose myself in the new squares and terraces of the brilliant brand-new Bayswater-and-Tyburn-Junction line; and in one and all of these districts the same truth comes across me. I stop before any house at hazard, and say, "O house, you are inhabited—O knocker, you are knocked at—O undressed flunkey, sunning your lazy calves as you lean against the iron railings, you are paid—by Snobs." It is a tremendous thought that; and it is almost sufficient to drive a benevolent mind to madness to think that perhaps there is not one in ten of those houses where the "Peerage" does not lie on the drawing-room table. Considering the harm that foolish lying book does, I would have all the copies of it burned, as the barber burned all Quixote's books of humbugging chivalry.

Look at this grand house in the middle of the square. The Earl of Loughcorrib lives there: he has fifty thousand a year. A *déjeuner dansant* given at his house last week cost, who knows how much? The mere flowers for the room and bouquets for the ladies cost four hundred pounds. That man in drab trousers, coming crying down the steps, is a dun: Lord Loughcorrib has ruined him, and won't see him: that is his Lordship peeping through the blind of his study at him now. Go thy ways, Loughcorrib: thou art a Snob, a heartless pretender, a hypocrite of hospitality; a rogue who passes forged notes upon society;—but I am growing too eloquent.

You see that fine house, No. 23, where a butcher's boy is ringing the area-bell. He has three mutton-chops in his tray. They are for the dinner of a very different and very respectable family; for Lady Susan Scraper, and her daughters, Miss Scraper and Miss Emily Scraper. The domestics, luckily for them, are on board wages

—two huge footmen in light blue and canary, a fat steady coach-man who is a Methodist, and a butler who would never have stayed in the family but that he was orderly to General Scraper when the General distinguished himself at Walcheren. His widow sent his por-trait to the United Service Club, and it is hung up in one of the back dressing-closets there. He is represented at a parlour window with red curtains; in the distance is a whirlwind, in which cannon are firing off; and he is pointing to a chart, on which are written the words "Walcheren, Tobago."

Lady Susan is, as everybody knows by referring to the "British Bible," a daughter of the great and good Earl Bagwig before men-tioned. She thinks everything belonging to her the greatest and best in the world. The first of men naturally are the Buckrams, her own race: then follow in rank the Scrapers. The General was the greatest general: his eldest son, Scraper Buckram Scraper, is at present the greatest and best; his second son the next greatest and best; and herself the paragon of women.

Indeed, she is a most respectable and honourable lady. She goes to church of course: she would fancy the Church in danger if she did not. She subscribes to the church and parish charities; and is a directress of many meritorious charitable institutions—of Queen Char-lotte's Lying-in Hospital, the Washerwomen's Asylum, the British Drummers' Daughters' Home &c. &c. She is a model of a matron.

The tradesman never lived who could say that his bill was not paid on the quarter-day. The beggars of her neighbourhood avoid her like a pestilence; for while she walks out, protected by John, that domestic has always two or three mendicity tickets ready for deserving objects. Ten guineas a year will pay all her charities. There is no respectable lady in all London who gets her name more often printed for such a sum of money.

Those three mutton-chops which you see entering at the kitchen-door will be served on the family-plate at seven o'clock this evening, the huge footman being present, and the butler in black, and the crest and coat-of-arms of the Scrapers blazing everywhere. I pity Miss Emily Scraper—she is still young—young and hungry. Is it a fact that she spends her pocket-money in buns? Malicious tongues say so; but she has very little to spare for buns, the poor little hungry soul! For the fact is, that when the footmen, and the ladies'-

maids, and the fat coach-horses, which are jobbed, and the six dinner-parties in the season, and the two great solemn evening-parties, and the rent of the big house, and the journey to an English or foreign watering-place for the autumn, are paid, my Lady's income has dwindled away to a very small sum, and she is as poor as you or I.

You would not think it when you saw her big carriage rattling up to the drawing-room, and caught a glimpse of her plumes, lappets, and diamonds, waving over her Ladyship's sandy hair and majestical hooked nose;—you would not think it when you hear "Lady Susan Scraper's carriage" bawled out at midnight so as to disturb all Belgravia:—you would not think it when she comes rustling into church, the obsequious John behind with the bag of Prayer-books. Is it possible, you would say, that so grand and awful a personage as that can be hard-up for money? Alas! so it is.

She never heard such a word as Snob, I will engage, in this wicked and vulgar world. And, O stars and garters! how she would start if she heard that she—she, as solemn as Minerva—she, as chaste as Diana (without that heathen goddess's unladylike propensity for field-sports)—that she too was a Snob!

A Snob she is, as long as she sets that prodigious value upon herself, upon her name, upon her outward appearance, and indulges in that intolerable pomposity; as long as she goes parading abroad, like Solomon in all his glory; as long as she goes to bed—as I believe she does—with a turban and a bird of paradise in it, and a Court train to her night-gown; as long as she is so insufferably virtuous and condescending; as long as she does not cut at least one of those footmen down into mutton-chops for the benefit of the young ladies.

I had my notions of her from my old schoolfellow—her son Sydney Scraper—a Chancery barrister without any practice—the most placid, polite, and genteel of Snobs, who never exceeded his allowance of two hundred a year, and who may be seen any evening at the "Oxford and Cambridge Club," simpering over the *Quarterly Review,* in the blameless enjoyment of his half-pint of port.

CHAPTER VIII

GREAT CITY SNOBS

There is no disguising the fact that this series of papers is making a prodigious sensation among all classes in this Empire. Notes of admiration (!), of interrogation(?), of remonstrance, approval, or abuse, come pouring into *Mr. Punch's* box. We have been called to task for betraying the secrets of three different families of De Mogyns; no less than four Lady Susan Scrapers have been discovered; and young gentlemen are quite shy of ordering half-a-pint of port and simpering over the *Quarterly Review* at the Club, lest they should be mistaken for Sydney Scraper, Esq. "What *can* be your antipathy to Baker Street?" asks some fair remonstrant, evidently writing from that quarter.

"Why only attack the aristocratic Snobs?" says one estimable correspondent: "are not the snobbish Snobs to have their turn?"— "Pitch into the University Snobs!" writes an indignant gentleman (who spelt *elegant* with two *l*'s).—"Show up the Clerical Snob," suggests another.—"Being at Meurice's Hotel, Paris, some time since," some wag hints, "I saw Lord B. leaning out of the window with his boots in his hand, and bawling out, 'Garçon, cirez-moi ces bottes.' Oughtn't he to be brought in among the Snobs?"

No; far from it. If his Lordship's boots are dirty, it is because he is Lord B., and walks. There is nothing snobbish in having only one pair of boots, or a favourite pair; and certainly nothing snobbish in desiring to have them cleaned. Lord B., in so doing, performed a perfectly natural and gentlemanlike action; for which I am so pleased with him that I should like to have him designed in a favourable and elegant attitude, and put at the head of this Chapter in the place of honour. No, we are not personal in these candid remarks. As Phidias took the pick of a score of beauties before he completed a Venus, so have we to examine, perhaps, a thousand Snobs, before one is expressed upon paper.

Great City Snobs are the next in the hierarchy, and ought to be considered. But here is a difficulty. The great City Snob is commonly most difficult of access. Unless you are a capitalist, you cannot visit him in the recesses of his bank parlour in Lombard Street. Unless you are a sprig of nobility there is little hope of seeing him at home. In a great City Snob firm there is generally one partner whose name is down for charities, and who frequents Exeter Hall; you may catch a glimpse of another (a scientific City Snob) at my Lord N——'s *soirées*, or the lectures of the London Institution; of a third (a City Snob of taste) at picture-auctions, at private views of exhibitions, or at the Opera or the Philharmonic. But intimacy is impossible, in most cases, with this grave, pompous, and awful being.

A mere gentleman may hope to sit at almost anybody's table—to take his place at my Lord Duke's in the country—to dance a quadrille at Buckingham Palace itself—(beloved Lady Wilhelmina Wagglewiggle! do you recollect the sensation we made at the ball of our late adored Sovereign Queen Caroline, at Brandenburg House, Hammersmith?) but the City Snob's doors are, for the most part, closed to him; and hence all that one knows of this great class is mostly from hearsay.

In other countries of Europe, the Banking Snob is more expansive and communicative than with us, and receives all the world into his circle. For instance, everybody knows the princely hospitalities of the Scharlaschild family at Paris, Naples, Frankfort, &c. They entertain all the world, even the poor, at their *fêtes*. Prince Polonia, at Rome, and his brother, the Duke of Strachino, are also remarkable for their hospitalities. I like the spirit of the first-named nobleman. Titles not costing much in the Roman territory, he has had the head clerk of the banking-house made a Marquis, and his lordship will screw a *bajocco* out of you in exchange as dexterously as any commoner could do. It is a comfort to be able to gratify such grandees with a farthing or two; it makes the poorest man feel that he can do good. The Polonias have intermarried with the greatest and most ancient families of Rome, and you see their heraldic cognisance (a mushroom *or* on an azure field quartered) in a hundred places in the city with the arms of the Colonnas and Dorias.

Our City Snobs have the same mania for aristocratic marriages. I like to see such. I am of a savage and envious nature,—I like to see these two humbugs which, dividing, as they do, the social empire of this kingdom between them, hate each other naturally, making truce and uniting, for the sordid interests of either. I like to see an old aristocrat, swelling with pride of race, the descendant of illustrious Norman robbers, whose blood has been pure for centuries, and who looks down upon common Englishmen as a free-born American does on a nigger,—I like to see old Stiffneck obliged to bow down his head and swallow his infernal pride, and drink the cup of humiliation poured out by Pump and Aldgate's butler. "Pump and Aldgate," says he, "your grandfather was a bricklayer and his hod is still kept in the bank. Your pedigree begin in a workhouse; mine can be dated from all the Royal palaces of Europe. I came over with the Conqueror; I am own cousin to Charles Martel, Orlando Furioso, Philip Augustus, Peter the Cruel, and Frederick Barbarossa. I quarter the Royal Arms of Brentford in my coat. I despise you, but I want money; and I will sell you my beloved daughter, Blanche Stiffneck, for a hundred thousand pounds, to pay off my mortgages. Let your son marry her and she shall become Lady Blanche Pump and Aldgate."

Old Pump and Aldgate clutches at the bargain. And a comfortable thing it is to think that birth can be bought for money. So you learn to value it. Why should we, who don't possess it, set a higher store on it than those who do? Perhaps the best use of that book, the "Peerage," is to look down the list, and see how many have bought and sold birth,—how poor sprigs of nobility somehow sell themselves to rich City Snobs' daughters, how rich City Snobs purchase noble ladies—and so to admire the double baseness of the bargain.

Old Pump and Aldgate buys the article and pays the money. The sale of the girl's person is blessed by a Bishop at St. George's, Hanover Square, and next year you read, "At Roehampton, on Saturday, the Lady Blanche Pump, of a son and heir."

After this interesting event, some old acquaintance, who saw young Pump in the parlour at the bank in the City, said to him, familiarly, "How's your wife, Pump, my boy?"

Mr. Pump looked exceedingly puzzled and disgusted, and after a pause, said, "*Lady Blanche Pump* is pretty well, I thank you."

"*Oh, I thought she was your wife!*" said the familiar brute, Snooks, wishing him good-bye; and ten minutes after, the story was all over the Stock Exchange, where it is told, when young Pump appears, to this very day.

We can imagine the weary life this poor Pump, this martyr to Mammon, is compelled to undergo. Fancy the domestic enjoyments of a man who has a wife who scorns him; who cannot see his own friends in his own house; who having deserted the middle rank of life, is not yet admitted to the higher; but who is resigned to rebuffs and delay and humiliation, contented to think that his son will be more fortunate.

It used to be the custom of some very old-fashioned clubs in this city, when a gentleman asked for change for a guinea, always to bring it to him in *washed silver:* that which had passed immediately out of the hands of the vulgar being considered "as too coarse to soil a gentleman's fingers." So, when the City Snob's money has been washed during a generation or so; has been washed into estates, and woods, and castles, and town-mansions, it is allowed to pass current as real aristocratic coin. Old Pump sweeps a shop, runs of messages, becomes a confidential clerk and partner. Pump the Second becomes chief of the house, spins more and more money, marries his son to an Earl's daughter. Pump Tertius goes on with the bank; but his chief business in life is to become the father of Pump Quartus, who comes out a full-blown aristocrat, and takes his seat as Baron Pumpington, and his race rules hereditarily over this nation of Snobs.

2 G[eorge] R[obert] Gleig

FROM *Story of the Battle of Waterloo,* 1847[1]

CHAPTER V
STATE OF BRUSSELS AND THE NETHERLANDS IN THE EARLY SUMMER OF 1815.

. . . During the spring and early summer of 1815 Brussels was thronged with visitors. As fresh troops arrived, and they came in as fast as the Governments which combined to form an army for the Duke of Wellington could equip them, fresh families, some of them wealthy and of good repute, arrived in their train. Many officers

1. London: John Murray, pp. 35–38, 59–64, 250–253. On June 3, 1847, Thackeray asked Murray for a copy of Gleig's book (see Gordon N. Ray, ed., *The Letters and Private Papers of William Makepeace Thackeray,* Cambridge, Mass.: Harvard University Press, 1945, vol. II, p. 294), and in chapter 28 of *Vanity Fair* refers to it in a footnote.

brought their wives, and some their very children, along with them; under the impression that war, though inevitable, was distant; and that it would be aggressive on their parts, not defensive. The same belief seemed to actuate noblemen and gentlemen who had no official connexion with the army. The Duke and Duchess of Richmond, the Duke and Duchess of Buccleugh, Lady Caroline Lamb, and many other persons of distinction, hired houses or apartments according as one or the other might be had; and, throwing open their saloons, rendered the second capital of the Netherlands a scene of continual hospitality and pleasant bustle. Meanwhile Louis XVIII. had established his court at Ghent. Though far from crowded, it was in the highest degree respectable, as well for the rank as for the talents of its members; and being reserved and very formal, it agreed admirably with the character of a city which, in all its architectural arrangements, if not in the order of its society, may be considered as belonging rather to the middle ages than to our own times.

Thus the din and bustle of military preparations were strangely intermingled with the pomp of fallen royalty and the gaieties of fashionable life; for the intercourse between Ghent and Brussels was constant, and the condition of society in one of these cities made itself felt in the other, while both exercised a marked influence over the manners of the camp.

While the larger towns were thus enlivened by the presence of princes, courtiers, officers of rank, and their families, there was not a village or hamlet between Binche and the sea-coast but swarmed with armed men. Every château, farm-house, and labourer's cottage, afforded accommodation to a greater or smaller number of soldiers—whose horses, if they happened to belong to the cavalry or artillery, filled the stables and choked up the cow-sheds. On what terms the Belgians lived with the soldiers of their own nation, and with the levies which came from Hanover, Brunswick, and Nassau, no very accurate record has been preserved; but between them and the British troops the best understanding prevailed. Portions, indeed, of the Duke's army seem to have made themselves perfectly at home among the Flemings. It is recorded of the Highland regiments in particular, that so completely had they become domesticated with the people on whom they were billeted, that it was no unusual thing to find a kilted warrior rocking the cradle while the mother of the little Fleming, which slept under its mountain of feathers, was abroad on her household affairs. . . .

Brussels, from the beginning of April to the middle of June, was the scene of great and untiring festivity. Dinners, soirées, balls, theatrical amusements, concerts—in which Catalani, then in her prime, played a prominent part—caused the streets of that beautiful and picturesque city to echo with sounds of gladness; while the fields and meadows around were alive all day long with military parades and reviews. There was not a grove or wood within six miles of the place but afforded shelter, as the summer advanced, to frequent encampments. The troops lay, for the most part, in quarters, or were distributed through the villages as they arrived; but the artillery, with the waggons and tumbrils belonging to it, was parked—and picquets slept, and sentries kept guard beside them. Moreover, the whole line of road from the sea-coast to the capital was kept in a state of constant bustle. Travellers hurrying to the focus of gaiety passed, at every stage, corps of infantry or cavalry, or guns on the march—and were enchanted, as darkness set in, with the spectacle, to them as new as it was striking, of bivouacs by the wayside such as Teniers delighted to represent. Nor were they more delighted than astonished to find that among the gayest of the gay in all the festive scenes to which they were introduced, the Duke and the principal officers of his army took the lead. *They* did not know—what to his followers in the Peninsula was a matter already well understood—that the Duke of Wellington never felt more thoroughly unembarrassed than when cares under which other men would have sunk demanded his attention; and that the mind which was found able to arrange plans for the preservation of Europe, could, while it worked, enter with perfect freedom and even zest into every scheme of fun or enjoyment which might be proposed to it. Yet so it was. . . .

CHAPTER VIII
CONCENTRATION OF THE ENGLISH AND PRUSSIAN ARMIES AT QUATRE BRAS AND LIGNY.

. . . It has been stated already that the first tidings communicated to the Duke of the attack by the French on Gen. Zieten's outposts were carried to him about three o'clock in the afternoon of the 15th, by the Prince of Orange. His Royal Highness evidently did not know whether the attack was a real or a feigned one, for he described the enemy as having occupied and subsequently abandoned Binche; and the Duke had too much respect for the genius of Napoleon to risk, on such uncertain tidings, a movement that might prove to be a false one. He, therefore, contented himself by directing the various divisions of his army to assemble at their respective alarm-posts. But no sooner was Gen. Müffling introduced as the bearer of intelligence that could be relied upon, than he put the whole of the troops in motion. All the corps lying to the left of Nivelles were directed to march on that point; they were to proceed, too, independently, under cover of the fortresses which the Duke's provident care had thrown up; and they did so without sustaining the slightest molestation. Moreover, so quietly was the operation planned and carried into effect, now that all fears of attack by the Mons road were removed, that in Brussels itself only a few vague rumours broke in upon the sense of security which, up to that moment, had pervaded all circles. There was no interruption to the common business of life; people bought and sold, went and came, as heretofore; and in the evening the notes of a well-arranged military band proclaimed where the Duchess of Richmond held her revels. Little guessed the majority of the fair and the brave who met that night under her Grace's auspices, that before another sun should have risen and set, the dance of life would by many be ended.

The reserve of the Anglo-Belgian army, consisting of the 5th and 6th English divisions, under Sir Thomas Picton and Sir Lowry Cole, of the Brunswick division, under the Duke of Brunswick, and the contingent of the Duke of Nassau, under Gen. Kruse, occupied quarters in and around Brussels. One brigade, indeed, the 7th, composed of the 2nd battalions 25th, 37th, and 78th regiments, of the 13th Veteran battalion, a foreign battalion of the same description of force, and the 2nd garrison battalion—in all, 3233 men— had been sent to garrison the various fortresses from Mons to Ostend. But the remainder, with its artillery, amounting in all to nine batteries, filled the town, or occupied the villages and hamlets adjacent to it, Gen. Kruse's Nassau brigade stretching off along the road to Louvain. Among these troops were three Highland regiments, the 42nd, 79th, and 92nd, which we stop to particularize—not because they surpassed their comrades in gallantry, but simply on account of a circumstance, unimportant in itself, which seems to connect them more than other corps with the transactions of this memorable night. The Duchess of Richmond, of whose ball so much notice has been taken, was the sister of the late and last Duke of Gordon. The Duke was Colonel of the 92nd regiment, which, because it had been raised upon his estates, was called the Gordon Highlanders; and the Duchess of Richmond, being proud of her brother and of her country, made arrangements for exhibiting to her guests that night a perfect specimen of the Highland fling. With this view she caused a selection to be made from among the non-commissioned officers of the above-mentioned corps, not only desiring such to be chosen as were most skilled in the mysteries of that national dance, but making a particular request that all should be, in point of personal appearance, excellent specimens of their race. The wishes of the high-born dame were carefully attended to. Preceded by their pipers, a little body of Highlanders marched that night into her Grace's hall, of whom it is not too much to assert, that Scotland could furnish nothing superior to them; and the admirable nature of their performance in reel, strathspey, and sword-dance, is still remembered by the fast-diminishing few who survive to speak of it. They also, like the ladies who beheld them and admired, were little aware of the brief interval which should elapse ere the instruments which then stirred them in the game would cheer them to the battle. Indeed there were but few in that bright assembly who guessed that danger was near; and they who knew it best, including the Duke and the officers of his personal staff, were in their manner the most entirely unembarrassed.

It had been hinted to the Generals of division and brigade, that, one by one, as the night drew on, they should take their leave. Orders likewise had been issued to the troops in and around Brussels to hold themselves in readiness to march at a moment's notice; and the consequence was, that without exactly anticipating the actual course of events, men packed their knapsacks, and officers arranged their baggage, ere they lay down. By and bye

General after General withdrew from the Duchess's party—some on the plea that their commands were far away—others, because duty or private business called them. The Duke remained till a late hour, and returned thanks after supper for the health of the Prince Regent, which was proposed by the Prince of Orange. He soon afterwards retired, and the company broke up.

There might have been one hour's quiet in the streets of Brussels. The rattle of carriages was over. Light after light had been extinguished in chamber and in hall, and sleep seemed to have established his dominion over the city, when a buglecall, heard first in the Place d'Armes, on the summit of the Montagne du Parc, and taken up and echoed back through various quarters of the town, roused all classes of people in a moment. From every window in the place heads were protruded, and a thousand voices desired to be informed if anything was the matter; for though they put the idea from them, few had lain down that night altogether free from uneasiness; and now the bugle's warning note seemed to speak to their excited imaginations of an enemy at the gates. Anxious, therefore, and shrill were the voices which demanded to be informed of the cause of this interruption to their repose. But there was little need to answer them in words: the bugle-call was soon followed by the rolling of drums and the screaming of bagpipes. By and bye regiments were seen, by the dim light of the stars, to muster in park, square, street, and alley—horses neighed—guns rumbled over the causeways—drivers shouted—and over all was heard, from time to time, the short quick word of command, which soldiers best love to hear, and obey with the greatest promptitude. The reserve, in short, was getting under arms, each brigade at its appointed alarm-post; and by and bye, one after another, as they were ready, they marched off in the direction of the forest of Soignies.

Many and heart-rending were the partings which occurred at two o'clock in the morning of the 16th of June, 1815. As has already been stated, Brussels swarmed at that time with visitors not of the military order; and the wives and families of British soldiers of all ranks made up no inconsiderable part of its population. They heard the bugle sound, and saw their husbands, and fathers, and brothers hurry to their stations with feelings such as they had never experienced till then. They had heard often enough of mustering for the conflict, and read, when the carnage was over, long lists of killed and wounded; but on former occasions the scene had been at a distance from them, and even if individually interested in the result they had no opportunity of realizing its horrors. Now they were upon the spot, clinging to the necks of those dearest to them, and knowing only this—that a battle was impending. It was piteous to see and agonizing to listen to the wild tokens of their alarm. Many a woman, cast in a more delicate mould than for the most part gives her shape to the private-soldier's wife, refused to be parted from her husband or her brother, and marched with him. One in particular—a bride of two months—threw herself on horseback, and rode on the flank of the regiment; and yet she was a fair, fragile girl, who, under any other circumstances, would have shrunk with horror from such an undertaking. That was a night never to be forgotten by such as witnessed the strange occurrences which marked its progress. All thought, all feeling seemed, among the non-combatants, to merge and lose themselves in the single idea of a battle at hand; and where no nobler impulse urged to acts of self-sacrifice, terror appeared to deprive them of their senses. . . .

CHAPTER XXXI   . . . .
STATE OF FEELING AND CONDITION OF THINGS
IN THE REAR.

All this while the confusion which reigned in Brussels, Malines, Antwerp, and the other cities nearest to the seat of war sets the power of description at defiance. As one body of fugitives after another escaped from the battle, and the wounded and their attendants began to pour in, Brussels became the scene of a consternation which was far more wild, and, as it seemed, far more reasonable, than that of the 16th. Who could doubt that the day was lost when they saw whole regiments of Belgian cavalry riding as if for life, and passing clean through the town? Who could refuse credit to the assertions of men in British uniforms, when they protested that their comrades were either killed or taken, and that they alone had escaped the general carnage? Moreover, such as took courage, or had the means of going forth to reconnoitre in the direction of Waterloo, encountered at every step objects which forced upon them the conviction that all was lost. From an early hour in the morning till late at night every road, track, bridle-path, and avenue that led through the forest of Soignies was crowded. Waggons laden with baggage or stores, sumpter-horses, ammunition carts, and cars drawn by bullocks jammed and crushed one against another in the eagerness of their drivers to escape. Many broke down or upset, thus blocking up the way against the crowds that followed, while in innumerable instances the drivers cut the animals loose, and, leaving the baggage to shift for itself, rode off. Then came streams of wounded with their attendants, the latter more numerous than the former, far more numerous than was necessary, of whom many dropped by the way-side, while others, retaining just strength enough to get out of the throng, crept into the wood and there sat down, some of them never to rise again. But the most hideous crash of all was when the Cumberland Hussars, fine looking men and well mounted, came galloping down the great avenue and shouting that the French were at their heels. No mercy was shown by these cowards to the helpless and the prostrate who came in their way. They rode over such as lacked time or strength to escape from them, and cut at the drivers of waggons who either did not or could not draw aside out of their way. Nor let the humiliating truth be concealed. In the noble army which stopped that day the torrent of violence which had burst upon Europe were more faint hearts than on any previous occasion had followed England's unconquered general to the field, and these—officers as well as privates—swelled the tide which rolled on, noisy and agitated, towards the capital, and would not be stayed.

The condition of that town during the night between the 16th and 17th, and the eagerness with which both strangers and inhabitants hastened during the course of the latter day to escape from it, have elsewhere been described. As the evening of the 17th drew on, and more certain intelligence from the army arrived, the panic moderated itself a little. They who yet lingered in the place ventured to hope for the best, and withdrew to their chambers, fearful indeed and very anxious, but not despairing. The dawn of the 18th saw them all afoot, and in spite of the heavy rain which fell the Parc was soon crowded. For a while all was still. No sound of firing came over the forest, neither were other signs

of war afforded to them, save in the occasional arrival of small
bodies of wounded from the field of Quatre Bras, and the hurried
visits of the medical attendants to such as already occupied the
hospitals. But by and bye there was a change. The roar of cannon
burst upon them suddenly; they knew that the battle was begun,
and from that moment terror became so predominant in every
bosom that the idea of its probably ending in the triumph of the
allies seems not to have occurred to any one. It may not be amiss
if we borrow the language of one who, having fled on the 17th
to Antwerp, saw and conversed on the evening of the 18th with
other fugitives who had succeeded in escaping only in the course
of the latter day.

"A hundred Napoleons had been vainly offered for a pair of
horses but a few hours after we left Brussels; and the scene of
confusion which it presented on Saturday evening surpassed all
conception. The certainty of the defeat of the Prussians, of their
retreat, and of the retreat of the British army, prepared the people
to expect the worst. Aggravated reports of disaster and dismay
continually succeeded to each other; the despair and lamentations
of the Belgians; the anxiety of the English to learn the fate of
their friends; the dreadful spectacle of the waggon-loads of wounded
coming in, and the terrified fugitives flying out in momentary expectation of the arrival of the French; the streets, the roads, the
canals covered with boats, carriages, waggons, horses, and crowds
of unfortunate people flying from this scene of horror and danger,
formed altogether a combination of tumult, terror, and misery
which cannot be described. Numbers even of ladies, unable to
procure any means of conveyance, set off on foot and walked in
the dark beneath the pelting storm to Malines; and the distress
of the crowds who now filled Antwerp it is utterly impossible to
conceive."

Thus it was even before the tidings of the commencement of the
battle arrived; the sound of firing augmented the terror a hundred-
fold in the capital, and the feeling soon spread with the intelligence
in which it had originated to all the cities near. Malines was
abandoned, as Brussels had been, by all who could command the
means of further flight. Even in Antwerp itself many did not feel
themselves secure, and therefore escaped as they best could, some

to Breda, others to Ostend. Among those who remained there was but one subject of thought that could interest. "Every faculty of our minds was absorbed in one feeling, one interest; we seemed like bodies without souls. Our persons and our outward senses were, indeed, present in Antwerp, but our whole hearts and souls were with the army.

"In the course of our wanderings (for no one could keep within doors) we met many people whom we knew, and had much conversation with many whom we did not know. At this momentous crisis one feeling actuated every heart, one thought engaged every tongue, one common interest bound together every human being. All ranks were confounded, all distinctions levelled, all common forms neglected. Gentlemen and servants, lords and common soldiers, British and foreigners were all upon an equality, elbowing each other without ceremony, and addressing each other without apology. Ladies accosted men they had never before seen with eager questions unhesitatingly; strangers conversed together like friends, and English reserve seemed no longer to exist. From morning till night the great Place de Maire was completely filled with people, standing under umbrellas and eagerly watching for news of the battle. So closely packed was this anxious crowd, that when viewed from the hotel windows nothing could be seen but one compact mass of umbrellas. As the day advanced the consternation became greater. The number of terrified fugitives from Brussels, upon whose faces were marked the deepest anxiety and distress, and who thronged into the town on horseback and on foot, increased the general dismay; while long rows of carriages lined the streets, filled with people who could find no place of shelter."

It was not, however, among the timid and the peaceful only that excitement prevailed in rear of the army to an extent which was positively painful. Every soldier who heard the sound of battle and felt himself so situated as to be incapable of sharing its perils with his comrades, fretted and chafed like a steed which a strong curb restrains; and many such there were. Not to speak of the continental troops, among some of whom an excellent spirit prevailed, there were English regiments doing garrison duty in the different fortresses; and others, still more distressingly situated, who, having arrived at Ostend on the previous day, were now in full march towards the front. These toiled and strained in the endeavour to reach the scene of action, more than the strength of the less robust members of each corps could endure, and they left in consequence numerous stragglers at most of the villages through which they passed. But not even the stoutest of them reached the field in time. They had borne the brunt of the American war. They had returned weak in numbers, but unshaken in discipline, from that ill-conducted contest, and burned to wipe out the remembrance of the failure before New Orleans in the encounter of a foe worthy of their renown. But they did not succeed. Night closed upon them just as they passed through the village of Waterloo; and ere they could reach the scene of strife the last shot had been fired.

3 *Charlotte Brontë*

FROM A Letter to W. S. Williams, August 14, 1848[1]

The first duty of an author is, I conceive, a faithful allegiance to Truth and Nature; his second, such a conscientious study of Art as shall enable him to interpret eloquently and effectively the oracles delivered by those two great deities. The Bells[2] are very sincere in their worship of Truth, and they hope to apply themselves to the consideration of Art, so as to attain one day the power of speaking the language of conviction in the accents of persuasion; though they rather apprehend that whatever pains they take to modify and soften, an abrupt word or vehement tone will now and then occur to startle ears polite, whenever the subject shall chance to be such as moves their spirits within them.

I have already told you, I believe, that I regard Mr. Thackeray as the first of modern masters, and as the legitimate high priest of Truth; I study him accordingly with reverence. He, I see, keeps the

1. Reprinted from Clement K. Shorter, *Charlotte Brontë and Her Circle*, New York: Dodd, Mead, 1896, pp. 413–414.
2. Pseudonym for the Brontë sisters.

mermaid's tail below water, and only hints at the dead men's bones and noxious slime amidst which it wriggles; *but,* his hint is more vivid than other men's elaborate explanations, and never is his satire whetted to so keen an edge as when with quiet mocking irony he modestly recommends to the approbation of the public his own exemplary discretion and forbearance. The world begins to know Thackeray rather better than it did two years or even a year ago, but as yet it only half knows him. His mind seems to me a fabric as simple and unpretending as it is deep-founded and enduring—there is no meretricious ornament to attract or fix a superficial glance; his great distinction of the genuine is one that can only be fully appreciated with time. There is something, a sort of "still profound," revealed in the concluding part of "Vanity Fair" which the discernment of one generation will not suffice to fathom. A hundred years hence, if he only lives to do justice to himself, he will be better known than he is now. A hundred years hence, some thoughtful critic, standing and looking down on the deep waters, will see shining through them the pearl without price of a purely original mind—such a mind as the Bulwers, etc., his contemporaries have *not*. Not acquirements gained from study, but the thing that came into the world with him—his inherent genius: the thing that made him, I doubt not, different as a child from other children, that caused him, perhaps, peculiar griefs and struggles in life, and that now makes him as a writer unlike other writers. Excuse me for recurring to this theme, I do not wish to bore you.

4 [*Robert Bell*]

FROM "Vanity Fair," *Fraser's Magazine*, September, 1848[1]

Every periodical has its white days and ambrosial memories. We have ours, and the great indigo book before us reminds us of one

1. Vol. XXXVIII, pp. 320–322, 324–327, 332–333.

of them. *Fraser's Magazine* was the nursery-bed in which Michael Angelo Titmarsh[1] quickened. Out of the 'Yellow-Plush Correspondence' grew the Jeameses and the Perkinses, the Crawleys, Dobbins, and Sharps. Transplanted into more open ground, Michael Angelo expanded with increased luxuriance; more salt was laid at the roots of his humour, which fattened and flourished accordingly.

But he is the same Michael Angelo still. The same characteristics may be traced throughout; the same quality of subtle observation, penetrating rarely below the epidermis, but taking up all the small vessels with microscopic vision; the same grotesque exaggeration, with truth at the bottom; the same constitutional instinct for seizing on the ridiculous aspect of things, for turning the 'seamy side' of society outwards, and for exposing false pretensions and the genteel ambition of *parvenus*. The task to which the natural bent of Michael Angelo's genius leads him is a disagreeable one, and often distressingly painful; but he never seems to be aware of that fact. He dissects his victims with a smile; and performs the cruellest of operations on their self-love with a pleasantry which looks provokingly very like good-nature. The peculiarities and eccentricities of matter and manner with which he started are here as trenchant as ever. No author ever advanced so far in reputation without advancing further in novelty of enterprise. He has never gone out of himself from the beginning, or out of the subjects over which he possesses so complete a mastery. He has never broken new pastures, but only taken a wider and more thoughtful survey of the old. Yet such are the inexhaustible resources of the soil, and such the skill with which he works them, that we are never conscious of the slightest sense of monotony. All is fresh, versatile, and original.

The follies, vices and meannesses of society are the game hunted down by Mr. Thackeray. He keeps almost exclusively amongst the middle-classes; not the fashionable circles, but the people who ape them. The distinction is important, since it gives him a larger scope with less restriction. It is by this standard he must be tested. We must always keep in mind that his *Vanity Fair* is not the Vanity Fair of the upper ranks, where a certain equanimity of breeding absorbs all crudenesses and angularities of character, but the Vanity Fair

1. One of Thackeray's pen-names.

of the vulgar great; who have no breeding at all. Into this picture all sorts of portraits are freely admissible. There is nothing too base or too low to be huddled up in a corner of the canvas. The most improbable combinations, the most absurd contrasts, are not out of place in this miscellaneous *mélange*. The life that is here painted is not that of high comedy, but of satiric farce; and it is the business of the artist to shew you all its deformities, its cringing affectations, its paltry pride, its despicable finery, its lying, treachery, and penury of soul in the broadest light. Starting from this point, and with this clear understanding, we shall be the better able to comprehend and estimate the nature of the entertainment prepared for us.

The people who fill up the motley scenes of *Vanity Fair*, with two or three exceptions, are as vicious and odious as a clever condensation of the vilest qualities can make them. The women are especially detestable. Cunning, low pride, selfishness, envy, malice, and all uncharitableness, are scattered amongst them with impartial liberality. It does not enter into the design of *Vanity Fair* to qualify these bitter ingredients with a little sweetness now and then; to shew the close neighbourhood of the vices and the virtues as it lies on the map of the human heart, that mixture of good and evil, of weakness and strength, which, in infinitely varied proportions, constitutes the compound individual. The parts here are all patented for set functions, and no lapse into their opposites ever compromises the integrity of the *rôle*. There is some reason in this. The special section of society painted in this book resembles, in more particulars than mere debauchery of life, the conduct of a masquerade where a character is put on as a disguise, and played out with the best skill of the actor, until drunkenness or the death-bed betrays his secret. It is a lie from first to last; and no class of people in the world stand in such need of consistency as liars. We must not quarrel with Mr. Thackeray, then, for not giving Rebecca Sharp an occasional touch of remorse or tenderness, for not suffering paternal Osborne to undergo a twitch of misgiving, and for bringing together a company of fools and rogues who cannot muster up amongst them a single grain of sincerity or good-feeling. He knows his sitters well, and has drawn them to the life. *Vanity Fair* is a movable wardrobe, without hearts or understandings beneath. But there still remains the question—important to all Art that addresses itself to the laudable business of scourging the foibles and criminalities of mankind—Is there any den of vice so utterly depraved, any round of intercourse so utterly hollow and deceitful, that there is not some redeeming feature lurking somewhere, under rags or tinsel? This revolting reflex of society is literally true enough. But it does not shew us the whole truth. Are there not women, even in *Vanity Fair,* capable of nobler things than are here set down for them? Are they all schemers or *intrigantes,* world-wise, shuffling, perfidious, empty-headed? With the exception of poor Amelia, whose pale lustre shines out so gently in the midst of these harpies, there is scarcely a woman in *Vanity Fair* from whom we should not shrink in private life as from a contagion. And poor Amelia goes but a short way to purify the foul atmosphere. The author has given her a heart, but no understanding. If he has made her patient and good, loving, trusting, enduring, he has also made her a fool. Her meekness under suffering, her innocent faith in the evils which she lacks sagacity to penetrate, constantly excite our pity; but the helpless weakness of her character forces the sentiment to the verge of that feeling to which pity is said to be akin.

We touch upon this obvious defect in this remarkable work because it lies upon the surface, and must not only challenge general observation, but is not unlikely to draw down in some quarters indiscriminating censure. Over-good people will be apt to shudder at a story so full of petty vices and grovelling passions. They will be afraid to trust it in the hands of young ladies and gentlemen, lest the unredeemed wickedness of its pictures should corrupt their morals, and send them into the world shut up in a crust of selfishness and suspicion. But this sort of apprehension, natural enough in its way, is manifestly founded upon a false and superficial estimate of the tendency of the work. Beneath the sneers and cynicism of *Vanity Fair* there is an important moral, which the large population of novel-readers, who skim hastily over the pages of a book, are almost sure to miss, although they are the very people of all the world to whom practically it ought to be most useful. The vices painted in this book lie about us as 'thick as leaves in Vallambrosa.' We tread amongst them every day of our lives. Mr. Thackeray exposes them for the benefit of mankind.

He shews them plainly in all their hideousness. He warns us off the infected spots. It is not enough to say that he never makes them tempting or successful, although he exhibits the attractions by which they sometimes prosper, and even goes so far as to give us a glimpse of the uneasy triumphs they sometimes achieve (more repulsive than the most ignominious failures); but that he produces upon the whole such a view of the egotism, faithlessness, and low depravities of the society he depicts, as to force us to look into the depths of a loathsome truth which the best of us are willing enough to evade, if we can. No doubt we pant for a little clear air in this pestiferous region; we feel oppressed by the weight of these loaded vapours, this stifling malaria. But who objects to Hogarth's 'Gin Lane' that it discloses a scene which offends his taste and shocks his sensibility? The moralist often effects the largest amount of good when he assails the nerves and faltering judgment of people who want the courage to follow out his labours to their final issues.

The defect is not in the moral of *Vanity Fair,* but in the artistical management of the subject. More light and air would have rendered it more agreeable and more healthy. The author's genius takes him off too much in the direction of satire. He has so quick an instinct for the ridiculous, that he finds it out even in the most pathetic passages. He cannot call up a tear without dashing it off with a sarcasm. Yet his power of creating emotion is equal to his wit, although he seems to have less confidence in it, or to have an inferior relish for the use of it. Hence the book, with a great capacity for tenderer and graver things, excels in keen ridicule, and grotesque caricature, and irresistible exaggerations of all sorts of social follies and delinquencies. The universal traits and general truths which he scatters about are accidental, not elementary; his men and women are expressly denizens of Russell Square and Park Lane; he keeps close to his text throughout; his heads are portraits, not passions; he describes less the philosophy of human action than the contrasts and collisions of a conventional world; and he seizes upon the small details which make up the whole business of the kind of life he paints with a minuteness, precision, and certainty, and throws them out with a sharpness of outline and depth of colour rarely if ever equalled. The sustaining power with which these influential trivialities are carried through a narrative of extraordinary length, and the tact with which they are selected and accummulated, display a knowledge of the 'frets and stops' of familiar experience, and an artistical faculty which will present as salient attractions to future readers as to ourselves. Alas! there will always be a Vanity Fair in this world, of which this crafty book will be recognised as the faithful image.

The story of *Vanity Fair* is subservient to the characterisation. There is not much action; the actual incidents are neither numerous nor startling; and the narrative flows on with surprising quietness, considering the periodical form of publication for which it was written, and which ordinarily demands an 'effect' of some sort at each monthly fall of the curtain. But the quantity and variety of the characters atone for the comparative stillness of the scenes through which they are carried.

. . . Sir Pitt Crawley is one of Mr. Thackeray's exaggerations; but we must make allowances for butts in such cases. There must be here and there a target to shoot at when the humour begins to flag, and we are in want of an excitement to revive our animal spirits. Sir Pitt answers the purpose to a miracle. His gross vulgarities and clownish ignorance—so highly improbable in a person of his descent, position, and opportunities— make capital side-play when-ever he is wanted to relieve the business of the scene.

. . . Nothing can be better than this rich satire upon a tapestried ancestry. Nor is it amiss to shew us the meanness and vulgarity that are so often crouched behind these gilt shields and transmitted heraldries; but the ridicule which overshoots its mark, misses its aim as completely as if the arrow had fallen short. No doubt there are white crows. Exceptional characters may be found in all ranks, but the business of true art is to generalise the features of society, not to pick out monstrosities. Sir Pitt Crawley is a man *per se*. There may be such a man in the world; but we have never met him or heard of him. His gross breeding, illiterateness, and cunning, his sly humours and roystering tastes, make up altogether a personage who at once amuses and disgusts you. It is impossible not to be entertained by the sayings and doings of this ribald sharper, who cuts his joke, and drinks with a tenant, and sells him up the next day; but it is equally impossible to reconcile such a person with the position he occupies, the circumstances by which he is surrounded, the duties to which he is called, and which he must fulfil more or less. He would at least have learned to spell, and have acquired some of the common-places of the life in which he habitually moves.

In direct contrast with Sir Pitt Crawley, as a work of art, we have the Marquis of Steyne, the only specimen of the upper ranks of the aristocracy drawn into the bustle of *Vanity Fair*. Here Mr. Thackeray has put out his powers with the most brilliant success. This gorgeous profligate, this cold-blooded voluptuary, this sumptuous man of wonderful energy and acuteness of intellect, absolutely grand in his sublime contempt for all ordinances of God and man, is a portrait of extraordinary merit. Here the excesses thrown into the characterisation only heighten its truth; instead of exaggerating it into a fancy piece, they intensify the reality, and shew the human demon in a glare of broad light that reveals every articulation of his frame. The Marquis of Steyne is a great conception, greatly developed. We recognise in him the unmistakeable lineaments of unrestrained power, of a giant will, of passions nursed in impunity, of brutal desires and luxury of taste. Set beside Sir Pitt Crawley, we at once distinguish the difference between caricature and high art.

In making the experiment of writing 'a novel without a hero,' Mr. Thackeray seems to have been forced into the necessity of throwing increased responsibility upon his heroine. Rebecca Sharp acts in both capacities. She is both heroine and hero. Her talents are masculine—her tact belongs to the other sex, and enables her to make the most of them. Born in poverty, and deriving her earliest experiences from equivocal associations, she springs up suddenly into life, armed at all points, and prepared for all difficulties. The diplomatic *finesse* and sleepless vigilance with which she employs her wiles and lures, and turns all the connexions she forms, and all the circles of society she frequents, into tools to work her own ends, are profoundly depicted. The progress of this woman makes one's honest flesh creep; but its truthfulness, to the slightest touches of gesture and innuendo, is incontestable. Her nature, utterly depraved at the core, is sentinelled by a presence of mind which never deserts her. She has the fascination and the poison of the snake. She is one of those persons in whom intuitive sagacity supplies the place of observation and experience; she adapts herself with facility to all circumstances, and shifts to the occasion as imperceptibly as the chameleon changes colour; she hoaxes, wheedles, menaces, always in the right places, always with the right people, and with never-failing success; she is equally triumphant in the meanest trick as in the most appalling crime; and carries herself through all with such ease and dexterity, as to provoke our admiration in spite of the abhorrence she inspires. A woman so odious, from whatever point of view we regard her, would be intolerable were it not for the skill with which her character is painted. It is this skill—surprising and highly-finished in its kind—that surrounds this consummate actress and heartless trickster with unflagging interest.

... If Mr. Thackeray had dealt in the vulgar way with this accomplished demirep, he would have cast her for some crushing punishment, instead of exhibiting her, after all her transgressions, presiding at a fashionable bazaar. But he has struck out a more impressive moral. It shews us a new shape of the world's deceptions—the life of guiltiness taking its last shelter under the garb of virtue and devotion. How much of this sort of iniquity is enacted about us every day! And how often are we deceived and cheated by the impudent lie! It is more than probable that if this clever, fascinating woman— who closely resembles Madame Laffarge, denuded of her spirituality —had been sentenced to a moral Botany Bay, she might have carried away with her a little morbid sympathy; but the author has effectually and wisely left her in a position which deepens the aversion she has all along inspired. Rebecca, in her booth at Vanity Fair, is an object from which we instinctively shrink with a sensation of repugnance, which we should certainly not have felt had she been consigned to beggary on the highway.

The history of Rebecca is thrown into strong contrast with that of Amelia Osborne, the gentlest of human beings. The two histories run side by side, and maintain opposition lines of interest with excellent effect. There is nothing new in the story of Amelia, nor in her character; but it is charmingly told, and appeals very piteously to one's sympathies from amidst the associations by which she is surrounded. ...

Looking back upon this story, we are struck more than ever by the simplicity of its conduct. It is not constructed upon a legitimate principle, or upon any principle at all. It is a novel without a plan, as without a hero. There are two distinct narratives running through it, which not only never interfere with each other, but frequently help each other on. Shoals of characters are drafted through its pages, but they never crowd or jostle each other, or produce the slightest confusion of action or obscurity of incident. The whole business of the fiction moves on before us, with as little reference to a beginning, middle, or end, as the progress of one's own life. The established usages of novels are entirely set aside. Instead of winding up with the merry marriage bells, as if all human interest in the personages of a story terminated in Doctors' Commons, the real interest does not fairly begin until the marriage bells have done their office. Nor is this interest kept up by fictitious means. There are no extraneous sources opened as we go along—no episodes to relieve the route—no superfluous characters to strew it with variety. The interest is progressive and complete to the end.

There is another merit in this story. It is free from over-refinement or elaboration. All is direct, palpable, and close. The touches exhibit the decisive hand of a true artist. There is never any necessity to repeat them, or to go back to clear up knots or mysteries in the narrative: there is nothing to clear up; it is all onward and straight-forward.

'A great book,' says the proverb, 'is a great evil;' and although we should be unwilling to lose a page of *Vanity Fair*, we may advise the author to keep within narrower limits in future. It is a gigantic undertaking to get through this massive volume, and in this age the consumption of time is a consideration. Inordinate length, however ably maintained, is an obstruction to enjoyment; and an author may be said to stand in his own light who produces a book that makes an unreasonable demand on the leisure of his readers. The attraction must be of a remarkable kind which can hold us in suspense over so huge an octavo; yet, large as this octavo is, we put it down with reluctance. The originality of the treatment, the freshness and fluency of the style, and the absence of peculiarities in the diction or terms of expression, inspire it with the charm of perpetual variety. No writer was ever less of a mannerist, and few writers have displayed within the compass of a single story more fertility of invention, or a more accurate knowledge of life.

5 William Makepeace Thackeray

A Letter to Robert Bell, September 3, 1848[1]

Although I have made a rule to myself never to thank critics yet I like to break it continually, and especially in the present instance for what I hope is the excellent article in Fraser.[2] It seems to me very just in most points as regards the author: some he questions as usual—If I had put in more fresh air as you call it my object would have been defeated—It is to indicate, in cheerful terms, that we are for the most part an abominably foolish and selfish people "desperately wicked" and all eager after vanities. Everybody is you see in that book,—for instance if I had made Amelia a higher order of woman there would have been no vanity in Dobbins falling in love with her, whereas the impression at present is that he is a fool for his pains that he has married a silly little thing and in fact has found out his error rather a sweet and tender one however, *quia multum amavit* I want to leave everybody dissatisfied and unhappy at the end of the story—we ought all to be with our own and all other stories. Good God dont I see (in that may-be cracked and warped looking glass in which I am always looking) my own weaknesses wickednesses lusts follies shortcomings? in company let us hope with better qualities about which we will pretermit discourse. We must lift up our voices about these and howl to a congregation of fools: so much at least has been my endeavour. You have all of you taken my misanthropy to task—I wish I could myself: but take the world by a certain standard (you know what I mean) and who dares talk of having any virtue at all? For instance Forster says After a scene with Blifil, the air is cleared by a laugh of Tom Jones—Why Tom Jones in my holding is as big a rogue as Blifil. Before God he is—I mean the man is selfish according to his nature as Blifil according to his. In fact I've a strong impression that we are most of us not fit for—never mind.

1. Reprinted, by permission of the publishers, from Gordon N. Ray, ed., *The Letters and Private Papers of William Makepeace Thackeray*, Cambridge, Mass.: Harvard University Press, 1945, vol. II, pp. 423–425. Copyright, 1945, by Hester Thackeray Ritchie Fuller and the President and Fellows of Harvard College.

2. See extracts on pp. 231–239 above.

Pathos I hold should be very occasional indeed in humourous works and indicated rather than expressed or expressed very rarely. In the passage where Amelia is represented as trying to separate herself from the boy—She goes upstairs and leaves him with his aunt 'as that poor Lady Jane Grey tried the axe that was to separate her slender life' I say that is a fine image whoever wrote it (& I came on it quite by surprize in a review the other day) that is greatly pathetic I think: it leaves you to make your own sad pictures—We shouldn't do much more than that I think in comic books—In a story written in the pathetic key it would be different & then the comedy perhaps should be occasional. Some day—but a truce to egotistical twaddle. It seems to me such a time ago that V F was written that one may talk of it as of some body elses performance. My dear Bell I am very thankful for your friendliness & pleased to have your good opinion.

6 John Cordy Jeaffreson

FROM *Novels and Novelists, From Elizabeth to Victoria*, 1858[1]

Thackeray's one single aim in literature has been to speak to men in plain language on questions of vital interest to society; not to create a lovely picture such as we might wish the world to resemble, but to give a chart of this actual life, with all its loveliness and all its terrors—this life wherein the sun sets daily, the summer is followed by the winter, youth leads on to old age, and birth is a step to decay. The men and women he puts before us are none of them "ideals," they are the veritable beings who adorn or dishonour our nature. He is not insensible to the charms of those conceptions of uniform, unfaltering excellence in which Dickens delights; but he says "it is not for me to *imagine,* I am to *speak of men as I find.*" So he gives us good women; but the best of them are jealous where their affections are concerned, and when tempted, will peep through key-holes

1. London: Hurst and Blackett, vol. II, pp. 276–281.

or tell fibs, and repent of their meanness as men never repent. He describes Amelia cherishing for long years the memory of a man whose selfish vain heart never deserved one pulse of her affection. The patient tenderness of the mother's love is contrasted with the selfishness of the child on whom it is lavished. His good men are not exempt from the personal disadvantages of awkward feet and clumsy features. If he is any where open to the charge of exaggerating certain features of his characters, and unwilling to give due prominence to others, it is when he is depicting the very bad. Barry Lindon, Esq. (the hero of the excellent "Memoirs of Barry Lindon, Esq.," a copy of Defoe, Fielding, and Smollett, far surpassing the originals), Bob Stubbs (that perfect specimen of the utterly mean in the "Fatal Boots") Becky Sharp, and Barnes Newcome may by some be instanced as caricatures of extreme villains, without any trace of redeeming virtue. But do we not in the world find that the vicious are much more consistent than the virtuous? That while there are none so good that they never sin, there are some so bad that they never by any accident fall for one single instant into the ways of holiness? This may be a sad view of life, but life has its sad features, which we do well to contemplate; it may be satire, but it is truth. What is satire save unpleasant truth? It is by his veracity that the satirist of all men stands.

When "Vanity Fair" had been generally read, the almost universal sentence at first was that the author had a painfully low estimate of human nature. Many who gave this judgment were at a loss when they were asked for their reasons for it. It was true that Thackeray had declared the world of fashion to be very vicious, that its men were too often selfish and sensual, its women too frequently frivolous and heartless; but in this he was not peculiar, for the dissipations and graceful godlessness of the upper ranks of society had long been the favourite subjects for novel readers and writers. Rawdon Crawleys, Lord Steynes, Becky Sharps, and contemptible dandified George Osbornes abound in the fictions of Bulwer, Disraeli, Trollope, and Gore, less forcibly drawn indeed, but intended by their creators to be full as wicked. Why then was censure poured on Thackeray for giving them as types of the society in which they moved, and which to some extent had created them? Suppose the representation to be unjust and libellous on humanity; still, why was the reproof bestowed on Thackeray alone, while his predecessors and companions in guilt were allowed to go scot free? The fact was society was uneasy, irritated, in a passion, and wanted to wreak its fury on the cause of its discomfort; and society never loses its temper unless a great moral purpose is to be served by it, and, as we all know, its most cruel acts of vengeance are only the fit expressions of a righteous indignation. The ladies were mortified by not finding at least one perfectly *faultless* woman in "the fair;" just as they would feel displeasure at not receiving any other compliment to which long custom has given them a certain vague right! So they said "Ah; poor man, he does not believe in the existence of good women!" The members of fashionable society generally were hurt—not by Mr. Thackeray's telling them they were miserable sinners (for they like to be reminded of that fact, and have from time immemorial paid people to repeat the gratifying intelligence)—but what they could not bear was to be told that they were essentially vulgar, disreputable, snobbish sinners. How natural was it for them to revile the plain-spoken prophet, to call him a sour embittered cynic, unable to admire the great, unable to pity the weak. Here was the real cause of offence. The satirist was no respecter of persons; the tyranny and infamy of a nobleman were described as truthfully as the vulgar ignorance of a waiting-man or lodging-house-keeper. St. James's and St. Giles's were alike vulgar; oftentimes the admired members of the most exclusive clubs were men to whom, starred and gartered though they might be, no true gentleman would give the hand of friendship. Society will bear almost any insult from a man of talent except an attack on its good taste; but he who presumes to question its delicacy and refinement must be prepared for the consequences. Miserable cynic, was its retort—"What! we yellow!—your eye is jaundiced; you have given us a picture, not of humanity, but of your own heart—no wonder that selfishness is in the front, and scorn in the back-ground!" And yet the book of this hateful, cold, callous man abounded with pathetic appeals for the desolate and distressed, like the following: "Oh! be humble, my brother, in your prosperity! Be gentle with those who are less lucky, if not more deserving. Think! what right have you to be scornful, whose virtue is a deficiency of temptation, whose success may be a chance, whose rank may be an ancestor's accident, whose prosperity is very likely a satire?"

But in art, Truth will prevail. Men read those much-abused yellow pamphlets that came out month after month; and strong men, men not given to emotion, least of all to religious excitement, laid them down with tearful eyes and full hearts; and they were not a few who prayed earnestly to the Almighty for mercy and help, and rose from their knees with a determination to be men of charity. Hitherto the novelists had made them exult in the splendid infamy and brilliant sin of the world. "Pelham" and "Henrietta Temple," had thrown such a halo of glory around debt and seductions and sinful desire, that few could read them without being ambitious of hell. It was Thackeray who tore from social depravity her twofold robe, one side of rags and one of spangled purple, and displayed her hateful proportions. So much for the demoralizing tendency of this writer! More need not be said of it, for the charge has long since been withdrawn by those who were foolish enough to advance it.

It was interesting to watch society as it slowly read its recantation of its first opinion of Thackeray, and magnanimously allowed that he was entitled to a high place in public esteem. "He was a gentleman 'by birth,'" was observed on all sides, and was remarked in newspapers by journalists who would have fired up if any one suggested that the *employés* of the press were not usually gentlemen. Then the fortune he inherited on coming of age was multiplied three and four times. "Had Mr. Thackeray not lost his noble patrimony," wrote Jeames, in one of the leading metropolitan papers, "still would there have been a mansion in the West End belonging to him, still, as now, would lines of coronetted carriages have crowded around his portals on nights of reception; but only as a distinguished leader of the world of fashion would he have been known—not as the greatest of living novelists, the poet, and the philosopher." We quote from memory, but most of our readers must have remembered passages as fulsome and ridiculous as the above in our public journals. Those who did not make their apologies for old neglect and abuse to the satirist, on the ground of not knowing that he was a gentleman "by birth," justified their former severity and subsequent softening, by avowing that the author had altered very much, that "Pendennis" and "Esmond" gave indications of benevolence and true humanity not to be found in "Vanity Fair," and that the creator of Colonel Newcome, was not the same man as he who placed old Sir Pitt Crawley and Miss Horrocks upon canvass; possibly the sun of prosperity had called into play a geniality of temper, which the cold chill of neglect and comparative penury had for a time repressed.

But it is needless to enumerate all the many amusing ways in which the world ate its words, and preserved its self-complacency. The recantation was made, and Mr. Thackeray is the favourite author of the day in the world of fashion. He is triumphant. There can be no doubt that just now he is regarded in some classes as having surpassed his great contemporary Charles Dickens. In our own minds also there is no doubt that ere long those admirers will reverse their decision, and will again return to their old allegiance to "Boz." We do not like to compare two such men as Thackeray and Dickens; but the remarks we have already made necessitate our doing so. For the genius of Charles Dickens, so varied, of such boundless resource, and so rich in almost every great poetic quality, we have a far higher esteem than we have for Thackeray's; as artists they are totally opposed, save that a warm heart animates every line they pen; the one has never drawn a character that is not an ideal; the other cautiously avoids crossing the limits of the actual. If Dickens had a bad heart, and his moral aim as a writer was just the reverse of what it is, his humour and imaginative powers would still secure him the high rank he holds in our literature. But Thackeray's success is almost solely owing to his moral influence. Much as we respect his intellectual powers, we have a far higher admiration of his heart—that noble courageous generosity for which language has no word. He is emphatically the true gentleman of our generation, who has appealed to our best and most chivalric sympathies, and raising us from the slough and pollution of the Regency has made us once more "a nation of gentlemen."

Mr. Thackeray has acquired fame, and is generally understood to have secured wealth with it. We wish that of the life he has yet before him between this and the grave, he would devote a portion of the leisure he does not require for money-taking, to writing his biography, as faithfully and philosophically as he has written his novels. The world will want it when he is gone. It will be instructive to watch the world dealing with his reputation when he is no longer one of it. We believe that his memory standing up in the past, in colossal calm, will be the object of more love, than the applauding world will ever give him during his life.

Charles Dickens
Bleak House
1853

1

An Editorial, *The Times,* March 28, 1851[1]

By way of recreation last night, after the fatigues of the anti-Papal debate, Lord John Russell broke the ground for his promised reform of the Chancery. The transition was much the same as that of the African hunter who, after shooting down a herd of wild elephants, takes up his gun to return the civilities his encampment has received from a neighbouring household of lions. Neither Pope nor Chancery, indeed, is very small game. In point of antiquity, in their apparently indestructible basis, in their thick incrustation of abuses, in the obstinacy with which they have defied all reform, and in the perplexities with which they are sure to embarrass the assailant, they are by no means dissimilar. To the common apprehension of Englishmen the Court of Chancery is a name of terror, a devouring gulf, a den whence no footsteps return. Ask why such a family was

1. P. 4.

ruined, why the representatives of a wealthy man are wanderers over
the face of the earth, why the butlers, and housekeepers, and gar-
deners of the kindest master in the world, in spite of ample legacies
in his will, are rotting on parish pay, why the best house in the
street is falling to decay, its windows all broken, and its very doors
disappearing, why such a one drowned himself, and another is dis-
graced,—you are just as likely as not to hear that a Chancery suit
is at the bottom of it. There is no word so terrible to an Englishman
as this. An honest, industrious man, accustomed to hard thrift and
slow accumulation, building his fortune course after course, and indulging in visions of futurity to compensate for much present self-
denial, will turn pale and sick at heart at the bare mention of
Chancery. A suit in that court is endless, bottomless, and insatiable.
Common notions of justice and law becomes childish follies before
the inscrutable mystery of a Chancery suit. Such is the ancient
court which our Premier ventures to threaten with innovation—a
court which in the estimation of most Englishmen, and with a view
to a large proportion of its actual results, is an organized iniquity,
an incurable evil, an inveterate wrong.

Of course the object is so to expedite proceedings in Chancery
that it shall no longer be what it is now—a mere bloodless arena
for mutual destruction. In its present form it belongs to a class
that usually disappears before the march of civilization, and only
re-appears when men are relapsing into barbarism. We once had
trial by wager, when a man who sought his just right might obtain
the satisfaction of being knocked on the head in due form of law.
We once had ordeals. In Caffre-land the suitors are placed in a
circle, surrounded by their tribes, and throw their assagais in turn
at one another. In the back States of America, when two gentlemen
have "a difficulty," they are placed a mile apart in a wood with
their rifles and bowie knives, and, at a given signal, creep within
range of one another, like two armies beating in one another's
pickets. In England, when revenge has overcome all other consid-
erations, a man determines to drag his enemy into Chancery, as he
would over a precipice, where both will perish. The instinct of self-
preservation must be very weak when a man spontaneously enters
those portals where hope is left behind, and where the only consolation of ruin is its certain community. A Chancery suit either starves

the education and spirit of youth, or consumes the energies of manhood, or makes a clean wreck of old age. It is the very grave of in-
heritances. When a peaceful man, therefore, is dragged into this
charnel-house of fortunes, this golgotha of estates, he feels simply
as if he were challenged to single combat. Now, spontaneous ruin
is almost as criminal as spontaneous death, and a man, in these
days, who brings his neighbour into Chancery does, in fact, propose to him a trial of spirit and of purse, which if duly persisted in
must infallibly ruin both parties, unless the property in contest be
very large indeed, the antagonists very good lives, and the question
more than usually determinable. As for a thousand pounds, it is but
as the dew of the morning under the burning sun of a Chancery suit.
We are afraid to say how high lawyers put the sum which is likely
to leave a surplus for the successful suitor. The evils of this system,
the iron hooks of this tremendous machine are the multiplicity of its
forms, the intricacy of its proceedings, the opportunities of vexatious
and malicious delay, the utter inadequacy of the staff, and the vast
number of incompatible duties imposed on the chief judge of the
court, who is made to combine, and of course partially to neglect,
duties that would find work for at least three officers, if not more, in
the place of the present Lord Chancellor.

The measure proposed by Lord John Russell for improving
the judicial staff in this court is one of many in which it is easy to
see some merit, and not difficult to detect great objections. The only
duty of which he would relieve the Lord Chancellor is the ecclesiastical patronage. This he proposes to vest in the office of which he is
himself just now the illustrious occupant. To ordinary minds it is
somewhat startling to hear one officer of the Crown proposing to take
away from another officer the best part of his patronage; but as the
ecclesiastical patronage of the Crown, in whatever hands it be vested,
is always administered according to the politics of the Prime Minister, it may as well be vested in him at once as in a lawyer of his
own appointment. There are, indeed, theories showing the appropri-
ateness of giving this patronage to the man whose official duties
put him in direct communication with the Lord-Lieutenants and the
magistracy, and whose legal practice must give him a wide acquaintance with the property and aristocracy of the country; but in matter
of fact we believe that Crown livings and dignities have now for a

long time been bestowed exactly as they would have been had they been vested in the Prime Minister—that is, with the same exclusive regard to the political opinions of the clergymen preferred, or of their Parliamentary friends. Though this is the only responsibility of which Lord John proposes to relieve the Lord Chancellor, the only permanent assistance he gives him is that of the Master of the Rolls, whom he proposes to associate with him, giving them the power to call in, whenever they please, one of the judges in the courts of law; any two of these to be competent to hear causes. In this arrangement, as far as we can see, the Master of the Rolls would become a sort of perpetual Lord Chancellor, not changing with the Ministry, and much less liable to interruptions and absence than the Lord Chancellor so called. As was observed last night, the Master of the Rolls would be very much missed from his own court. Any approach to a permanent judge in the Court of Chancery is so much to be desired that we willingly abstain at present from criticising a proposal which it certainly takes some time to follow through all its bearings.

2 [Charles Dickens]

FROM "On Duty with Inspector Field," *Household Words*, June 14, 1851[1]

How goes the night? Saint Giles's clock is striking nine. The weather is dull and wet, and the long lines of street-lamps are blurred, as if we saw them through tears. A damp wind blows, and rakes the pieman's fire out, when he opens the door of his little furnace, carrying away an eddy of sparks.

Saint Giles's clock strikes nine. We are punctual. Where is Inspector Field? Assistant Commissioner of Police is already here, enwrapped in oil-skin cloak, and standing in the shadow of Saint Giles's steeple. Detective Serjeant, weary of speaking French all day

1. American ed., vol. III, pp. 265–267.

to foreigners unpacking at the Great Exhibition, is already here. Where is Inspector Field?

Inspector Field is, to-night, the guardian genius of the British Museum. He is bringing his shrewd eye to bear on every corner of its solitary galleries, before he reports "all right." Suspicious of the Elgin marbles, and not to be done by cat-faced Egyptian giants, with their hands upon their knees, Inspector Field, sagacious, vigilant, lamp in hand, throwing monstrous shadows on the walls and ceilings, passes through the spacious rooms. If a mummy trembled in an atom of its dusty covering, Inspector Field would say, "Come out of that, Tom Green. I know you!" If the smallest "Gonoph" about town were crouching at the bottom of a classic bath, Inspector Field would nose him with a finer scent than the ogre's, when adventurous Jack lay trembling in his kitchen copper. But all is quiet, and Inspector Field goes warily on, making little outward show of attending to anything in particular, just recognising the Icthyosaurus as a familiar acquaintance, and wondering, perhaps, how the detectives did it in the days before the Flood.

Will Inspector Field be long about this work? He may be half-an-hour longer. He sends his compliments by Police Constable, and proposes that we meet at Saint Giles's Station House, across the road. Good. It were as well to stand by the fire, there, as in the shadow of Saint Giles's steeple.

Anything doing here to-night? Not much. We are very quiet. A lost boy, extremely calm and small, sitting by the fire, whom we now confide to a constable to take home, for the child says that if you show him Newgate Street, he can show you where he lives—a raving drunken woman in the cells, who has screeched her voice away, and has hardly power enough left to declare, even with the passionate help of her feet and arms, that she is the daughter of a British officer, and, strike her blind and dead, but she'll write a letter to the Queen! but who is soothed with a drink of water—in another cell, a quiet woman with a child at her breast, for begging—in another, her husband in a smock-frock, with a basket of watercresses —in another, a pickpocket—in another, a meek tremulous old pauper man who has been out for a holiday, "and has took but a little drop, but it has overcome him arter so many months in the house"—and that's all, as yet. Presently, a sensation at the Station House door. Mr. Field, gentlemen!

Inspector Field comes in, wiping his forehead, for he is of a burly figure, and has come fast from the ores and metals of the deep mines of the earth, and from the Parrot Gods of the South Sea Islands, and from the birds and beetles of the tropics, and from the Arts of Greece and Rome, and from the Sculptures of Nineveh, and from the traces of an elder world, when these were not. Is Rogers ready? Rogers is ready, strapped and greatcoated, with a flaming eye in the middle of his waist, like a deformed Cyclops. Lead on, Rogers, to Rats' Castle!

How many people may there be in London, who, if we had brought them deviously and blindfold, to this street, fifty paces from the Station House, and within call of Saint Giles's church, would know it for a not remote part of the city in which their lives are passed? How many, who amidst this compound of sickening smells, these heaps of filth, these tumbling houses, with all their vile contents, animate and inanimate, slimily overflowing into the black road, would believe that they breath *this* air? How much Red Tape may there be, that could look round on the faces which now hem us in—for our appearance here has caused a rush from all points to a common centre—the lowering foreheads, the sallow cheeks, the brutal eyes, the matted hair, the infected, vermin-haunted heaps of rags—and say "I have thought of this. I have not dismissed the thing. I have neither blustered it away, nor frozen it away, nor tied it up and put it away, nor smoothly said pooh, pooh! to it, when it has been shown to me"?

This is not what Rogers wants to know, however. What Rogers wants to know, is, whether you *will* clear the way here, some of you, or whether you won't; because if you don't do it right on end, he'll lock you up! What! *You* are there, are you, Bob Miles? You haven't had enough of it yet, haven't you? You want three months more, do you? Come away from that gentleman! What are you creeping round there for?

"What am I a doing, thinn, Mr. Rogers?" says Bob Miles, appearing, villainous, at the end of a lane of light, made by the lantern.

"I'll let you know pretty quick, if you don't hook it. WILL you hook it?"

A sycophantic murmur rises from the crowd. "Hook it, Bob, when Mr. Rogers and Mr. Field tells you! Why don't you hook it, when you are told to?"

The most importunate of the voices strikes familiarly on Mr. Rogers's ear. He suddenly turns his lantern on the owner.

"What! *You* are there, are you, Mister Click? You hook it too—come?"

"What for?" says Mr. Click, discomfited.

"You hook it, will you!" says Mr. Rogers with stern emphasis.

Both Click and Miles *do* "hook it," without another word, or, in plainer English, sneak away.

"Close up there, my men!" says Inspector Field to two constables on duty who have followed. "Keep together gentlemen; we are going down here. Heads?"

Saint Giles's church strikes half-past ten. We stoop low, and creep down a precipitous flight of steps into a dark close cellar. There is a fire. There is a long deal table. There are benches. The cellar is full of company, chiefly very young men in various conditions of dirt and raggedness. Some are eating supper. There are no girls or women present. Welcome to Rats' Castle, gentlemen, and to this company of noted thieves!

"Well, my lads! How are you, my lads! What have you been doing to-day? Here's some company come to see you, my lads! *There's* a plate of beefsteak, Sir, for the supper of a fine young man! And there's a mouth for a steak, Sir! Why, I should be too proud of such a mouth as that, if I had it myself! Stand up and show it, Sir! Take off your cap. There's a fine young man for a nice little party, Sir! An't he?"

Inspector Field is the bustling speaker. Inspector Field's eye is the roving eye that searches every corner of the cellar as he talks. Inspector Field's hand is the well-known hand that has collared half the people here, and motioned their brothers, sisters, fathers, mothers, male and female friends, inexorably, to New South Wales. Yet Inspector Field stands in this den, the Sultan of the place. Every thief here, cowers before him, like a schoolboy before his schoolmaster. All watch him, all answer when addressed, all laugh at his jokes, all seek to propitiate him. This cellar-company alone—to say nothing of the crowd surrounding the entrance from the street above, and making the steps shine with eyes—is strong enough to murder us all, and willing enough to do it; but, let Inspector Field have a mind to pick out one thief here, and take him; let him produce that ghostly truncheon from his pocket, and say, with his business-air, "My lad, I want you!" and all Rats' Castle shall be stricken with paralysis, and not a finger move against him, as he fits the handcuffs on! . . .

Saint Giles's church clock, striking eleven, hums through our hand from the dilapidated door of a dark outhouse as we open it, and are stricken back by the pestilent breath that issues from within. Rogers, to the front with the light, and let us look!

Ten, twenty, thirty—who can count them! Men, women, children, for the most part naked, heaped upon the floor like maggots in a cheese! Ho! In that dark corner yonder! Does any body lie there? Me Sir, Irish me, a widder with six children. And yonder? Me Sir, Irish me, with me wife and eight poor babes. And to the left there? Me Sir, Irish me, along with two more Irish boys as is me friends. And to the right there? Me Sir and the Murphy fam'ly, numbering five blessed souls. And what's this, coiling, now, about my foot? Another Irish me, pitifully in want of shaving, whom I have awakened from sleep—and across my other foot lies his wife—and by the shoes of Inspector Field lie their three eldest—and their three youngest are at present squeezed between the open door and the wall. And why is there no one on that little mat before the sullen fire? Because O'Donovan, with wife and daughter, is not come in yet from selling Lucifers! Nor on the bit of sacking in the nearest corner? Bad luck! Because that Irish family is late to-night, a-cadging in the streets!

They are all awake now, the children excepted, and most of them sit up, to stare. Wheresoever Mr. Rogers turns the flaming eye, there is a spectral figure rising, unshrouded, from a grave of rags. Who is the landlord here?—I am, Mr. Field, says a bundle of ribs and parchment against the wall, scratching itself.—Will you spend this money fairly, in the morning, to buy coffee for 'em all?—Yes Sir, I will!—O he'll do it Sir, he'll do it fair. He's honest; cry the spectres. And with thanks and Good Night sink into their graves again.

Thus, we make our New Oxford Streets, and our other new streets, never heeding, never asking where the wretches whom we clear out, crowd. With such scenes at our doors, with all the plagues of Egypt tied up with bits of cobweb in kennels so near our homes, we timorously make our Nuisance Bills and Boards of Health, nonentities, and think to keep away the Wolves of Crime and Filth, by our electioneering ducking to little vestrymen, and our gentlemanly handling of Red Tape!

3 Charles Dickens

FROM "Memoranda and Number Plans for *Bleak House*"[1]

[Leaf XIII, left]
Krook's cat   *Yes*.[2]
The Smallweeds in connexion with the house in the Court.
Sir Leicester Dedlock?—*And the cousins?   Yes*   *Yes*
Lady Dedlock?   *Yes*

Yes.*
Finds that Mr Tulkinghorn has discovered her secret?
Their interview at night, at Chesney Wold?   *Yes**
Wind up with Esther's Narrative?

No—Frenchwoman.   *Lay
that ground.*

[Leaf XIII, right]
(*Bleak House*————*No. XIII.*)

1. Reprinted, by permission of the editors, *Renaissance and Modern Studies,* University of Nottingham, and of the Director and Secretary of the Victoria and Albert Museum, from H. P. Sucksmith, "Dickens at Work on *Bleak House:* A Critical Examination of his Memoranda and Number Plans," *Renaissance and Modern Studies,* vol. IX, 1965, pp. 77–80. Sucksmith explains (p. 48) that there is a separate leaf of manuscript notes for each serial "number" of *Bleak House* and that each leaf is divided into a left and a right hand side. On the left are memoranda for the number being written, and on the right, "plans," under chapter headings, referring to events and characters.

2. "Words underscored *once* in the MS are indicated by italics, *twice* by italics and underlining, *three times* by italics, underlining, and asterisk."—Sucksmith, work cited, p. 49.

chapter XXXIX.
Attorney and client.

Vholes—Symond's Inn
The respectability of the Vholes Legion.   Make man-
eating unlawful, and you starve the Vholeses.
Richards' decline—*carry on*.
Guppy and Tony—Court—Smallweeds in possession.
Carry on to next.

chapter XL.
National and Domestic.

Coodle and Doodle.   No Govt. without Coodle or Doodle.
Only two men in the country.
Volumnia.   *Debilitated cousin.*   *country house**
Electioneering.   Sir Leicester—658 gentlemen in a
bad way.
Carry through Rouncewell and Rosa, to Tulking-
horn's story. So to next.

chapter XLI.
In Mr Tulkinghorn's Room.

—?—Tulkinghorn's room at night.   Lady Dedlock comes
to him there.
Begin grim shadow on him

chapter XLII.
In Mr Tulkinghorn's chambers.

Lincolns Inn Fields–Tulkinghorn coming back at dusk–
London bird.
Begin with Snagsby, and
work up to—*Frenchwoman.*
[Leaf XIV, left]
Mr and Mrs Chadband?   *No*
Allan Woodcourt?   *Yes.*   Return
Skimpole?—family?   *Yes.*
Boythorn.—*about him, but not himself*
Mr Jarndyce.   *Yes—And his love for Esther to be now
brought out*
George—and Bagnets?   No.   *Next No.*

(Bleak House.————No. XIV.)

chapter XLIII.
Esther's Narrative.

Skimpole family at home—borders of Somers Town.

Polygon

Beauty Daughter, Sentiment daughter, Comedy Daughter
Angry baker—such an absurd figure.

Sir Leicester calls—?—on Mr Jarndyce
(through Skimpole)
)—?—'Guardian, Lady Dedlock is my
mother

*Boythorn and Miss
Barbary.*   *chapter XLIV.*
The Letter and the Answer.

Send Charley *'for the letter.'*
'I have brought the answer guardian'

chapter XLV.
In trust

Esther to—Plymouth—no—*Deal*—Ada's letter
Allan *Woodcourt* comes back
Had to be thought of, like the dead

chapter XLVI.
Stop him!

Tom all alone's—Night and morning.
Allan—Jenny—Jo—Jo tells that he was taken away
by Mr Bucket—Allan takes him

[Leaf XV, left]
Mr Tulkinghorn to be shot (Pointing Roman)
George to be taken by Bucket.   *Yes?**
Jo?   Yes.   Kill him.*
Allan?—And Richard?   Not *Richard*
Mr Guppy?   *No.*
Smallweeds   *No.*
Lead up to murder through Chesney Wold?   *No.* Through
Mrs Bucket?   *No*   house in town.

Snagsbys? *Mr. Slightly*
Chadbands? *Not yet.*

[Leaf XV, right]
(*Bleak House.* ————*No. XV.*)
chapter XLVII.
Jo's will

Esther.
λ 'If it could be written wery large as I didn't go to do it'—
our father.

Dead my Lords and gentlemen

chapter XLVIII.
Closing in.
Gather up Ironmaster and Rosa
Lady Dedlock and Mr Tulkinghorn
If it said now, Don't go home!   *High and mighty street.*
Shot.   *Pointing Roman*

chapter XLIX.
Dutiful Friendship.
The old girl's birthday.
George
Mr Bucket
Making things pleasant
Hundred Pound reward—Sir Leicester—
Handcuffs—and hat over his eyes.   *George taken.*

4 [Henry Fothergill Chorley]

"Bleak House," *The Athenaeum,*
September 17, 1853[1]

This novel shows progress on the part of its writer in more ways
than one,—and thus merits close attention now that it is completed.
Ready sympathy has not been denied to it during its progress,—for

1. Pp. 1087–1088.

in the Preface Mr. Dickens announces his belief "that he has never had so many readers as in 'Bleak House.'"

There is progress in art to be praised in this book,—and there is progress in exaggeration to be deprecated. At its commencement the impression made is strange. Were its opening pages in anywise accepted as representing the world we live in, the reader might be excused for feeling as though he belonged to some orb where eccentrics, Bedlamites, ill-directed and disproportioned people were the only inhabitants. Esther Summerson, the narrator, is, in her surpassingly sweet way, little less like ordinary persons than are Krook and Skimpole. Her own story was of itself sadly romantic enough—the provident beneficence of Mr. Jarndyce to her was sufficiently unlike Fortune's usual dealings with those born as she was—to have sufficed for the marvels of one number. But on her mysterious summons to town to join the delightful wards in Chancery with whom she makes an instant and cordial friendship, she is thrown, on the very moment of arrival, into company with a sharp-witted and coxcombical limb of the law, in Guppy,—with an over-weening philanthropist, who lets everything at home go to rack and ruin for the sake of her foreign mission, in Mrs. Jellyby,—with an infuriated madman who has a mysterious lodger and a demoniacal cat, in Krook,—and with a ruefully fantastic Chancery victim in poor little Miss Flite. Nay, when she gets to the house of her guardian, he too, must needs be marked out as a curiosity by his whimsical manner of wreaking his vexation at sin, sorrow and meanness, on the weather,—while his guest happens to be none other than such a rare specimen of the man of imagination as Mr. Harold Skimpole.—Here is "the apple-pie made of quinces" with a ven-geance, if there ever was such a thing!—Granting the simple heroine of Mr. Dickens to possess the immediate power of the daguerreotype in noting at once the minutest singularities of so many exceptional people—granting her, further, in its fullest extent, the instantaneous influence for good in word and in deed which she exercises over every person with whom she is brought into contact,—it surely befalls few such angels of experience, simplicity and overflowing kindness to enter Life through the gate of usefulness down a highway lined with figures so strange as the above. The excuse of Esther's creator, we suppose, lies in the supposed necessity of catching his public at the outset, by exhibiting a rare set of figures in readiness for the coming harlequinade. But in 'Bleak House' they stand in one another's way; and seeing that, as the narrative advances, they are reinforced by such a cast-iron *Lady Bountiful* as Mrs. Pardiggle, with her terrible children—such as horrible *Darby* and *Joan* as the two old Smallweeds,—such a greasy, preaching *Mawworm* as Mr. Chadband—such a *Boanerges* as Mr. Boythorn—such an uxurious admirer of his wife's two former husbands as Mr. Bayham Badger,—we must protest against the composition of the company, not merely on the ground of the improbability of such an assemblage, but from the sense of fatigue which the manœuvres of such singular people cannot fail to cause.

This resolution to startle, besides being bad in itself, leads the novelist, even though he have of the richest *cornucopia* of humours at his disposal, into two faults,—both of which may be seriously objected against 'Bleak House.' First, from noticing mere peculiarities, he is beguiled into a cruel consideration of physical defects,— from the unnatural workings of the mind, the step to the painful agonies of the body is a short one. The hideous palsy of Grandfather Smallweed, and the chattering idiocy of his wife, belong to the coarse devices which are losing their hold on the popular taste even at the minor theatres.—The death of Krook—attacked as an impossible catastrophe, and defended by our novelist on medical testimony— would be false and repugnant in point of Art, even if it were scientifically true. We would not willingly look into fiction for the phenomena of *elephantiasis,* or for the hopeless writhings of those who suffer and perish annually in the slow sharp pains of cancer. Again,—in his determination to exhibit snub minds and pimpled tempers, principles that squint, and motives that walk on club-feet (analogous to the mis-shapen figures which ought not to come too frequently even from the professed caricaturist's pencil)—it is difficult, perhaps, for the novelist to avoid touching on another forbidden ground, to abstain from that sharpness of individual portraiture which shall make certain of his *dramatis personæ* recognizable as reproductions of living people. This is not a remark, like our former one, to be substantiated by instances; we will not spread a sore under pretence of exhibiting it.—But the charge has been laid so widely and so universally against 'Bleak House,' that it cannot be wholly ignored by any faithful analyst. We will assume that Mr. Dickens may not have desired to inflict personal pain on any one—friend or foe. We will concede that the motion of the hand which sketched in this or the other known person in 'Bleak House' may, in the first instance, have been involuntary.—The more need is there of strong, grave, friendly protest against devices of style and manner which may lead kindly-natured men so much further than they would care to go.

Thus much recorded as regards the progress in exaggerations which we conceive 'Bleak House' to exhibit,—we now turn to the admirable things which this last tale by Mr. Dickens contains.—And first, though he has been thereby led away from his great Chancery case further than may have been his original intention, we must signalize the whole machinery by which Lady Dedlock's private history is gradually brought to day—as admirable in point of fictitious con-struction,—an important advance on anything that we recollect in our author's previous works. Not a point is missed,—not a person left without part or share in the gradual disclosure—not a pin dropped that is not to be picked up for help or for harm to somebody. The great catastrophe is, after all, determined as much by the distant jealousy of Mrs. Snagsby, the fretful law-stationer's wife, as by the more intimate vengeance of the discarded lady's maid. Capital, too,— of an excellence which no contemporary could reach,—is the manner in which Mr. Bucket the detective officer is worked into the very centre and core of the mystery, until we become almost agreed with Sir Leicester Dedlock in looking on him as a superior being in right of his cool resource and wondrous knowledge. Nor has Mr. Dickens wrought up any scene more highly and less melo-dramatically than those of the night-ride into the country in which the over-perfect Esther is included—and of the despairing affectionate, hopeless expectation of the deserted husband in the town-house. It is curious, however, to observe how completely our novelist's power has failed him on the threshold of the dank grave-yard, where the proud and desperate lady lies down to die of remorse and shame,—how despotically he has chosen to forget that such a catastrophe could not really have been hushed up in the manner hinted at in his closing chapters. We are not sorry to be spared a second inquest over the body of the faithless woman, having assisted at like rites over the corpse of the outcast lover of her youth,—we can dispense with the excitement of the trial of Mademoiselle Hortense, the murderess, and the horrors of her execution,—but such events there must have been;—and to have overlooked them so completely as Mr. Dickens has done in winding up his story, is an arbitrary exercise of his art, made all the more striking by the minute painting with which other parts of the narrative are wrought.

In his own particular walk—apart from the exaggerations complained of, and the personalities against which many have protested—Mr. Dickens has rarely, if ever, been happier than in 'Bleak House.' Poor miserable Mr. Jellyby, with all hope, life, and energy washed out of him by the flow of his wife's incessant zeal—the dancing-school in which the African missionary's daughter finds her mission—the cousins who cluster round Sir Leicester Dedlock, giving an air of habitation to the great house, by filling up its empty corners,—could have been hit off by no one else so well. Then, with all his inanity, pomposity, and prejudice in favour of his order, the Lincoln-shire baronet is a true gentleman:—we are not only told this, we are made to feel it. His wife is a comparative failure: a second edition of *Mrs. Dombey*,—with somewhat of real stateliness super-added. Trooper George is new:—and here, again, Mr. Dickens is masterly, in preserving (though with some exaggeration) the simplicity, sentimentality, and credulity of the original nature which made the man a roamer,—and which have a strong and real life in many a barrack and in many a ship of war. Mr. Snagsby "puts too fine a point" on his intimations concerning the spectre that destroys his home peace, somewhat too ceaselessly. The queerest catch-word may be used too mercilessly, even for a farce,—much more for a novel.—Perhaps among all the waifs and strays, the beggars and the outcasts, in behalf of whose humanity our author has again and again appealed to a world too apt to forget their existence, he has never produced anything more rueful, more pitiable, more complete than poor Jo. The dying scene, with its terrible morals and impetuous protest, Mr. Dickens has nowhere in all his works excelled. The book would live on the strength alone of that one sketch from the swarming life around us. Mr. Bucket is a jewel among detectives:—and the mixture of professional enjoyment and manly, delicate consideration in his great scene with Sir Leicester Dedlock, is marked and carried through with a master's hand. Esther is, as we have hinted, too precociously good, to perpetually self-present, and too helpful to everyone around her to carry a sense of reality:—nor are her virtues made more probable by the fact that she is the chronicler of her own perfection,—though with disclaimers manifold. She does not, it is true, profess less profession than did *Harriet Byron* before her:—yet *Harriet Byron*, as the centre of a galaxy of admiring relations, loving neighbours, and revering domestics, is a "being of the mind" as clear and as complete as most other fictitious gentle-women of our acquaintance.

It may be thought, that in the above attempt to sum up the merits and defects of this unequal tale, more account should have been made of what may be called its main argument, the great Chancery suit. But of that we spoke when announcing the publication of its opening number . . . and those who, with us, then anticipated scenes which might rival the Pickwick trial, or combinations such as should keep that mighty mystery of Iniquity and Equity perpetually before the reader, must have been disappointed,—since at an early period the fortunes of Richard and Ada pass into the place of second interests, while the first concern and sympathy are given to Lady Dedlock's secret: so that the matter has not the importance which Mr. Dickens could have given it, had it pleased him so to do. The statements made in his Preface, by way of justification, will make many regret that he should have been fascinated away from his master-purpose, even by such a tempting "passage of arms," as the silent strife betwixt the haughty woman of fashion and the deep, astute, and ruthless arbiter of her destiny, "the old man, Tulking-horn."

 5

FROM "Charles Dickens," *Blackwood's Edinburgh Magazine,* April, 1855[1]

In Mr. Dicken's last great work (an adjective which cannot apply in any sense to his very last one, *Hard Times*), he makes a beginning

1. Vol. LXXVII, pp. 461–465.

as pleasant as in *Copperfield*; but great as are the merits of *Bleak House*, we cannot be persuaded into the same thorough liking for it as we entertain for its predecessor. Here we are again on the perilous standing-ground of social evil; and the sketch of workhouse tyranny in *Oliver Twist*, and the miserable picture of the miserable school in *Nickleby*, are transcended by this last exposition of a still wider and more extensive desolation. Had the lesson been unlearned, or the truth less universally known, this must have been a very telling revelation of the long-acknowledged evils of Chancery litigation; and even admitting that Mr. Dickens comes late into the field, it is not to be denied that, for the purposes of his story, he makes very effective use of his suit in Chancery. Not to speak of Miss Flite and Gridley, the earlier victims, who are introduced rather to support the argument than to help the narrative, the manner in which the fatal Jarndyce case engulfs and swallows up poor Richard Carstone is at once extremely well managed, and a quite legitimate use of a public evil. Poor Richard! his flightiness and youthfulness, his enthusiasm and discontent, and that famous and most characteristic argument of his, by which he proves that, in not making some extravagant purchase he meditated, he has saved so much, and has consequently such a sum additional to spend, are very true—sadly true, and to the life. Poor Ada is a sweet slight sketch, not aiming at very much, but Mr. Dickens has been ambitious in Esther. Esther begins very well, but, alas! falls off sadly as she goes on. In her extreme unconsciousness Esther is too conscious by half: we see her going about, rattling her basket of keys, and simpering with a wearisome sweetness. Yes, we are grieved to say it; but it is with a simper that Miss Esther Summerson recalls those loving and applauding speeches which she is so sweetly surprised that everybody should make to her. We are sometimes reminded of the diary of Miss Fanny Burney in reading that of Esther; each of these ladies exhibits a degree of delightful innocence and confusion in recording the compliments paid to them, which it is edifying to behold. But Esther, though her historian does great things for her, is not so clever as Fanny; and as there is no affection so disagreeable as the affectation of ingenuous simplicity, we feel considerably tired of Esther before she comes to an end. Nevertheless we must make a protest in behalf of this young lady, little as she interests us: we cannot be content with this style of unceremonious transfer from one suitor to another, which so many modern heroines are subjected to. This, which is becoming quite a favourite arrangement in fiction, especially patronised, to increase the wonder, by lady novelists, does not seem to us to be particularly flattering even to the bridegroom, promoted at the eleventh hour to the post of honour; but how much less flattering to the bride, thus quietly disposed of, let the first heroine of spirit, threatened with such an insult, declare indignantly, by casting adrift *both* the wooers, who barter her between them. Perhaps Esther deserves the indignity, and she certainly does not seem to resent it; but before she loses or gives up *all* the honours accorded to her sex, we must make our stand in behalf of the unfortunate piece of perfection called a heroine. Take our novels as a criterion, and how much of the love-making of the present day is done by the ladies? Oh age of chivalry! oh knightly worshippers of beauty, throned and unapproachable! What has become of all the reverence and duty of your magnanimous bestowal, the sacred honours you gave to woman's weakness, and all the noble fruits it bore?

We are somewhat at a loss to find why so many pseudo-philanthropists come in to the first stage of this tale, for it does not seem enough reason for their introduction that they are simply to play upon the benevolence of Mr. Jarndyce, and thence to disappear into their native gloom. Altogether the author seems to have intended making more of Jarndyce, and his immediate surroundings, in his first design—else why the momentary vision of Mrs Pardiggle, and the elaborate sketch of Boythorne, of whom so very little is made afterwards? Mrs Jellyby, too, disappears placidly, though she leaves a very sufficient representative in her daughter, whose various adventures and simple girlish character make a pleasant variety in the tale. Then there is Skimpole, a sketch, which *looks* almost too near the life, of the fashionable amiable phase of the most entire and unalloyed selfishness. The poor boy Joe is a very effective picture though we fail to discover a sufficient reason for his introduction; and the household of Snagsby, in spite of the clandestine virtues of its good little master, is far from an agreeable one. We cannot omit, either, to remark the horrible catastrophe of the book, a pure outrage upon imagination. It is not of the slightest importance to us if a case of spontaneous combustion occurs somewhere every week or every day, but we know it is quite out of the range of healthful and sound invention, a monstrous and fantastic horror;— worthy of it, and of their relationship to its victim, are the revolting family of Smallweeds. Is this humour? or is it worthy to be offered to a trustful public in any guise? Yet many of these pages, which Mr Dickens can fill so well, are given over to disgust and impatience, that our author may bring before us this miserable family, and prove to us what he can do in the way of exaggerated and uninstructive caricature. We have another quarrel with Mr Dickens— one of long standing, dating back to the period of his first work: the "shepherd" of Mr Weller's widow, the little Bethel of Mrs Nubbles, have effloresced in *Bleak House* into a detestable Mr Chadband, an oft-repeated libel upon the preachers of the poor. This is a very vulgar and common piece of slander, quite unworthy of a true artist. Are we really to believe, then, that only those who are moderately religious are true in their profession?—that it is good to be in earnest in every occupation but one, the most important of all, as it happens? What a miserable assumption is this! Mr Dickens' tender charity does not disdain to embrace a good many equivocal people—why then so persevering an aim at a class which offends few and harms no man? Not very long since, we ourselves, who are no great admirers of English dissent, happened to go into a very humble little meeting-house—perhaps a Bethel— where the preacher, at his beginning, we are ashamed to say, tempted our unaccustomed faculties almost to laughter. Here was quite an opportunity for finding a Chadband, for the little man was round and ruddy, and had a shining face—his grammar was not perfect, moreover, and having occasion to mention a certain Scripture town, he called it Cana*r* of Galilee; but when we had listened for half an hour, we had no longer the slightest inclination to laugh at the humble preacher. This unpretending man reached to the heart of his subject in less time than we have taken to tell of it; gave a bright, clear, individual view of the doctrine he was considering, and urged it on his hearers with homely arguments which were as little ridiculous as can be supposed. Will Mr Dickens permit us to advise him, when he next would draw a "shepherd," to study his figure from the life? Let him choose the least little chapel on his way, and take his chance for a successful sitting: we grant him he may find a Chadband, but we promise him he has at least an equal chance of finding an apostle instead.

We are glad to turn from those disagreeable people to the lofty household which adds its state and grandeur to this novel, and we can give nothing but commendation, and that of the highest, to the family of Sir Leicester Dedlock. Lady Dedlock, haughty, imperious, beautiful, elevated to a higher world, above suspicion, like the wife of Cæsar, by the reverential admiration of her husband, is admirably introduced; and the woman's heart weeping behind these disguises— the old secret history so slowly unfolded, the womanish impulses so sudden and stormy, the womanish horror and yet defiance of shame, are nobly developed as the tale goes on. How did her ladyship's daughter chance to have so mild and tame a nature? The fire and passion of Lady Dedlock are things of a very different rank and order from any emotion of Esther Summerson's. The whole house, from the grey-haired pompous ancient gentleman himself—a true gentleman, and tenderly revealed to us, in the end, with the old chivalry alive and noble under these grand pretences of his— down to the debilitated cousin, is worthy of its author. In this sphere he has done nothing so dignified and so perfect. The accessories and dependents of the family are all touched with equal delicacy. What can be better in its way than George, his friends, and his story?— or that stout-hearted trooper's wife, with her far-travelled umbrella and her grey cloak?

In the very highly wrought and tragical pursuit of Lady Dedlock, Mr Dickens makes use of materials long since collected. Strangely different in its superficial garb from the romance of the past is the romance of to-day; yet who ever traced a picturesque fugitive, warned by spectres, and pressed by armed pursuers, with interest more breathless and absorbed than that with which we follow Bucket as *he* follows the faint trace of this unhappy lady? The dash of the horses along the midnight road—the breathless and silent excitement to which the pursuers reach at last, and then the sudden discovery and climax so simply told, form a wonderful picture. And most pathetic is that other scene, where poor Sir Leicester lies in his chamber, listening for their return. These scenes are full of delicacy and power, and are very great efforts, conceived and carried out with unfaltering force.

It is very ungrateful, after all this, and acknowledging to the full how excellently this portion of *Bleak House* is accomplished, to yield to the temptation given us in the conclusion, and suffer our dissatisfaction with that to overshadow the book with all its admirable qualities; but we are obliged to say that we think Esther a failure, and, when she has only herself to talk about, are glad to be done with the complaisant history. Mr Dickens is evidently ambitious of achieving a heroine—witness his vehement endeavour to make something of Ruth Pinch, his careful elaboration of Dolly Varden, and even the pains he has taken with Dora. It is a laudable ambition, for heroines are a sadly featureless class of well-intentioned young women in these days—but we cannot say that the effort is successful in Esther Summerson. In the ordinary type of heroines—in the Agnes Wickfield, the Ada, the Kate Nickleby—Mr Dickens is very generally successful. These young ladies are pretty enough, amiable enough, generous enough, to fill their necessary places with great credit and propriety, but to produce an individual woman is another and quite a different matter. We have a strong impression that, except for the highest and most commanding genius, a woman of a high ideal, and yet of a distinct individual character, is almost an impossible achievement. We have female writers in these days of very considerable talents and pretensions, but which of them can make a man? Vague pieces of perfection figure in a woman's novel for the heroes, and indistinct visions of beauty and sweetness represent, for the most part, the heroines of a man. That it should be so is according to all the rules of nature, which in every case leaves a haze of mutual attraction and ignorance upon the twain representatives of creation—a haze which nothing short of the highest eminence can look over and into, and not always even that. Perhaps the greatest of all Sir Walter's claims to a sovereign place (especially now, when we are so much wiser than Sir Walter, and complain that his stories are only stories, and not dissections of human motive and purpose), is the wonderful impersonation of Jeanie Deans, a picture which, in our judgment, is quite unequalled, thoroughly idealised, yet as true as daylight, and as perfect a woman as ever woman was; but as Jeanie, noble as she is, could never have been her historian's love and ladye, even she does not quite enter into the class of heroines, a perfect example of which is one of the highest criterions of genius.

George Eliot
Middlemarch
1871-72

﹈ *1* [*George Eliot*]

FROM "Silly Novels by Lady Novelists," *The Westminster Review,* October, 1856[1]

Silly Novels by Lady Novelists are a genus with many species, determined by the particular quality of silliness that predominates in them—the frothy, the prosy, the pious, or the pedantic. But it is a mixture of all these—a composite order of feminine fatuity, that produces the largest class of such novels, which we shall distinguish as the *mind-and-millinery* species. The heroine is usually an heiress, probably a peeress in her own right, with perhaps a vicious baronet, an amiable duke, and an irresistible younger son of a marquis as lovers in the foreground, a clergyman and a poet sighing for her in the middle distance, and a crowd of undefined adorers dimly indicated beyond. Her eyes and her wit are both dazzling; her nose and her morals are alike free from any tendency to irregularity; she has a superb *contralto* and a superb intellect; she is perfectly

1. Vol. LXVI, pp. 243–245.

well dressed and perfectly religious; she dances like a sylph, and reads the Bible in the original tongues. Or it may be that the heroine is not an heiress—that rank and wealth are the only things in which she is deficient; but she infallibly gets into high society, she has the triumph of refusing many matches and securing the best, and she wears some family jewels or other as a sort of crown of righteousness at the end. Rakish men either bite their lips in impotent confusion at her repartees, or are touched to penitence by her reproofs, which, on appropriate occasions, rise to a lofty strain of rhetoric; indeed, there is a general propensity in her to make speeches, and to rhapsodize at some length when she retires to her bedroom. In her recorded conversations she is amazingly eloquent, and in her unrecorded conversations, amazingly witty. She is understood to have a depth of insight that looks through and through the shallow theories of philosophers, and her superior instincts are a sort of dial by which men have only to set their clocks and watches, and all will go well. The men play a very subordinate part by her side. You are consoled now and then by a hint that they have affairs, which keeps you in mind that the working-day business of the world is somehow being carried on, but ostensibly the final cause of their existence is that they may accompany the heroine on her "starring" expedition through life. They see her at a ball, and are dazzled; at a flower-show, and they are fascinated; on a riding excursion, and they are witched by her noble horsemanship; at church, and they are awed by the sweet solemnity of her demeanour. She is the ideal woman in feelings, faculties, and flounces. For all this, she as often as not marries the wrong person to begin with, and she suffers terribly from the plots and intrigues of the vicious baronet; but even death has a soft place in her heart for such a paragon, and remedies all mistakes for her just at the right moment. The vicious baronet is sure to be killed in a duel, and the tedious husband dies in his bed requesting his wife, as a particular favour to him, to marry the man she loves best, and having already dispatched a note to the lover informing him of the comfortable arrangement. Before matters arrive at this desirable issue our feelings are tried by seeing the noble, lovely, and gifted heroine pass through many *mauvais moments,* but we have the satisfaction of knowing that her sorrows are wept into embroidered pocket-handkerchiefs, that her fainting form reclines on the very best upholstery, and that whatever vicissitudes she may undergo, from being dashed out of her carriage to having her head shaved in a fever, she comes out of them all with a complexion more blooming and locks more redundant than ever.

We may remark, by the way, that we have been relieved from a serious scruple by discovering that silly novels by lady novelists rarely introduce us into any other than very lofty and fashionable society. We had imagined that destitute women turned novelists, as they turned governesses, because they had no other "ladylike" means of getting their bread. On this supposition, vacillating syntax and improbable incident had a certain pathos for us, like the extremely supererogatory pin-cushions and ill-devised nightcaps that are offered for sale by a blind man. We felt the commodity to be a nuisance, but we were glad to think that the money went to relieve the necessitous, and we pictured to ourselves lonely women struggling for a maintenance, or wives and daughters devoting themselves to the production of "copy" out of pure heroism,—perhaps to pay their husband's debts or to purchase luxuries for a sick father. Under these impressions we shrank from criticising a lady's novel: her English might be faulty, but we said to ourselves her motives are irreproachable; her imagination may be uninventive, but her patience is untiring. Empty writing was excused by an empty stomach, and twaddle was consecrated by tears. But no! This theory of ours, like many other pretty theories, has had to give way before observation. Women's silly novels, we are now convinced are written under totally different circumstances. The fair writers have evidently never talked to a tradesman except from a carriage window; they have no notion of the working-classes except as "dependents;" they think five hundred a-year a miserable pittance; Belgravia and "baronial halls" are their primary truths; and they have no idea of feeling interest in any man who is not at least a great landed proprietor, if not a prime minister. It is clear that they write in elegant boudoirs, with violet-coloured ink and a ruby pen; that they must be entirely indifferent to publishers' accounts, and inexperienced in every form of poverty except poverty of brains. It is true that we are constantly struck with the want of verisimilitude in their representations of the high society in which they seem to live; but then they betray no closer acquaintance with any other form of life. If their peers and peeresses are improbable, their literary men, tradespeople, and cottagers are impossible; and their intellect seems to have the peculiar impartiality of reproducing both what they *have* seen and heard, and what they have *not* seen and heard, with equal unfaithfulness. . . .

"Be not a baker if your head be made of butter," says a homely proverb, which being interpreted, may mean, let no woman rush into print who is not prepared for the consequences. We are aware that our remarks are in a very different tone from that of the reviewers who, with perennial recurrence of precisely similar emotions, only paralleled, we imagine, in the experience of monthly nurses, tell one lady novelist after another that they "hail" her productions "with delight." We are aware that the ladies at whom our criticism is pointed are accustomed to be told, in the choicest phraseology of puffery, that their pictures of life are brilliant, their characters well drawn, their style fascinating, and their sentiments lofty. But if they are inclined to resent our plainness of speech, we ask them to reflect for a moment on the chary praise, and often captious blame, which their panegyrists give to writers whose works are on the way to become classics. No sooner does a woman show that she has genius or effective talent, than she receives the tribute of being moderately praised and severely criticised. By a peculiar thermometric adjustment, when a woman's talent is at zero, journalistic approbation is at the boiling pitch; when she attains mediocrity, it is already at no more than summer heat; and if ever she reaches excellence, critical enthusiasm drops to the freezing point. Harriet Martineau, Currer Bell, and Mrs. Gaskell have been treated as cavalierly as if they had been men. And every critic who forms a high estimate of the share women may ultimately take in literature, will, on principle, abstain from any exceptional indulgence towards the productions of literary women. For it must be plain to every one who looks impartially and extensively into feminine literature, that its greatest deficiencies are due hardly more to the want of intellectual power than to the want of those moral qualities that contribute to literary excellence—patient diligence, a sense of the responsibility involved in publication, and an appreciation of the sacredness of the writer's art. In the majority of women's books you see that kind of facility which springs from the absence of any high standard; that fertility in imbecile combination or feeble imitation which a little self-criticism would check and reduce to barrenness; just as with a total want of musical ear people will sing out of tune, while a degree more melodic sensibility would suffice to render them silent. The foolish vanity of wishing to appear in print, instead of being counterbalanced by any consciousness of the intellectual or moral derogation implied in futile authorship, seems to be encouraged by the extremely false impression that to write *at all* is a proof of superiority in a woman. On this ground, we believe that the average intellect of women is unfairly represented by the mass of feminine literature, and that while the few women who write well are very far above the ordinary intellectual level of their sex, the many women who write ill are very far below it. So that, after all, the severer critics are fulfilling a chivalrous duty in depriving the mere fact of femine authorship of any false prestige which may give it a delusive attraction, and in recommending women of mediocre faculties—as at least a negative service they can render their sex—to abstain from writing.

The standing apology for women who become writers without any special qualification is, that society shuts them out from other spheres of occupation. Society is a very culpable entity, and has to answer for the manufacture of many unwholesome commodities, from bad pickles to bad poetry. But society, like "matter," and Her Majesty's Government, and other lofty abstractions, has its share of excessive blame as well as excessive praise. Where there is one woman who writes from necessity, we believe there are three women who write from vanity; and, besides, there is something so antiseptic in the mere healthy fact of working for one's bread, that the most trashy and rotten kind of feminine literature is not likely to have been produced under such circumstances. "In all labour there is profit;" but ladies' silly novels, we imagine, are less the result of labour than of busy idleness.

Happily, we are not dependent on argument to prove that Fiction is a department of literature in which women can, after their kind, fully equal men. A cluster of great names, both living and dead, rush to our memories in evidence that women can produce novels not only fine, but among the very finest;—novels, too, that have a precious speciality, lying quite apart from masculine aptitudes and experience. No educational restrictions can shut women out from the materials of fiction, and there is no species of art which is so free from rigid requirements. Like crystalline masses, it may take any form, and yet be beautiful; we have only to pour in the right elements—genuine observation, humour, and passion. But it is precisely this absence of rigid requirement which constitutes the fatal seduction of novel-writing to incompetent women. Ladies are not wont to be very grossly deceived as to their power of playing on the piano; here certain positive difficulties of execution have to be conquered, and incompetence inevitably breaks down. Every art which has its absolute *technique* is, to a certain extent, guarded from the intrusions of mere left-handed imbecility. But in novel-writing there are no barriers for incapacity to stumble against, no external criteria to prevent a writer from mistaking foolish facility for mastery. And so we have again and again the old story of La Fontaine's ass, who puts his nose to the flute, and, finding that he elicits some sound, exclaims, "Moi, aussi, je joue de la flute;"—a fable which we commend, at parting, to the consideration of any feminine reader who is in danger of adding to the number of "silly novels by lady novelists."

2 George Eliot

FROM *Quarry for Middlemarch*[1]

Remarks on the History & Treatment of Delirium Tremens. By John Ware, M.D. Boston, 1831

Dr Ware first dogmatically taught that *delirium tremens* is a paroxysm of poisoning by alcohol, which in a majority of cases lasts only a given time, & terminates favourably in a critical sleep. He says, "The natural tendency of the paroxysm is to terminate in a

1. Anna Theresa Kitchel, ed., Berkeley, Calif.: University of California Press, © 1950 by The Regents of the University of California. Reprinted from *Nineteenth Century Fiction*, Volume IV, by permission of The Regents, pp. 35–36, 43, 45–46, 52–54, 56–57, 62–63.

spontaneous & salutary sleep at the end of a certain period—viz. sixty to seventy-two hours; & even in the reports of cases which have been submitted to the public as evidences of the efficacy of various modes of practice, sleep has not actually taken place sooner than it would have done in the natural course of the disease. . . . The termination of a paroxysm of delirium tremens is always, as has been already mentioned, in *profound* sleep. . . . Sleep, however, is not always to be regarded as indicating the speedy termination of the paroxysm, since it is not uncommon for patients to sleep a little—from a few minutes to an hour, for instance—on each day of the delirium." Dr Ware maintained that in a large proportion of cases with-drawal of the accustomed stimulants had nothing to do with the accessions of the paroxysm, that the disease occurs also in individuals whose habit of drinking has never been suspended at all . . . up to the commencement of the delirium.

vide. Bacon's advancement of learning
      Stowe's London—medical schools?

* * *

DATES

1830 opening of Liverpool & Manchr. Railway, April
"   George IV died, June 26—Whigs come in
"   French Revolution,* July, 27, 28, 29,
"   Parliament Dissolved,† July 24
"   King & Queen decline to visit the city, Nov. 9. Funds fall.
"   Mr. Brougham's motion for Reform   Nov. 16
"   Tory amendment carried. Machine breaking
"   x (Writs returnable for
1831 Parliament dissolved April 22 & gen. election. Reopened.
     June 21
"   x First cases of Cholera
"   (Paganini) Reform Bill thrown out by the Lords Oct. 7
"   Bristol Riots Oct. 29
     Reintrod. 3d time Dec. 12
1832 Cholera appears at Rotherhithe & London Feb. & Sep.
     R.B. read in the Lords, Mar. Motion against it carried May 7‡
"   Reform Bill passed, June 7.
"   Capl. Punishment for sheep & cattle stealing abolished.
"   First Nos. of Chambers' Journal & Penny Mag.

1833 Reformed Parliament, election Jan.
" Thanksgiving for departure of Cholera, Ap. 14

* * *

RELATIONS TO BE DEVELOPED

1 of Dorothea to Mr. Casaubon
2 " Lydgate to Rosamond
3 " Fred Vincy to Mary Garth
4 " The Vincys to Old Featherstone
5 " Dorothea to Will Ladislaw
6 " Lydgate to Bulstrode
7 " Bulstrode to John Raffles
8 " Celia to Sir James
9 " Ladislaw to Mr Brooke
10 " Caleb Garth to Mr Brooke etc.
11 " Mr Farebrother to all, except Sir J. & Mr Brooke

PRIVATE DATES

Dorothea married, 1827. Featherstone dies & Ladislaw comes to
Tipton, Ap. 1830. Celia married May
Lydgate's marriage 1830—July or August
Mr Brooke tries for Parliament May 1831
Mr Casaubon's death, 1831. March
Celia's baby born, 1831—April
Dorothea's second marriage, 1832 Jan. or Feb.
Child born, 1833
Rosamond's baby born, June 1, 1831
Bulstrode buys Stone Court, June or July 1831
Raffles comes back, July 1831
Raffles dies, Aug. 1832. Two years after Lydgate's marriage.

"   "   "

Mr Casaubon's Death, March 1831
Dorothea settled at Lowick again June 1831
Bulstrode & Raffles at Stone Court, end of June 1831
Fred Vincy's adventure & choice July 1831
Lydgate's disclosure of trouble to Rosd. Aug.

* * *

SKETCH I.

Bulstrode, when young, was a banker's clerk in London & member of a dissenting church to wh. a wealthy couple living at Highbury also belonged. The husband had a business in the city, & on Bulstrode becoming an intimate offered him a place as clerk & accountant; which would be more profitable than his actual situation. Bulstrode accepted & found that the business was a pawnbroker's connected with the receipt of stolen goods.

Preliminary conversations had warned him that the wife was unacquainted with the nature of the business, & the facts were gradually opened to him as necessities which had crept into the management & could not be done away with.

Bulstrode showed ability, & became a confidential associate, wining his way at the same time with the pious wife on the ground of his gifts & divine grace.

SKETCH II.

The couple had had three children, but the two sons had died, & this bereavement made them relent towards the daughter who had run away from them to go on the stage, & had married.

But this daughter had disappeared, & they knew no means of recovering her except by advertisement, which had hitherto failed, but was persevered in.

Meanwhile, the husband died, & after a short time Bulstrode won the favour of the widow, who, however, before she made the settlements preliminary to her second marriage, was increasingly anxious to find her daughter & her daughter's possible offspring. Bulstrode, on the other hand, thought this extremely undesirable, as a possible diversion of her property into a less useful channel.

If she married him, he intended

SKETCH III.

as occasion served, to draw away the capital from the criminal business & use it more irreproachably. But the advertising could not be evaded, or an apparent sympathy with the widow's wish.

Still there was no result. But at this stage of affairs a man named Raffles who had early been in service at Highbury but was now a subordinate in the city business was sent on some occasion to Dieppe, & there saw a young couple with their child, the man apparently in a reduced state from sickness, the woman closely resembling the girl whom Raffles had known as the pawnbroker's daughter & whom he knew to have been advertised for. She was holding her baby in her arms & showed a wedding ring.

Raffles came forward & said, "I beg pardon, ma'am, but was your name

SKETCH IV.

Sarah Yorke? & did your parents live at Highbury?" She coloured, was startled & said "Yes." But Raffles then drew back, saying, "I thought so," & left them. He knew that the marriage was pending between Bulstrode & the widow York, & hence debated with himself to which of the two he should carry his information. He determined for Bulstrode, conjecturing that he should get more money there for silence than in the other direction for speech, & in no case should he lose the claim for speech ultimately.

Bulstrode told Raffles that he himself would mention the matter: it was necessary to inquire into things & be cautious, for the sake of the widow's feelings. On certain hints from Raffles, he observed that R. had done a good

SKETCH V.

service which should be well rewarded if he remained silent. After this, the advertising ceased, & Bulstrode married the widow, but not before Raffles had so presented the question to Bulstrode that he had secured a large sum in acquittance & had gone off to America.

Not long after the marriage the widow died, Bulstrode wound up the business & sought a position in the provinces; having among other changes, left the dissenting body & found all the edification he needed in the evangelical party of the Establishment.

The child of that couple is Will Ladislaw whose father is the son of Mr Casaubon's aunt Julia & her Polish husband, & inherits from the latter artistic faculties. In his extremity of illness & poverty he makes himself known to Mr Casaubon, having family guarantees, & from that time

SKETCH VI.

Mr Casaubon provides for the mother & Will, the father having shortly died. Will's mother, Sarah York, had run away from home to go on the stage under peculiar circumstances, not only following a bent in opposition to her mother's dissenting tastes, but proximately determined by learning from a spiteful rejected suitor that her father's trade was dishonorable. Hence the choice of her husband's friends as sources of help, rather than her own, was doubly determined.

[The idea which governs the plot about Bulstrode is, that there is nothing which the law can lay hold of to make him responsible for: the Nemesis is wrought out by the public opinion determined against him.]

* * *

WILL LADISLAW & DOROTHEA

An offence springs up between Mr Brooke & Will
Will, going on as editor of the Pioneer, comes to Lowick to see the Farebrothers, & has an interview with Dorothea. They part with a sense of being divided by destiny.

Dorothea has projects about filling her life: tells Sir James & Celia that she will never be married again—Celia's boy will have everything. She will go on some heroic errand of carrying away emigrants etc. Meanwhile, the cholera. Will does not go away & gets more intimate with Mrs. Lydgate. Learns the nature of Mr Casaubon's codicil; also about his mother's family from Bulstrode. There is another meeting & parting between him & Dorothea. She finds him with Mrs Lydgate. Scene between her & Will—anger, jealousy, reproach, ending in Dorothea's passionate avowal, & declaration that she will never marry him. Will reproaches Rosamond with having ruined his happiness. Rosamond alarmed lest Dorothea should tell Lydgate. Dorothea goes to R. having conquered her jealousy by pity, & hears that Will has been true to her.

* * *

COURSE OF PART VII.

1 Mr Farebrother makes advances to Lydgate—refused.
2 Lydgate trying to get rid of his house: Rosd. thwarts him
3 Difficulties increase   Sir Godwin's letter comes
4 Lydgate goes to the billiard room. Fred Vincy is there: Mr Farebrother comes to fetch him.
5 Fred Vincy & he walk together
6 Lydgate begins to think of applying to Bulstrode. Bulstrode's efforts to free himself & wish to quit Middlemarch—business with Caleb Garth.
7 Lydgate sounds Bulstrode
8 Caleb Garth picks up Raffles. Takes him to Stone Court. Raffles tells him the secrets
9 Caleb calls on Bulstrode, who tells him Raffles is there & declines further transactions. Bulstrode suspects the reasons. Caleb reassures him as to secrecy. Execution in Lydgate's house
10 Bulstrode having called in Lydgate, neglects his orders, & causes Raffles to take alcohol etc.
11 Bulstrode calls on Lydgate & gives him £1000 or £500 (?)
12 Lydgate out of his difficulties. Scandal. Outbursts of Mr Hawley against Bulstrode

CONDITIONS

_____

_____

Return of Will Ladislaw: reasons for his return. Time at which it happens.
What becomes of Bulstrode's arrangements as to property, especially Stone Court?
   How Fred & Mary get married.
About Dorothea's money, over & above her own 700 a year.
                    Times
The death of Raffles about 21st. March
Bambridge's return 26th.
Meeting on Sanitary Reform, April 10th.
Return of Will Ladislaw

3 George Eliot

FROM Letters to John Blackwood[1]

(July 24, 1871)

Thanks for the prompt return of the M.S., which arrived this morning. I have just been making a calculation of the pages and I find, on a liberal estimate, that this second portion is about 190 pp. of the size you usually give to my novels—I think, 25 lines per page, is it not? "Miss Brooke" being about 150 pp. the two parts together would be equal to the larger volumes of Adam Bede and The Mill, which are at least 350 pp. if my memory may be trusted.

Mr. Lewes has been saying that it may perhaps be well to take in a portion of Part II at the end of Part I. But it is too early for such definite arrangements. I don't see how I can leave anything out, because I hope there is nothing that will be seen to be irrelevant to my design, which is to show the gradual action of ordinary causes rather than exceptional, and to show this in some directions which have not been from time immemorial the beaten path—the Cremorne walks and shows of fiction. But the best intentions are good for nothing until execution has justified them. And you know I am always compassed about with fears. I am in danger in all my designs of parodying dear Goldsmith's satire on Burke, and think of refining when novel readers only think of skipping.

* * *

(January 18, 1872)

It is like your kindness to write me your encouraging impressions on reading the Third Book. I suppose it is my poor health that just now makes me think my writing duller than usual. For certainly

---

1. Reprinted, by permission of the publisher, from Gordon S. Haight, ed., *The George Eliot Letters*, New Haven: Yale University Press, 1954–55, vol. V, pp. 168–169, 236–237, 249, 296–297. Blackwood was the publisher of *Middlemarch*.

the reception of the First Book by my old readers is quite beyond my most daring hopes. One of them, who is a great champion of Adam Bede and Romola, told Mr. Lewes yesterday that he thought Middlemarch surpassed them. All this is very wonderful to me. I am thoroughly comforted as to the half of the work which is already written—but there remains the terror about the *un*written. Mr. Lewes is much satisfied with the Fourth Book, which opens with the continuation of the Featherstone drama. I wanted for the sake of quantity, to add a chapter to the Third Book, instead of opening the Fourth with it. But Mr. Lewes objects on the ground of effectiveness. . . .

I felt something like a shudder when Sir Henry Maine asked me last Sunday whether this would not be a very long book—saying, when I told him it would be four good volumes, that that was what he had calculated. However it will not be longer than Thackeray's books, if so long. And I don't see how the sort of thing I want to do could have been done briefly.

* * *

(February 21, 1872)

Thanks for the list of sales since February 12th. Things are encouraging and the voices that reach us are enthusiastic. But you can understand how people's interest in the book heightens my anxiety that the remainder should be up to the mark.

I want to get the Fourth Book into print and shall send the M.S. when the printers are free from the magazine. It has caused me some uneasiness that the Third Part is two sheets less than the First. But Mr. Lewes insisted that the death of old Featherstone was the right point to pause at, and he cites your approbation of the Part as a proof that effectiveness is secured in spite of diminished quantity. Still it irks me to ask 5/- for a smaller amount than that already given at the same price. Perhaps I must regard the value as made up solely by effectiveness, and certainly the book will be long enough.

* * *

(August 4, 1872)

I shall send Part VII in a few days, as I wish to see it in print that I may be better able to judge of quantities. It will perhaps be desirable to make a few excisions in order to introduced a little further development and leave larger room in the last Part. Since Mr. Lewes tells me that the Spectator considers me the most melancholy of authors, it will perhaps be a welcome assurance to you that there is no unredeemed tragedy in the solution of the story.

Mr. Lewes examines the newspapers before I see them, and cuts out any criticisms which refer to me, so as to save me from these spiritual chills—though alas, he cannot save me from the physical chills which retard my work more seriously. I had hoped to have the manuscript well out of my hands before we left this place at the end of the month, but the return of my dyspeptic troubles makes me unable to reckon on such a result.

It will be a good plan, I think to quicken the publication towards the end, but we feel convinced that the slow plan of publication has been of immense advantage to the book in deepening the impression it produces. Still, I shudder a little to think what a long book it will be—not so long as Vanity Fair or Pendennis, however, according to my calculation.

4 [*Sidney Colvin*]

"Middlemarch," *The Fortnightly Review,* January 1, 1873[1]

Fifteen months of pausing and recurring literary excitement are at an end; and "Middlemarch," the chief English book of the immediate present, lies complete before us. Now that we have the book as a whole, what place does it seem to take among the rest with which its illustrious writer has enriched, I will not say posterity, because

1. Vol. XIII (new series), pp. 142–147.

for posterity every present is apt in turn to prove itself a shallow judge, but her own generation and us who delight to honour her?

In the sense in which anything is called ripe because of fulness and strength, I think the last of George Eliot's novels is also the ripest. "Middlemarch" is extraordinarily full and strong, even among the company to which it belongs. And though I am not sure that it is the property of George Eliot's writing to satisfy, its property certainly is to rouse and attach, in proportion to its fulness and strength. There is nothing in the literature of the day so rousing —to the mind of the day there is scarcely anything so rousing in all literature—as her writing is. What she writes is so full of her time. It is observation, imagination, pathos, wit and humour, all of a high class in themselves; but what is more, all saturated with modern ideas, and poured into a language of which every word bites home with peculiar sharpness to the contemporary consciousness. That is what makes it less safe than it might seem at first sight to speak for posterity in such a case. We are afraid of exaggerating the meaning such work will have for those who come after us, for the very reason that we feel its meaning so pregnant for ourselves. If, indeed, the ideas of to-day are certain to be the ideas of to-morrow and the day after, if scientific thought and the positive synthesis are indubitably to rule the world, then any one, it should seem, might speak boldly enough to George Eliot's place. For the general definition of her work, I should say, is precisely this—that, among writers of the imagination, she has taken the lead in expressing and discussing the lives and ways of common folks—*votum, timor, ira, voluptas*—in terms of scientific thought and the positive synthesis. She has walked between two epochs, upon the confines of two worlds, and has described the old in terms of the new. To the old world belong the elements of her experience, to the new world the elements of her reflection on experience. The elements of her experience are the "English Provincial Life" before the Reform Bill—the desires and alarms, indignations and satisfactions, of the human breast in county towns and villages, farms and parsonages, manor-houses, counting-houses, surgeries, streets and lanes, shops and fields, of midlands unshaken in their prejudices and unvisited by the steam-engine. To the new world belong the elements of her reflection; the many-sided culture which looks back upon prejudice with analytical amusement; the philosophy which declares the human family deluded in its higher dreams, dependent upon itself, and bound thereby to a closer if a sadder brotherhood; the habit in regarding and meditating physical laws, and the facts of sense and life, which leads up to that philosophy and belongs to it; the mingled depth of bitterness and tenderness in the human temper of which the philosophy becomes the spring.

Thus there is the most pointed contrast between the matter of these English tales and the manner of their telling. The matter is antiquated in our recollections, the manner seems to anticipate the future of our thoughts. Plenty of other writers have taken humdrum and narrow aspects of English life with which they were familiar, and by delicacy of perception and justness of rendering have put them together into pleasant works of literary art, without running the matter into a manner out of direct correspondence with it. But this procedure of George Eliot's is a newer thing in literature, and infinitely harder to judge of, than the gray and tranquil harmonies of that other mode of art. For no writer uses so many instruments in riveting the interest of the cultivated reader about the characters, and springs of character, which she is exhibiting. First, I say, she has the perpetual application of her own intelligence to the broad problems and conclusions of modern thought. That, for instance, when Fred Vincy, having brought losses upon the Garth family, feels his own dishonour more than their suffering, brings the reflection how *"we are most of us brought up in the notion that the highest motive for not doing a wrong is something irrespective of the beings who would suffer the wrong."* That again, a few pages later, brings the humorous allusions to Caleb Garth's classification of human employments, into business, politics, preaching, learning, and amusement, as one which *"like the categories of more celebrated men, would not be acceptable in these more advanced times."* And that makes it impossible to describe the roguery of a horsedealer without suggesting that he *"regarded horse-dealing as the finest of the arts, and might have argued plausibly that it had nothing to do with morality."*

Next, this writer possesses, in her own sympathetic insight into the workings of human nature, a psychological instrument which will be perpetually displaying its power, its subtlety and trenchancy, in passages like this which lays bare the working of poor Mrs. Bulstrode's faithful mind upon the revelation of her husband's guilt: "Along with her brother's looks and words, there darted into her mind the idea of some guilt in her husband. Then, under the working of terror, came the image of her husband exposed to disgrace; *and then, after an instant of scorching shame in which she only felt the eyes of the world, with one leap of her heart she was at his side in mournful but unreproaching fellowship with shame and isolation.*" Of the same trenchancy and potency, equally subtle and equally sure of themselves, are a hundred other processes of analysis, whether applied to serious crises—like that prolonged one during which Bulstrode wavers before the passive murder which shall rid him of his one obstacle as an efficient servant of God—or to such trivial crises as occur in the experiences of a Mrs. Dollop or a Mrs. Taft, or others who, being their betters, still belong to the class of "well-meaning women knowing very little of their own motives." And this powerful knowledge of human nature is still only one of many instruments for exposing a character and turning it about. What the character itself thinks and feels, exposed by this, will receive a simultaneous commentary in what the modern analytic mind has to remark upon such thoughts and feelings: see a good instance in the account (. . . Book III.) of Mr. Casaubon's motives before marriage and experiences after it.

Then, the writer's studies in science and physiology will constantly come in to suggest for the spiritual processes of her personages an explanation here or an illustration there. For a stroke of overwhelming power in this kind, take what is said in one place of Bulstrode—that "he shrank from a direct lie with an intensity disproportionate to the number of his more indirect misdeeds. *But many of these misdeeds were like the subtle muscular movements which are not taken account of in the consciousness, though they bring about the end that we fix in our minds and desire. And it is only what we are vividly conscious of that we can vividly imagine to be seen by Omniscience.*"

And it is yet another instrument which the writer handles when she seizes on critical points of physical look and gesture in her personages, in a way which is scientific and her own. True, there are many descriptions, and especially of the beauty and gestures of

Dorothea—and these are written with a peculiarly loving and as it were watchful exquisiteness—which may be put down as belonging to the ordinary resources of art. But look at Caleb Garth; he is a complete physiognomical study in the sense of Mr. Darwin, with the "deepened depression in the outer angle of his bushy eyebrows, which gave his face a peculiar mildness;" with his trick of "broadening himself by putting his thumbs into his arm-holes," and the rest. Such are Rosamond's ways of turning her neck aside and patting her hair when she is going to be obstinate. So, we are not allowed to forget "a certain massiveness in Lydgate's manner and tone, corresponding with his physique;" nor indeed, any point of figure and physiognomy which strike the author's imagination as symptomatic. Symptomatic is the best word. There is a medical strain in the tissue of the story. There is a profound sense of the importance of physiological conditions in human life. But further still, I think, there is something like a medical habit in the writer, of examining her own creations for their symptoms, which runs through her descriptive and narrative art and gives it some of its peculiar manner.

So that, apart from the presence of rousing thought in general maxims and allusions, we know now what we mean when we speak of the fulness and strength derived, in the dramatic and narrative part of the work, from the use of so many instruments as we have seen. Then comes the question, do these qualities satisfy us as thoroughly as they rouse and interest? Sometimes I think they do, and sometimes not. Nothing evidently can be more satisfying, more illuminating, than that sentence which explained, by a primitive fact in the experimental relations of mind and body, a peculiar kind of bluntness in the conscience of the religious Bulstrode. And generally, wherever the novelist applies her philosophy or science to serious purposes, even if it may be applied too often, its effect seems to me good. But in lighter applications I doubt if the same kind of thing is not sometimes mistaken. The wit and humour of this writer every one of us knows and has revelled in; I do not think these want to gain body from an elaborate or semi-scientific language. In the expression of fun or common observation, is not such language apt to read a little technical and heavy, like a kind of intellectual slang? I do not think the delightful fun about Mrs. Garth and Mary and the children gains by it. I doubt if it is in place when it is applied to the mental processes of Mrs. Dollop or Mr. Bambridge. And when, for example, we are asked to consider what would have happened if Fred Vincy's "prophetic soul had been urged to particularize," that is what I mean by something like a kind of intellectual slang.

But all this only concerns some methods or processes of the writer, picked from random points in the development of her new story and its characters. What of these in themselves? Well, there comes back the old sense, of a difference to the degree to which we are roused, attached, and taught, and the degree to which we are satisfied. The book is full of high feeling, wisdom, and acuteness. It contains some of the most moving dramatic scenes in our literature. A scene like that of Dorothea in her night of agony, a scene like that in which the greatness of her nature ennobles for a moment the smallness of Rosamond's, is consummate alike in conception and in style. The characters are admirable in their vigour and individuality, as well as in the vividness and fulness of illustration with which we have seen that they are exhibited. Dorothea with her generous ardour and ideal cravings; Mr. Brooke with his good-natured viewy incoherency and self-complacence; Celia with her narrow worldly sense seasoned by affectionateness; Chettam with his honourable prejudices; Ladislaw with his dispersed ambitions, and the dispositions and susceptibilities of his origin; Casaubon with his learning which is lumber, his formalism and inaccessibility of character, his distrust of himself and other people; Lydgate with his solid ambitions which fail, and his hollow which succeed; Rosamond "with that hard slight thing called girlishness," and all the faults which can underlie skin-deep graces; Bulstrode with the piety designed in vain to propitiate the chastisement of destiny; the witty unscrupulous rattle of Mrs. Cadwallader; the Garth household, the Farebrother household, the Vincys, the country bankers and country tradesmen, the rival practitioners, the horse-dealer, the drunkard who is the ghost of Bulstrode's ancient sin—all these are living and abiding additions to every one's circle of the familiar acquaintances that importune not. But as one turns them over in one's mind or talk, them and and their fortunes in the book, with laughter or sympathy or pity or indignation or love, there will arise all sorts of questionings, debatings, such as do not arise after a reading which has left the mind satisfied. One calls in question this or that point in the conduct of the story; the attitude which the writer personally assumes towards her own creation; the general lesson which seems to underlie her scheme; above all, the impression which its issue leaves upon oneself.

The questions one asks are such as, within limits like these, it would be idle to attempt to solve, or even to state, except in the most fragmentary way. Are not, for instance, some points in the story a little coarsely invented and handled? At the very outset, is not the hideous nature of Dorothea's blind sacrifice too ruthlessly driven home to us, when it ought to have been allowed to reveal itself by gentler degrees? Is it not too repulsive to talk of the moles on Casaubon's face, and to make us loathe the union from the beginning? Is not the formalism and dryness of Casaubon's nature a little overdone in his first conversation and his letter of courtship? Or again, is not the whole intrigue of Ladislaw's birth and Bulstrode's guilt, the Jew pawnbroker and Raffles, somewhat common and poor? The story is made to hinge twice, at two important junctures, upon the incidents of watching by a death-bed. Is that scant invention, or is it a just device for bringing out, under nearly parallel circumstances, the opposite characters of Mary Garth and of Bulstrode—her untroubled and decisive integrity under difficulties, his wavering conscience, which, when to be passive is already to be a murderer, permits itself at last in something just beyond passiveness? Or, to shift the ground of question, does not the author seem a little unwarrantably hard upon some of her personages and kind to others? Fred and Rosamond Vincy, for instance—one would have said there was not so much to choose. The author, however, is on the whole kind to the brother, showing up his faults but not harshly, and making him in the end an example of how an amiable spendthrift may be redeemed by a good man's help and a good girl's love. While to the sister, within whose mind "there was not room enough for luxuries to look small in," she shows a really merciless animosity, and gibbets her as an example of how an unworthy wife may degrade the career of a man of high purposes and capacities. Celia, too, who is not really so very much higher a character, the author makes quite a pet of in comparison, and puts her in situations where all her small virtues tell; and so on. Minute differences of character for better or worse may justly be shown, of course, as producing vast differences of effect under the impulsion of circumstances. Still, I do not think it is altogether fancy to find wanting here the impartiality of the greatest creators toward their mind's offspring.

Then, for the general lesson of the book, it is not easy to feel quite sure what it is, or how much importance the author gives it. In her prelude and conclusion both, she seems to insist upon the design of illustrating the necessary disappointment of a woman's nobler aspirations in a society not made to second noble aspirations in a woman. And that is one of the most burning lessons which any writer could set themselves [sic] to illustrate. But then, Dorothea does not suffer in her ideal aspirations from yielding to the pressure of social opinion. She suffers in them from finding that what she has done, in marrying an old scholar in the face of social opinion, was done under a delusion as to the old scholar's character. "Exactly," is apparently the author's drift; "but it is society which so nurtures women that their ideals cannot but be ideals of delusion." Taking this as the author's main point (and I think prelude and conclusion leave it still ambiguous), there are certainly passages enough in the body of the narrative which point the same remonstrance against what society does for women. *"The shallowness of a water-nixie's soul may have a charm till she becomes didactic:"* that describes the worthlessness of what men vulgarly prize in women. *"In the British climate there is no incompatibility between scientific insight and furnished lodgings. The incompatibility is chiefly between scientific ambition and a wife who objects to that kind of residence."* That points to the rarity of a woman, as women are brought up, who prefers the things of the mind to luxury. *" 'Of course she is devoted to her husband,' said Rosamond, implying a notion of necessary sequence which the scientific man regarded as the prettiest possible for a woman."* That points with poignant irony to the science, as to the realities of society and the heart, of men whose science is solid in other things.

It is perhaps in pursuance of the same idea that Dorothea's destiny, after Casaubon has died, and she is free from the consequences of a first illusory ideal, is not made very brilliant after all. She cannot be an Antigone or a Theresa. She marries the man of her choice, and bears him children; but we have been made to feel all along that he is hardly worthy of her. There is no sense of triumph in it; there is rather a sense of sadness in a subdued and restricted, if not now a thwarted destiny. In this issue there is a deep depression; there is that blending of the author's bitterness with her profound tenderness of which I have already spoken. And upon this depends, or with it hangs together, that feeling of uncertainty and unsatisfiedness as to the whole fable and its impression which remains with the reader when all is done. He could spare the joybells —the vulgar upshot of happiness for ever after—Sophia surrendered to the arms of her enraptured Jones—if he felt quite sure of the moral or intellectual point of view which had dictated so chastened and subdued a conclusion. As it is, he does not feel clear enough about the point of view, the lesson, the main moral and intellectual outcome, to put up with that which he feels to be uncomfortable in the combinations of the story, and flat in the fates of friends and acquaintances who have been brought so marvellously near to him.

That these and such like questionings should remain in the mind, after the reading of a great work of fiction, would in ordinary phrase be said to indicate that, however great the other qualities of the work, it was deficient in qualities of art. The fact is, that this writer brings into her fiction so many new elements, and gives it pregnancy and significance in so many unaccustomed directions, that it is presumptuousness to pronounce in that way as to the question of art. Certainly, it is possible to write with as little illusion, or with forms of disillusion much more cynical, as to society and its dealings and issues, and yet to leave a more harmonious and definite artistic impression than is here left. French writers perpetually do so. But then George Eliot, with her science and her disillusion, has the sense of bad and good as the great French literary artists have not got it, and is taken up, as they are not, with the properly moral elements of human life and struggling. They exceed in all that pertains to the passions of the individual; she cares more than they do for the general beyond the individual. That it is by which she rouses—I say rouses, attaches, and elevates—so much more than they do, even if her combinations satisfy much less. Is it, then, that a harmonious and satisfying literary art is impossible under these conditions? Is it that a literature, which confronts all the problems of life and the

world, and recognises all the springs of action, and all that clogs the
springs, and all that comes from their smooth or impeded working,
and all the importance of one life for the mass,—is it that such a
literature must be like life itself, to leave us sad and hungry?

5 [Henry James]

"Middlemarch," The Galaxy, March, 1873[1]

"Middlemarch" is at once one of the strongest and one of the
weakest of English novels. Its predecessors as they appeared might
have been described in the same terms; "Romola," is especially a
rare masterpiece, but the least *entraînant* of masterpieces. "Romola"
sins by excess of analysis; there is too much description and too little drama; too much reflection (all certainly of a highly imaginative
sort) and too little creation. Movement lingers in the story, and
with it attention stands still in the reader. The error in "Middlemarch" is not precisely of a similar kind, but it is equally detrimental
to the total aspect of the work. We can well remember how keenly
we wondered, while its earlier chapters unfolded themselves, what
turn in the way of form the story would take—that of an organized,
moulded, balanced composition, gratifying the reader with a sense of
design and construction, or a mere chain of episodes, broken into
accidental lengths and unconscious of the influence of a plan. We
expected the actual result, but for the sake of English imaginative
literature which, in this line is rarely in need of examples, we hoped
for the other. If it had come we should have had the pleasure of
reading, what certainly would have seemed to us in the immediate
glow of attention, the first of English novels. But that pleasure has
still to hover between prospect and retrospect. "Middlemarch" is
a treasure-house of details, but it is an indifferent whole.

Our objection may seem shallow and pedantic, and may even be
represented as a complaint that we have had the less given us rather
than the more. Certainly the greatest minds have the defects of

1. Vol. XV, pp. 424–428. *The Galaxy* was an American periodical.

their qualities, and as George Eliot's mind is preëminently contemplative and analytic, nothing is more natural than that her manner should be discursive and expansive. "Concentration" would doubtless have deprived us of many of the best things in the book—of Peter Featherstone's grotesquely expectant legatees, of Lydgate's medical rivals, and of Mary Garth's delightful family. The author's purpose was to be a generous rural historian, and this very redundancy of touch, born of abundant reminiscence, is one of the greatest charms of her work. It is as if her memory was crowded with antique figures, to whom for very tenderness she must grant an appearance. Her novel is a picture—vast, swarming, deep-colored, crowded with episodes, with vivid images, with lurking master-strokes, with brilliant passages of expression; and as such we may freely accept it and enjoy it. It is not compact, doubtless; but when was a panorama compact? And yet, nominally, "Middlemarch" has a definite subject —the subject indicated in the eloquent preface. An ardent young girl was to have been the central figure, a young girl framed for a larger moral life than circumstance often affords, yearning for a motive for sustained spiritual effort and only wasting her ardor and soiling her wings against the meanness of opportunity. The author, in other words, proposed to depict the career of an obscure St. Theresa. Her success has been great, in spite of serious drawbacks. Dorothea Brooke is a genuine creation, and a most remarkable one when we consider the delicate material in which she is wrought. George Eliot's men are generally so much better than the usual trowsered offspring of the female fancy, that their merits have perhaps overshadowed those of her women. Yet her heroines have always been of an exquisite quality, and Dorothea is only that perfect flower of conception of which her predecessors were the less unfolded blossoms. An indefinable moral elevation is the sign of these admirable creatures; and of the representation of this quality in its superior degrees the author seems to have in English fiction a monopoly. To render the expression of a soul requires a cunning hand; but we seem to look straight into the unfathomable eyes of the beautiful spirit of Dorothea Brooke. She exhales a sort of aroma of spiritual sweetness, and we believe in her as in a woman we might providentially meet some fine day when we should find ourselves doubting of the immortality of the soul. By what unerring mechanism this effect is produced—whether by fine strokes or broad ones, by description or by narration, we can hardly say; it is certainly the great achievement of the book. Dorothea's career is, however, but an episode, and though doubtless in intention, not distinctly enough in fact, the central one. The history of Lydgate's *menage*, which shares honors with it, seems rather to the reader to carry off the lion's share. This is certainly a very interesting story, but on the whole it yields in dignity to the record of Dorothea's unresonant woes. The "love-problem," as the author calls it, of Mary Garth, is placed on a rather higher level than the reader willingly grants it. To the end we care less about Fred Vincy than appears to be expected of us. In so far as the writer's design has been to reproduce the total sum of life in an English village forty years ago, this common place young gentleman, with his somewhat meagre tribulations and his rather neutral egotism, has his proper place in the picture; but the author narrates his fortunes with a fulness of detail which the reader often finds irritating. The reader indeed is sometimes tempted to complain of a tendency which we are at loss exactly to express—a tendency to make light of the serious elements of the story and to sacrifice them to the more trivial ones. Is it an unconscious instinct or is it a deliberate plan? With its abundant and massive ingredients "Middlemarch" ought somehow to have depicted a weightier drama. Dorothea was altogether too superb a heroine to be wasted; yet she plays a narrower part than the imagination of the reader demands. She is of more consequence than the action of which she is the nominal centre. She marries enthusiastically a man whom she fancies a great thinker, and who turns out to be but an arid pedant. Here, indeed, is a disappointment with much of the dignity of tragedy; but the situation seems to us never to expand to its full capacity. It is analyzed with extraordinary penetration, but one may say of it, as of most of the situations in the book, that it is treated with too much refinement and too little breadth. It revolves too constantly on the same pivot; it abounds in fine shades, but it lacks, we think, the great dramatic *chiaroscuro*. Mr. Casaubon, Dorothea's husband (of whom more anon) embittered, on his side, by matrimonial disappointment, takes refuge in vain jealousy of his wife's relations with an interesting young cousin of his own and registers this sentiment in a codicil to his will, mak-

ing the forfeiture of his property the penalty of his widow's marriage
with this gentleman. Mr. Casaubon's death befalls about the middle
of the story, and from this point to the close our interest in Dorothea
is restricted to the question, will she or will [*sic*] not marry Will Ladislaw? The question is relatively trivial and the implied struggle
slightly factitious. The author has depicted the struggle with a sort
of elaborate solemnity which in the interviews related in the two
last books tends to become almost ludicrously excessive.

The dramatic current stagnates; it runs between hero and heroine
almost a game of hair-splitting. Our dissatisfaction here is provoked
in a great measure by the insubstantial character of the hero. The
figure of Will Ladislaw is a beautiful attempt, with many finely-com-
pleted points; but on the whole it seems to us a failure. It is the
only eminent failure in the book, and its defects are therefore the
more striking. It lacks sharpness of outline and depth of color; we
have not found ourselves believing in Ladislaw as we believe in Dorothea, in Mary Garth, in Rosamond, in Lydgate, in Mr. Brooke and
Mr. Casaubon. He is meant, indeed, to be a light creature (with a
large capacity for gravity, for he finally gets into Parliament), and
a light creature certainly should not be heavily drawn. The author,
who is evidently very fond of him, has found for him here and there
some charming and eloquent touches; but in spite of these he remains vague and impalpable to the end. He is, we may say, the one
figure which a masculine intellect of the same power as George
Eliot's would not have conceived with the same complacency; he
is, in short, roughly speaking, a woman's man. It strikes us as an
oddity in the author's scheme that she should have chosen just this
figure of Ladislaw as the creature in whom Dorothea was to find her
spiritual compensations. He is really, after all, not the ideal foil to
Mr. Casaubon which her soul must have imperiously demanded,
and if the author of the "Key to all Mythologies" sinned by lack of
order, Ladislaw too has not the concentrated fervor essential in the
man chosen by so nobly strenuous a heroine. The impression once
given that he is a *dilettante* is never properly removed, and there is
slender poetic justice in Dorothea's marrying a *dilettante*. We are
doubtless less content with Ladislaw, on account of the noble, almost
sculptural, relief of the neighboring figure of Lydgate, the real hero
of the story. It is an illustration of the generous scale of the author's

picture and of the conscious power of her imagination that she has given us a hero and heroine of broadly distinct interests—erected, as it were, two suns in her firmament, each with its independent solar system. Lydgate is so richly successful a figure that we have regretted strongly at moments, for immediate interests' sake, that the current of his fortunes should not mingle more freely with the occasionally thin-flowing stream of Dorothea's. Toward the close, these two fine characters are brought into momentary contact so effectively as to suggest a wealth of dramatic possibility between them; but if this train had been followed we should have lost Rosamond Vincy —a rare psychological study. Lydgate is a really complete portrait of a *man*, which seems to us high praise. It is striking evidence of the altogether superior quality of George Eliot's imagination that, though elaborately represented, Lydgate should be treated so little from what we may roughly (and we trust without offence) call the sexual point of view. Perception charged with feeling has constantly guided the author's hand, and yet her strokes remain as firm, her curves as free, her whole manner as serenely impersonal, as if, on a small scale, she were emulating the creative wisdom itself. Several English romancers—notably Fielding, Thackeray, and Charles Reade—have won great praise for their figures of women: but they owe it, in reversed conditions, to a meaner sort of art, it seems to us, than George Eliot has used in the case of Lydgate; to an indefinable appeal to masculine prejudice—to a sort of titillation of the masculine sense of difference. George Eliot's manner is more philosophic—more broadly intelligent, and yet her result is as concrete or, if you please, as picturesque. We have no space to dwell on Lydgate's character; we can but repeat that he is a vividly consistent, manly figure—powerful, ambitious, sagacious, with the maximum rather than the mimimum of egotism, strenuous, generous, fallible, and altogether human. A work of the liberal scope of "Middlemarch" contains a multitude of artistic intentions, some of the finest of which become clear only in the meditative after-taste of perusal. This is the case with the balanced contrast between the two histories of Lydgate and Dorothea. Each is a tale of matrimonial infelicity, but the conditions in each are so different and the circumstances so broadly opposed that the mind passes from one to the other with that supreme sense of the vastness and variety of human life, under aspects apparently similar, which it belongs only to the greatest novels to produce. The most perfectly successful passages in the book are perhaps those painful fireside scenes between Lydgate and his miserable little wife. The author's rare psychological penetration is lavished upon this veritably mulish domestic flower. There is nothing more powerfully real than these scenes in all English fiction, and nothing certainly more *intelligent*. Their impressiveness, and (as regards Lydgate) their pathos, is deepened by the constantly low key in which they are pitched. It is a tragedy based on unpaid butchers' bills, and the urgent need for small economies. The author has desired to be strictly real and to adhere to the facts of the common lot, and she has given us a powerful version of that typical human drama, the struggles of an ambitious soul with sordid disappointments and vulgar embarrassments. As to her catastrophe we hesitate to pronounce (for Lydgate's ultimate assent to his wife's worldly programme is nothing less than a catastrophe). We almost believe that some terrific explosion would have been more probable than his twenty years of smothered aspiration. Rosamond deserves almost to rank with Tito in "Romola" as a study of a gracefully vicious, or at least of a practically baleful nature. There is one point, however, of which we question the consistency. The author insists on her instincts of coquetry, which seems to us a discordant note. They would have made her better or worse —more generous or more reckless; in either case more manageable. As it is, Rosamond represents, in a measure, the fatality of British decorum.

In reading, we have marked innumerable passages for quotation and comment; but we lack space and the work is so ample that half a dozen extracts would be an ineffective illustration. There would be a great deal to say on the broad array of secondary figures, Mr. Casaubon, Mr. Brooke, Mr. Bulstrode, Mr. Farebrother, Caleb Garth, Mrs. Cadwallader, Celia Brooke. Mr. Casaubon is an excellent invention; as a dusky *repoussoir* to the luminous figure of his wife he could not have been better imagined. There is indeed something very noble in the way in which the author has apprehended his character. To depict hollow pretentiousness and mouldy egotism with so little of narrow sarcasm and so much of philosophic sympathy, is to be a rare moralist as well as a rare story-teller. The whole portrait of Mr. Casaubon has an admirably sustained greyness of tone in which the shadows are never carried to the vulgar black of coarser artists. Every stroke contributes to the unwholesome, helplessly sinister expression. Here and there perhaps (as in his habitual diction), there is a hint of exaggeration; but we confess we like fancy to be fanciful. Mr. Brooke and Mr. Garth are in their different lines supremely genial creations; they are drawn with the touch of a Dickens chastened and intellectualized. Mrs. Cadwallader is, in another walk of life, a match for Mrs. Poyser, and Celia Brooke is as pretty a fool as any of Miss Austen's. Mr. Farebrother and his delightful "womankind" belong to a large group of figures begotten of the superabundance of the author's creative instinct. At times they seem to encumber the stage and to produce a rather ponderous mass of dialogue; but they add to the reader's impression of having walked in the Middlemarch lanes and listened to the Middlemarch accent. To but one of these accessory episodes— that of Mr. Bulstrode, with its multiplex ramifications—do we take exception. It has a slightly artificial cast, a melodramatic tinge, unfriendly to the richly natural coloring of the whole. Bulstrode himself—with the history of whose troubled conscience the author has taken great pains—is, to our sense, too diffusely treated; he never grasps the reader's attention. But the touch of genius is never idle or vain. The obscure figure of Bulstrode's comely wife emerges at the needful moment, under a few light strokes, into the happiest reality.

All these people, solid and vivid in their varying degrees, are members of a deeply human little world, the full reflection of whose antique image is the great merit of these volumes. How bravely rounded a little world the author has made it—with how dense an atmosphere of interests and passions and loves and enmities and strivings and failings, and how motley a group of great folk and small, all after their kind, she has filled it, the reader must learn for himself. No writer seems to us to have drawn from a richer stock of those long-cherished memories which one's later philosophy makes doubly tender. There are few figures in the book which do not seem to have grown mellow in the author's mind. English readers may fancy they enjoy the "atmosphere" of "Middlemarch;" but we maintain that to relish its inner essence we must—for reasons too numerous to detail—be an American. The author has commissioned herself to be real, her native tendency being that of an idealist, and the intellectual result is a very fertilizing mixture. The constant presence of thought, of generalizing instinct, of *brain*, in a word, behind her observation, gives the latter its great value and her whole manner its high superiority. It denotes a mind in which imagination is illumined by faculties rarely found in fellowship with it. In this respect—in that broad reach of vision which would make the worthy historian of solemn fact as well as wanton fiction—George Eliot seems to us among English romancers to stand alone. Fielding approaches her, but to our mind, she surpasses Fielding. Fielding was didactic—the author of "Middlemarch" is really philosophic. These great qualities imply corresponding perils. The first is the loss of simplicity. George Eliot lost hers some time since: it lies buried (in a splendid mausoleum) in "Romola." Many of the discursive portions of "Middlemarch" are, as we may say, too clever by half. The author wishes to say too many things, and to say them too well; to recommend herself to a scientific audience. Her style, rich and flexible as it is, is apt to betray her on these transcendental flights; we find, in our copy, a dozen passages marked "obscure." "Silas Marner" has a delightful tinge of Goldsmith—we may almost call it: "Middlemarch" is too often an echo of Messrs. Darwin and Huxley. In spite of these faults—which it seems graceless to indicate with this crude rapidity—it remains a very splendid performance. It sets a limit, we think, to the development of the old-fashioned English novel. Its diffuseness, on which we have touched, makes it too copious a dose of pure fiction. If we write novels so, how shall we write History? But it is nevertheless a contribution of the first importance to the rich imaginative department of our literature.

Thomas Hardy
Jude the Obscure
1895

1 A[lgernon] C[harles] Swinburne

A Letter to Thomas Hardy, November 5, 1895[1]

Thank you most sincerely for the gift of 'Jude.' The tragedy—if I may venture an opinion—is equally beautiful and terrible in its pathos. The beauty, the terror, and the truth, are all yours, and yours alone. But (if I may [say] so) how cruel you are! Only the great and awful father of 'Pierrette' and 'L'Enfant Maudit' was ever so merciless to his children. I think it would hardly be seemly to enlarge on all that I admire in your work—or on half of it. The man who can do such work can hardly care about criticism or praise, but I will risk saying how thankful we should be (I know that I may speak for other admirers as cordial as myself) for another admission into an English paradise 'under the greenwood tree.' But if you prefer to be—or to remain—ποιητῶν τραγικώτατος;[2] no doubt

---

1. Reprinted, by permission of the publisher, from Cecil Y. Lang, ed., *The Swinburne Letters,* New Haven: Yale University Press, 1959–62, vol. VI, p. 91.
2. "most tragic of poets"

you may; for Balzac is dead, and there has been no such tragedy in fiction—on anything like the same lines—since he died.

2 Jeannette L. Gilder

FROM "Thomas Hardy Makes a New Departure," *The World,* December 8, 1895[1]

What has happened to Thomas Hardy? What has gone wrong with the hand that wrote "Far from the Madding Crowd?" I am shocked, appalled by this story, "Jude, the Obscure." . . . It is almost the worst book I have ever read. I only know of one of Balzac's that is as bad. To think that such a story as this should be written by Thomas Hardy, one of the few really great writers of modern fiction! What has twisted this brilliant mind? What caused those clear eyes to see so darkly?

I thought that "Tess of the D'Urbervilles" was bad enough, but that is milk for babes compared to this. No wonder that Harper's Magazine could not print it all.[2] The only wonder is that it could print any of it, knowing all that was there. In the book, apparently, there has been no expurgating.

Heaven knows what has come over Thomas Hardy that he should write in this way. The story would seem to advocate free love and the abolition of the marriage tie, if we judge by its arguments, but how can a man argue for free love with words and show its terrible consequences as does Mr. Hardy?

"For a novel," says Mr. Hardy, "addressed by a man to men and women of full age, which attempts to deal unaffectedly with the fret and fever, derision and disaster that may press in the wake of the strongest passion known to humanity, and to point without a mincing of words the tragedy of unfulfilled aims, I am not aware

1. *The World* was an American newspaper.
2. *Jude the Obscure* had first appeared, in a less "shocking" version, as a serial in *Harper's Magazine.*

that there is anything in the handling to which exception can be taken."[1]

NO NEWSPAPER WOULD PRINT IT

More's the pity, Mr. Hardy, more's the pity! It is the "handling" of it that is the horror of it. The daily press is not accused of squeamishness by either its friends or its enemies. It is accused by the latter of printing questionable articles in its columns. And yet I do not believe that there is a newspaper in England or America that would print this story of Thomas Hardy's as it stands in the book. Aside from its immorality, there is its coarseness, which is beyond belief. Unnecessary coarseness that does not add one iota to the value of the story. Brutal, horrible coarseness inconceivable in a man of Mr. Hardy's great gifts and earlier performance.

COARSENESS AND BRUTALITY

As for the people in this terrible story, there is only one with any semblance to reality, and he is Phillotson, the husband of Sue. As for Jude, he is a beast, and so is Arabella. She is an impossible person, and little Jude, "Father Time," is an absurdity. It may have been weak in Phillotson to consent to his young wife leaving him for another man, but there was not much else for him to do. He knew that she did not care for him and that she did care for Jude. She was making his life a hell, and hers too, for that matter, so he gave her her freedom. Some husbands would have considered her deranged and locked her up in an asylum, but Phillotson took her at her word and let her go. . . .

LOVE AND PIG-STICKING

Mr. Hardy's mind seems to be grovelling all through this story. He goes out of his way to write of nastiness. When Jude first sees Arabella she is with a group of girls kneeling beside a brook "with buckets and platters beside them containing heaps of pig's chitterlings, which they were washing in the water." Arabella spying Jude on the other side of the stream, playfully threw a bit of pig's "innards" at him and struck him on the ear.

1. This quotation from Hardy's preface is slightly garbled.

This was the beginning of her courtship of that susceptible young man. They get married, and one of the first domestic scenes described is a pig killing. Mr. Hardy's mind seems to run to pigs—animal and human. . . .

TOO FILTHY TO PRINT

The singular thing is that Jude, though a drunkard and a libertine, wanted to be a preacher. A stonecutter by trade, he learned Greek and Latin in his leisure moments, and hoped to get a university education that he might take orders and enter the Church. He seems to have been a sort of Jekyll and Hyde, with the Hyde uppermost.

As far as the writing goes, no one can find fault with Mr. Hardy. He is a master of the art of story-telling. Even with such a story as this he holds the reader's attention, though filling him with disgust. I thought before I read the book that it might be interesting to compare the expurgated with the unexpurgated story, as it was with "Trilby," but after reading it I find that this is impossible. The latter could not be printed here, and I assuredly would not wish to call attention to such things.

No one will be the better for having read this book, but many will be the worse for it. When I finished the story, I opened the windows and let in the fresh air, and I turned to my book-shelves and I said: "Thank God for Kipling, and Stevenson, Barrie and Mrs. Humphry Ward. Here are four great writers who have never trailed their talents in the dirt."

3 M[argaret] O[liphant] W. O[liphant]

FROM "The Anti-Marriage League," *Blackwood's Edinburgh Magazine,* January, 1896[1]

I do not know . . . for what audience Mr Hardy intends his last work, which has been introduced, as he tells us, for the last twelve months, into a number of decent houses in England and America,

1. Vol. CLIX, pp. 137–142.

with the most shameful portions suppressed. How they could be suppressed in a book whose tendency throughout is so shameful I do
not understand; but it is to be hoped that the conductors and readers of 'Harper's Magazine' were so protected by ignorance as not to
understand what the writer meant then—though he now states it
with a plainness beyond mistake. I hesitate to confess that until the
publication of Mr Hardy's last book, 'Tess,' I was one of those who
had not been convinced of the extent of his power, or of the
amount of real genius he possessed. The difference between that
book and the former books from his hand was, it appeared to me,
very great. It marked the moment of his supposed emancipation
from prejudices of modesty which had previously held him (more or
less, and sometimes rather less than more) from full enunciation
of what was in him. And certainly the result of the *débordement* was
very remarkable. To demonstrate that a woman, twice fallen from
the woman's code of honour and purity, was by that fact proved to
be specially and aggressively pure, was a task for a Hercules, and
Mr Hardy has no more succeeded in doing this than others have
done before him; but the rustic landscape, the balmy breathing of
the cows, looming out of the haze in the mystery of the dawn—the
rapture of the morning in the silent fields, the large figures of the
men and women shaping out of the mist and dews—were things to
call forth the enthusiasm of admiration with which indeed they were
received. But I suppose Mr Hardy, like so many people, deceived by
a simplicity which clings to genius, even when most self-conscious,
was not aware what it was which procured him this fame, and ingenuously believed it to be the worser part, the doctrine he preached,
and the very hideous circumstances of guilt, unjustified even by passion, of his theme, and not these better things—which thus uplifted
him suddenly to the skies.

This perhaps explains, or partially explains, the tremendous downfall of the present book, which, by following 'Tess,' accentuates its
own grossness, indecency, and horror. Nothing, I think, but a theory
could explain the wonderful want of perception which induces a man
full of perceptions to make a mistake so fundamental; but it is done
—and thus unconsciously affords us the strangest illustration of what
Art can come to when given over to the exposition of the unclean.
The present writer does not pretend to a knowledge of the works

of Zola, which perhaps she ought to have before presuming to say
that nothing so coarsely indecent as the whole history of Jude in his
relations with his wife Arabella has ever been put in English print
—that is to say, from the hands of a Master. There may be books
more disgusting, more impious as regards human nature, more foul
in detail, in those dark corners where the amateurs of filth find
garbage to their taste; but not, we repeat, from any Master's hand.
It is vain to tell us that there are scenes in Shakespeare himself
which, if they were picked out for special attention, would be offensive to modesty. There is no need for picking out in the work now
referred to. Its faults do not lie in mere suggestion, or any *double
entendre,* though these are bad enough. In the history of Jude, the
half-educated and by no means uninteresting hero in whose early
self-training there is much that is admirable—Mr Hardy has given
us a chapter in what used to be called the conflict between vice and
virtue. The young man, vaguely aspiring after education, learning,
and a position among the scholars and students of the land, with a
piteous ignorance of the difficulties before him, yet that conviction
of being able to triumph over them, which, as we know, has often in
real life succeeded in doing so—is really an attractive figure at his
outset. He is virtuous by temperament, meaning no evil; bent upon
doing more than well, and elevating himself to the level which appears to him the highest in life. But he falls into the hands of a
woman so completely animal that it is at once too little and too
much to call her vicious. She is a human pig, like the beast whom in a
horrible scene she and her husband kill, quite without shame or
consciousness of any occasion for shame, yet not even carried away
by her senses or any overpowering impulse for their gratification,
so much worse than the sow, that it is entirely on a calculation of
profit that she puts forth her revolting spell. After the man has been
subjugated, a process through which the reader is required to follow
him closely (and Jude's own views on this subject are remarkable),
he is made for the rest of his life into a puppet flung about between
them by two women—the fleshly animal Arabella and the fantastic
Susan, the one ready to gratify him in whatever circumstances they
may meet, the other holding him on the tiptoe of expectation, with
a pretended reserve which is almost more indecent still. In this
curious dilemma the unfortunate Jude, who is always the puppet,

always acted upon by the others, never altogether loses our esteem. He is a very poor creature, but he would have liked much better to do well if they would have let him, and dies a virtuous victim of the eternal feminine, scarcely ever blamable, though always bearing both the misery and the shame.

We can with difficulty guess what is Mr Hardy's motive in portraying such a struggle. It can scarcely be said to be one of those attacks upon the institution of Marriage, which is the undisguised inspiration of some of the other books before us. It is marriage indeed which in the beginning works Jude's woe; and it is by marriage, or rather the marrying of himself and others, that his end is brought about. We rather think the author's object must be, having glorified women by the creation of Tess, to show after all what destructive and ruinous creatures they are, in general circumstances and in every development, whether brutal or refined. Arabella, the first—the pig-dealer's daughter, whose native qualities have been ripened by the experiences of a barmaid—is the Flesh, unmitigated by any touch of human feeling except that of merciless calculation as to what will be profitable for herself. She is the native product of the fields, the rustic woman, exuberant and overflowing with health, vanity, and appetite. The colloquy between her and her fellows in their disgusting work, after her first almost equally disgusting interview with Jude, is one of the most unutterable foulness—a shame to the language in which it is recorded and suggested; and the picture altogether of the country lasses at their outdoor work is more brutal in depravity than anything which the darkest slums could bring forth, as are the scenes in which their good advice is carried out. Is it possible that there are readers in England to whom this infamy can be palatable, and who, either in inadvertence or in wantonness, can *make it pay?* Mr Hardy informs us he has taken elaborate precautions to secure the double profit of the serial writer, by subduing his colours and diminishing his effects, in the presence of the less corrupt, so as to keep the perfection of filthiness for those who love it. It would be curious to compare in this unsavoury traffic how much of the sickening essence of his story Mr Hardy has thought his first public could stomach, and how many edifying details he has put in for the enlightenment of those who have no squeamish scruples to get over. The transaction is insulting to the public, with

whom he trades the viler wares under another name, with all the
suppressed passages restored, as old-book dealers say in their cata-
logues, recommending their ancient scandal to the amateurs of the
unclean. It is not the first time Mr Hardy has adopted this expedient. If the English public supports him in it, it will be to the shame
of every individual who thus confesses himself to like and accept
what the author himself acknowledges to be unfit for the eyes—not
of girls and young persons only, but of the ordinary reader,—the
men and women who read the Magazines, the public whom we address in these pages. That the prophets should prophesy falsely is
not the most important fact in national degradation: it is only
when the people love to have it so that the climax is attained.

The other woman—who makes virtue vicious by keeping the
physical facts of one relationship in life in constant prominence by
denying, as Arabella does by satisfying them, and even more skil-
fully and insistently than Arabella—the fantastic *raisonneuse,* Susan
[*sic*], completes the circle of the unclean. She marries to save herself from trouble; then quits her husband, to live a life of perpetual
temptation and resistance with her lover; then marries, or professes
to marry him, when her husband amiably divorces her without the
reason he supposes himself to have; and then, when a selfish conscience is tardily awakened, returns to the husband, and ends in
ostentatious acceptance of the conditions of matrimony at the moment when the unfortunate Jude, who has also been recaptured by
the widowed Arabella, dies of his cruel misery. This woman we are
required to accept as the type of high-toned purity. It is the women
who are the active agents in all this unsavoury imbroglio: the story
is carried on, and life is represented as carried on, entirely by their
means. The men are passive, suffering, rather good than otherwise,
victims of these and of fate. Not only do they never dominate, but
they are quite incapable of holding their own against these remorse-
less ministers of destiny, these determined operators, managing all
the machinery of life so as to secure their own way. This is one of
the most curious developments of recent fiction. It is perhaps natural
that it should be more or less the case in books written by women,
to whom the mere facility of representing their own sex acts as a
primary reason for giving them the chief place in the scene. But it
has now still more markedly, though much less naturally, become

the method with men, in the hands of many of whom women have returned to the *rôle* of the temptress given to them by the old monkish sufferers of ancient times, who fled to the desert, like Anthony, to get free of them, but even there barely escaped with their lives from the seductions of the sirens, who were so audacious as to follow them to the very scene of the macerations and miseries into which the unhappy men plunged to escape from their toils. In the books of the younger men, it is now the woman who seduces—it is no longer the man.

This, however, is a consideration by the way. I have said that it is not clear what Mr Hardy's motive is in the history of Jude: but, on reconsideration, it becomes more clear that it is intended as an assault on the stronghold of marriage, which is now beleaguered on every side. The motto is, "The letter killeth"; and I presume this must refer to the fact of Jude's early and unwilling union to Arabella, and that the lesson the novelist would have us learn is, that if marriage were not exacted, and people were free to form connections as the spirit moves them, none of these complications would have occurred, and all would have been well. "There seemed to him, vaguely and dimly, something wrong in a social ritual which made necessary the cancelling of well-formed schemes involving years of thought and labour, of foregoing a man's one opportunity of showing himself superior to the lower animals, and of contributing his units of work to the general progress of his generation, because of a momentary surprise by a new and transitory instinct which had nothing in it of the nature of vice, and could be only at the most called weakness." This is the hero's own view of the circumstances which, in obedience to the code of honour prevalent in the country-side, compelled his marriage. Suppose, however, that instead of upsetting the whole framework of society, Jude had shown himself superior to the lower animals by not yielding to that new and transitory influence, the same result could have been easily attained: and he might then have met and married Susan and lived happy ever after, without demanding a total overthrow of all existing laws and customs to prevent him from being unhappy. Had it been made possible for him to have visited Arabella as long as the new and transitory influence lasted, and then to have lived with Susan as long as she pleased to permit him to do so, which was the best that could happen were marriage abolished, how would that have altered the circumstances? When Susan changed her mind would he have been less unhappy? When Arabella claimed him again would he have been less weak?

Mr Hardy's solution of the great insoluble question of what is to be the fate of children in such circumstances brings this nauseous tragedy suddenly and at a stroke into the regions of pure farce— which is a surprise of the first quality, only too grotesque to be amusing. There are children, as a matter of course: a weird little imp, the son of Arabella, and two babies of Susan's. What is the point of the allegory which Mr Hardy intends us to read in the absurd little gnome, nicknamed Old Father Time, who is the off-spring of the buxom country lass, is a secondary subject upon which we have no light: but it is by the means of this strange creature that the difficulty is settled. In a moment of dreadful poverty and depression, Susan informs her step-son, whom she loves and is very kind to, of the severe straits in which she is. The child—he is now fourteen—asks whether himself and the others are not a great burden upon the parents who are already so poor; and she consents that life would be easier without them. The result is that when she comes in after a short absence she can find no trace of the children, until she perceives what seems to be, at first, suits of their clothes hanging against the wall, but discovers to be the children them-selves, all hanged, and swinging from the clothes-pegs: the elder boy having first hanged them and then himself to relieve the parent's hands. Does Mr Hardy think this is really a good way of disposing of the unfortunate progeny of such connections? does he recom-mend it for general adoption? It is at least a clean and decisive cut of the knot, leaving no ragged ends; but then there is no natural provision in families of such a wise small child to get its progenitors out of trouble. I read, not long ago, a book in which a young lady of extreme loveliness and genius, to whom it had occurred to begin her life in an irregular manner, confessed to her lover, when fortunate fate brought him to her side after a long separation, by way of mak-ing a clean breast of all small peccadilloes before their reunion— that she had killed the baby. He thought no worse of her, and they lived happy ever after. It is no doubt startling at the first glance. But is this to be the way? Mr Hardy knows, no doubt as everybody does, that the children are a most serious part of the question of the abolition of marriage. Is this the way in which he considers it would be resolved best?

4 Edmund Gosse

"Mr. Hardy's New Novel," *Cosmopolis,* January, 1896[1]

Among the novelists who, with so remarkable a vitality and variety, have illustrated the latest generation of English thought and feeling, three, by general consent, have attracted the most enthusiastic attention of men of letters. Mr. George Meredith, Mr. Thomas Hardy, the late Mr. Stevenson—these are certainly the names which occur, before any others, to the historian of literature as he reaches the fourth quarter of the ninetenth century. These three have, in no small measure, already entered into their rest; if, which every reader deprecates, Mr. Meredith and Mr. Hardy should write no more, these three, at least, have become classical. Other eminent novelists of our day may have surpassed them in wide popularity, others may possess a more strenuous moral purpose, a greater fluidity of invention, a more ebullient flood of narrative, but those men and women have thir reward. The Authors' Club bends, awe-stricken, before the enormous volume of their "sales." But pure literary renown, sapped though it is by the commercial spirit, is still a commanding element. Still a great number of English novelists, and many of them with no small success, hear the voice yet speaking which said two hundred years ago:

> "Travaillez pour la gloire, et qu'un sordide gain
> Ne soit jamais l'objet d'un illustre écrivain,"

and among these we say Meredith, Hardy, Stevenson, as one hundred and fifty years ago we might have said Richardson, Fielding, Sterne.

When so high a position as this has been definitely secured by a

1. Vol. I, pp. 60–69.

living writer, it seems to me futile, if not impertinent, to continue, in speaking of his successive books, that strain of purely indulgent eulogy which is the agreeable mode in criticism when welcoming the work of a man who by meritorious production is conquering a place in literature. There is something either patronising or obsequious, surely, in speaking of Mr. Meredith, for instance, with a less judicious freedom than we use in the consideration of Thackeray or Balzac. We do not hold it artistic to admire every excrescence on the strongly individualised work of the dead; we ought not to suppose that there is any disrespect in admitting that the psychology of Stevenson is sometimes puerile, or that the pertinacious euphuism of Mr. Meredith often painfully clouds the lucidity of his intelligence. We take our favourites as we find them, and, because they are great, we neither expect them to be, nor declare that they are, faultless. Nor is Mr. Hardy, although the author of pages and scenes indescribably felicitous, one of those monsters that the world ne'er saw, a perfect writer. In "Jude the Obscure," he has aimed, in all probability, higher than he ever aimed before, and it is not to be maintained that he has been equally successful in every part of his design.

Before these pages find a reader, everybody will be familiar with "Jude the Obscure," and we may well be excused, therefore, from repeating the story in detail. It will be remembered that it is a study of four lives, a rectangular problem in failures, drawn with almost mathematical rigidity. The tragedy of these four persons is constructed in a mode almost as geometrical as that in which Dr. Samuel Clarke was wont to prove the existence of the Deity. It is difficult not to believe that the author set up his four ninepins in the wilds of Wessex, and built up his theorem round them. Here is an initial difficulty. Not quite thus is theology or poetry conveniently composed; we like to conceive that the relation of the parts was more spontaneous, we like to feel that the persons of a story have been thrown up in a jet of enthusiasm, not put into a cave of theory to be slowly covered with stalactite. In this I may be doing Mr. Hardy an injustice, but a certain hardness in the initial conception of "Jude the Obscure" cannot, I believe, be denied. Mr. Hardy is certainly to be condoled with upon the fact that his novel, which has been seven years in the making, has appeared at last at a moment when a sheaf of "purpose" stories on the "marriage question" (as it is called) have just been irritating the nerves of the British Patron. No serious critic, however, will accuse Mr. Hardy of joining the ranks of these deciduous troublers of our peace.

We come, therefore, without prejudice to his chronicle of four unnecessary lives. There are the poor village lad, with his longing for the intellectual career; the crude village beauty, like a dahlia in a cottage-garden; the neurotic, semi-educated girl of hyper-sensitive instincts; and the dull, earthy, but not ungenerous schoolmaster. On these four failures, inextricably tied together and dragging one another down, our attention is riveted—on Jude, Arabella, Sue, and Phillotson. Before, however, we discuss their characteristics, we may give a little attention to the scene in which these are laid. Mr. Hardy, as all the world knows, has dedicated his life's work to the study of the old province of Wessex. It is his as Languedoc belongs to M. Ferdinand Fabre, or the Isle of Man to Mr. Hall Caine. That he is never happy outside its borders is a commonplace; it is not quite so clearly perceived, perhaps, that he is happiest in the heart of it. When Mr. Hardy writes of South Wessex (Dorsetshire) he seldom goes wrong; this county has been the theatre for all his most splendid successes. From Abbot's Cornal to Budmouth Regis, and wherever the wind blows freshly off Egdon Heath, he is absolute master and king. But he is not content with such a limited realm; he claims four other counties, and it must be confessed that his authority weakens as he approaches their confines.

"Jude the Obscure" is acted in North Wessex (Berkshire) and just across the frontier, at Christminster (Oxford), which is not in Wessex at all. We want our novelist back among the rich orchards of the Hintocks, and where the water-lilies impede the lingering river at Shottsford Ash. Berkshire is an unpoetical county, "meanly utilitarian," as Mr. Hardy confesses; the imagination hates its concave, loamy cornfields and dreary, hedgeless highways. The local history has been singularly tampered with in Berkshire; it is useless to speak to us of ancient records where the past is all obliterated, and the thatched and dormered houses replaced by modern cottages. In choosing North Wessex as the scene of a novel Mr. Hardy wilfully deprives himself of a great element of his strength. Where there are no prehistoric monuments, no ancient buildings, no mossed

314 · The English Novel

and immemorial woodlands, he is Samson shorn. In Berkshire, the change which is coming over England so rapidly, the resignation of the old dreamy elements of beauty, has proceeded further than anywhere else in Wessex. Pastoral loveliness is to be discovered only here and there, while in Dorsetshire it still remains the master-element. All this combines to lessen the physical charm of "Jude the Obscure" to those who turn from it in memory to "Far from the Madding Crowd" and "The Return of the Native."

But, this fortuitous absence of beauty being acknowledged, the novelist's hand shows no falling off in the vigour and reality of his description. It may be held, in fact, to be a lesser feat to raise before us an enchanting vision of the valley of the Froom, than successfully to rivet our attention on the prosaic arable land encircling the dull hamlet of Marygreen. Most attractive Mr. Hardy's pictures of purely country life have certainly been—there is no picture in "Jude" to approach that of the life on the dairy farm in "Tess"—but he has never treated rural scenes with a more prodigious mastery and knowledge. It is, in fact, in knowledge, that Mr. Hardy's work of this class is so admirable. Mere observation will not produce this illusion of absolute truth. That it is not enough to drive in an open carriage through the rural districts was abundantly proved, in the face of Europe, by M. Zola's deplorable fiasco of "La Terre." The talent of M. Zola, long unduly exalted, now perhaps as unduly decried, covers so wide a ground of human experience that a failure in one direction proves no want of skill in another, but as a student of the peasant his incompetence is beyond question. Curiously enough—and doubtless by a pure accident—there are not a few passages of "Jude the Obscure" which naturally excite comparison with similar scenes in "La Terre." The parallel is always in Mr. Hardy's favour; his vision of the peasant is invariably more distinct, and more convincing than M. Zola's. He falls into none of the pitfalls laid for the Parisian romancier, and we are never more happy than when he allows us to overhear the primitive Wessex speech. Our only quarrel with Mr. Hardy, indeed, in this respect, is that he grows now impatient of retailing to us the axiomatic humour, the crafty and narrow dignity of the villager.

To pass from the landscape to the persons, two threads of action seem to be intertwined in "Jude the Obscure." We have, first of all, the contrast between the ideal life the young peasant of scholarly instincts wished to lead, and the squalid real life into which he was fated to sink. We have, secondly, the almost rectilinear puzzle of the sexual relations of the four principal characters. Mr. Hardy has wished to show how cruel destiny can be to the eternal dream of youth, and he has undertaken to trace the lamentable results of unions in a family exhausted by intermarriage and poverty. Some collision is apparent between these aims; the first seems to demand a poet, the second a physician. The Fawleys are a decayed and wasted race, in the last of whom, Jude, there appears, with a kind of flicker in the socket, a certain intellectual and artistic brightness. In favourable surroundings, we feel that this young man might have become fairly distinguished as a scholar, or as a sculptor. But at the supreme moment, or at each supreme moment, the conditions hurl him back into insignificance. When we examine clearly what these conditions are, we find them to be instinctive. He is just going to develop into a lad of education, when Arabella throws her hideous missile at him, and he sinks with her into a resigned inferiority.

So far, the critical court is with Mr. Hardy; these scenes and their results give a perfect impression of truth. Later on, it is not quite evident whether the claim on Jude's passions, or the inherent weakness of his inherited character, is the source of his failure. Perhaps both. But it is difficult to see what part Oxford has in his destruction, or how Mr. Hardy can excuse the rhetorical diatribes against the university which appear towards the close of the book. Does the novelist really think that it was the duty of the heads of houses to whom Jude wrote his crudely pathetic letters to offer him immediately a fellowship? We may admit to the full the pathos of Jude's position—nothing is more heart-rending than the obscurity of the half-educated—but surely, the fault did not lie with Oxford.

The scene at Commemoration (Part vi.) is of a marvellous truth and vividness of presentment, but it would be stronger, and even more tragic, if Mr. Hardy did not appear in it as an advocate taking sides with his unhappy hero. In this portion of his work, it seems to me, Mr. Hardy had but to paint—as clearly and as truthfully as he could—the hopes, the struggles, the disappointments of Jude, and of these he has woven a tissue of sombre colouring, indeed, and even of harsh threads, but a tapestry worthy of a great imaginative writer. It was straightforward poet's work in invention and observation, and he has executed it well.

But in considering the quadruple fate of the four leading characters, of whom Jude is but one, we come to matter of a different order. Here the physician, the neuropathist, steps in, and takes the pen out of the poet's hand. Let us for a moment strip to its barest nomination this part of the plot. Jude, a neurotic subject in whom hereditary degeneracy takes an idealist turn, with some touch, perhaps, of what the new doctors call megalomania, has been warned by the local gossips not to marry. But he is physically powerful and attractive, and he engages the notice of Arabella, a young woman of gross instincts and fine appearance, who seduces and marries him. He falls from his scholastic dream to the level of a labourer, and is only saved by the fact that Arabella wearies of him and leaves him. He goes to Oxford, and, gradually cultivating the dream again, seems on the first rung of the ladder of success, when he comes across his own cousin Sue, and loves her. But she has promised to marry Phillotson, a weary middle-aged schoolmaster, and marry him she will, although she loves Jude, and has forced him to compromise her. But she finds Phillotson intolerable, and leaves him to join Jude, only to find herself equally unhappy and unsatisfying, dragging Jude once more down to mediocrity. Arabella crosses Jude's life again, and jealousy forces Sue to some semblance of love for Jude. Sue becomes the mother of several children, who are killed in a fit of infantile mania by a boy, the son of Jude and Arabella, whose habitual melancholy, combined with his hereditary antecedents, has prepared us for an outbreak of suicide, if not of murder. This horrible event affects Sue by producing religious mania. She will live no longer with Jude, although both couples have got their divorce, but fatally returns to be the slave of her detested schoolmaster, while Jude, in a paroxysm of drunken abandonment, goes back to Arabella and dies.

It is a ghastly story, especially when reduced to this naked skeleton. But it does not appear to me that we have any business to call in question the right of a novelist of Mr. Hardy's extreme distinction to treat what themes he will. We may wish—and I for my part cordially wish—that more pleasing, more charming plots than this could take his fancy. But I do not feel at liberty to challenge his discretion. One thing, however, the critic of comparative literature must note. We have, in such a book as "Jude the Obscure," traced the full circle of propriety. A hundred and fifty years ago, Fielding and Smollett brought up before us pictures, used expressions, described conduct, which appeared to their immediate successors a little more crude than general reading warranted. In Miss Burney's hands and in Miss Austen's, the morals were still further hedged about. Scott was even more daintily reserved. We came at last to Dickens, where the clamorous passions of mankind, the coarser accidents of life, were absolutely ignored, and the whole question of population seemed reduced to the theory of the gooseberry bush. This was the *ne plus ultra* of decency; Thackeray and George Eliot relaxed this intensity of prudishness; once on the turn, the tide flowed rapidly, and here is Mr. Hardy ready to say any mortal thing that Fielding said, and a good deal more too.

So much we note, but to censure it, if it calls for censure, is the duty of the moralist and not the critic. Criticism asks how the thing is done, whether the execution is fine and convincing. To tell so squalid and so abnormal a story in an interesting way is in itself a feat, and this, it must be universally admitted, Mr. Hardy has achieved. "Jude the Obscure" is an irresistible book; it is one of those novels into which we descend and are carried on by a steady impetus to the close, when we return, dazzled, to the light of common day. The two women, in particular, are surely created by a master. Every impulse, every speech, which reveals to us the coarse and animal, but not hateful Arabella, adds to the solidity of her portrait. We may dislike her, we may hold her intrusion into our consciousness a disagreeable one, but of her reality there can be no question: Arabella lives.

It is conceivable that not so generally will it be admitted that Sue Bridehead is convincing. Arabella is the excess of vulgar normality; every public bar and village fair knows Arabella, but Sue is a strange and unwelcome product of exhaustion. The *vita sexualis* of Sue is the central interest of the book, and enough is told about it to fill the specimen tables of a German specialist. Fewer testimonies will be given to her reality than to Arabella's because hers is much the rarer case. But her picture is not less admirably drawn; Mr. Hardy has, perhaps, never devoted so much care to the portrait of a woman. She is a poor, maimed "degenerate," ignorant of herself and of the perversion of her instincts, full of febrile, amiable illusions, ready to dramatise her empty life, and play at loving though she cannot love. Her adventure with the undergraduate has not taught her what she is; she quits Phillotson still ignorant of the source of her repulsion; she lives with Jude, after a long, agonising struggle, in a relation that she accepts with distaste, and when the tragedy comes, and her children are killed, her poor extravagant brain slips one grade further down, and she sees in this calamity the chastisement of God. What has she done to be chastised? She does not know, but supposes it must be her abandonment of Phillotson, to whom, in a spasm of self-abasement, and shuddering with repulsion, she returns without a thought for the misery of Jude. It is a terrible study in pathology, but of the splendid success of it, of the sustained intellectual force implied in the evolution of it, there cannot, I think, be two opinions.

One word must be added about the speech of the author and of the characters in "Jude the Obscure." Is it too late to urge Mr. Hardy to struggle against the jarring note of rebellion which seems growing upon him? It sounded in "Tess," and here it is, more roughly expressed, further acerbated. What has Providence done to Mr. Hardy that he should rise up in the arable land of Wessex and shake his fist at his Creator? He should not force his talent, should not give way to these chimerical outbursts of philosophy falsely so called. His early romances were full of calm and lovely pantheism; he seemed in them to feel the deep-hued country landscapes full of rural gods, all homely and benign. We wish he would go back to Egdon Heath and listen to the singing in the heather. And as to the conversations of his semi-educated characters, they are really terrible. Sue and Jude talk a sort of University Extension jargon that breaks the heart. "The mediævalism of Christminster must go, be sloughed off, or Christminster will have to go," says Sue, as she sits in a pair of Jude's trousers, while Jude dries her petticoat at his garret-fire. Hoity-toity, for a minx! the reader cries, or, rather, although he firmly believes in the existence of Sue, and in the truth of the episode, he is convinced that Mr. Hardy is mistaken in what he heard her say. She *could* not have talked like that.

A fact about the infancy of Mr. Hardy has escaped the interviewers and may be recorded here. On the day of his birth, during a brief absence of his nurse, there slipped into the room an ethereal creature, known as the Spirit of Plastic Beauty. Bending over the cradle she scattered roses on it, and as she strewed them she blessed the babe. "He shall have an eye to see moral and material loveliness, he shall speak of richly-coloured pastoral places in the accent of Theocritus, he shall write in such a way as to cajole busy men into a sympathy with old, unhappy, far-off things." She turned and went, but while the nurse still delayed, a withered termagant glided into the room. From her apron she dropped toads among the rose-leaves, and she whispered: "I am the genius of False Rhetoric, and led by me he shall say things ugly and coarse, not recognizing them to be so, and shall get into a rage about matters that call for philosophic calm, and shall spoil some of his best passages with pedantry and incoherency. He shall not know what things belong to his peace, and he shall plague his most loyal admirers with the barbaric contortions of his dialogue." So saying, she put out her snaky tongue at the unoffending babe, and ever since, his imagination, noble as it is, and attuned to the great harmonies of nature, is liable at a moment's notice to give a shriek of discord. The worst, however, which any honest critic can say of "Jude the Obscure" is that the fairy godmother seems, for the moment, to have relaxed her guardianship a little unduly.

5 *Thomas Hardy*

FROM Letters to Edmund Gosse[1]

(November 10, 1895)

Your review (of *Jude the Obscure*) is the most discriminating that has yet appeared. It required an artist to see that the plot is almost geometrically constructed—I ought not to say *constructed*, for, beyond a certain point, the characters necessitated it, and I simply

1. "The Life of Thomas Hardy," by Florence Emily Hardy and by the permission of the Hardy Estate, St. Martin's Press, Inc., The Macmillan Company of Canada, Ltd., and Macmillan & Co., Ltd., 1962, pp. 40–43.

let it come. As for the story itself, it is really sent out to those into whose souls the iron has entered, and has entered deeply at some time of their lives. But one cannot choose one's readers.

It is curious that some of the papers should look upon the novel as a manifesto on 'the marriage question' (although, of course, it involves it), seeing that it is concerned first with the labours of a poor student to get a University degree, and secondly with the tragic issues of two bad marriages, owing in the main to a doom or curse of hereditary temperament peculiar to the family of the parties. The only remarks which can be said to bear on the *general* marriage question occur in dialogue, and comprise no more than half a dozen pages in a book of five hundred. And of these remarks I state . . . that my own views are not expressed therein. I suppose the attitude of these critics is to be accounted for by the accident that, during the serial publication of my story, a sheaf of 'purpose' novels on the matter appeared.

You have hardly an idea how poor and feeble the book seems to me, as executed, beside the idea of it that I had formed in prospect.

I have received some interesting letters about it already—yours not the least so. Swinburne writes, too enthusiastically for me to quote with modesty. . . .

P.S. One thing I did not answer. The 'grimy' features of the story go to show the contrast between the ideal life a man wished to lead, and the squalid real life he was fated to lead. The throwing of the pizzle, at the supreme moment of his young dream, is to sharply initiate this contrast. But I must have lamentably failed, as I feel I have, if this requires explanation and is not self-evident. The idea was meant to run all through the novel. It is, in fact, to be discovered in *everybody's* life, though it lies less on the surface perhaps than it does in my poor puppet's.

* * *

(November 20, 1895)

I am keen about the new magazine. How interesting that you should be writing this review for it! I wish the book were more worthy of such notice and place.

You are quite right; there is nothing perverted or depraved in Sue's nature. The abnormalism consists in disproportion, not in inversion, her sexual instinct being healthy as far as it goes, but unusually weak and fastidious. Her sensibilities remain painfully alert notwithstanding, as they do in nature with such women. One point illustrating this I could not dwell upon: that, though she has children, her intimacies with Jude have never been more than occasional, even when they were living together (I mention that they occupy separate rooms, except towards the end), and one of her reasons for fearing the marriage ceremony is that she fears it would be breaking faith with Jude to withhold herself at pleasure, or altogether, after it; though while uncontracted she feels at liberty to yield herself as seldom as she chooses. This has tended to keep his passion as hot at the end as at the beginning, and helps to break his heart. He has never really possessed her as freely as he desired.

Sue is a type of woman which has always had an attraction for me, but the difficulty of drawing the type has kept me from attempting it till now.

Of course the book is all contrasts—or was meant to be in its original conception. Alas, what a miserable accomplishment it is, when I compare it with what I meant to make it!—*e.g.* Sue and her heathen gods set against Jude's reading the Greek testament; Christminster academical, Christminster in the slums; Jude the saint, Jude the sinner; Sue the Pagan, Sue the saint; marriage, no marriage; &c., &c.

As to the 'coarse' scenes with Arabella, the battle in the schoolroom, etc., the newspaper critics might, I thought, have sneered at them for their Fieldingism rather than for their Zolaism. But your everyday critic knows nothing of Fielding. I am read in Zola very little, but have felt akin locally to Fielding, so many of his scenes having been laid down this way, and his home near.

Did I tell you I feared I should seem too High-Churchy at the end of the book where Sue recants? You can imagine my surprise at some of the reviews.

* * *

(January 4, 1896)

For the last three days I have been tantalized by a difficulty in getting *Cosmopolis* and had only just read your review when I received your note. My sincere thanks for the generous view you take of the book, which to me is a mass of imperfections. We have both been amused—or rather delighted—by the sub-humour (is there such a word?) of your writing. I think it a rare quality in living essayists, and that you ought to make more of it—I mean write more in that vein than you do.

But this is apart from the review itself, of which I will talk to you when we meet. The rectangular lines of the story were not premeditated, but came by chance: except, of course, that the involutions of four lives must necessarily be a sort of quadrille. The only point in the novel on which I feel sure is that it makes for morality; and that delicacy or indelicacy in a writer is according to his object. If I say to a lady 'I met a naked woman', it is indelicate. But if I go on to say 'I found she was mad with sorrow', it ceases to be indelicate. And in writing Jude my mind was fixed on the ending.

5 - 2 0 0